The Puzzle of Christianity

The Puzzle of Christianity

PETER VARDY

WILLIAM
COLLINS

William Collins
An imprint of HarperCollins*Publishers*
1 London Bridge Street
London
SE1 9GF

WilliamCollinsBooks.com

First published in the United Kingdom by in 2016 by William Collins

19 18 17 16

10 9 8 7 6 5 4 3 2 1

A catalogue record for this book is available from the British Library

ISBN 978-0-00-820424-2
Ebook ISBN 978-0-00-820425-9
Audiobook ISBN 978-0-00-820426-6

Typeset by Palimpsest Book Production Limited, Falkirk, Stirlingshire
Printed and bound in Great Britain by Clays Ltd, St Ives plc

To Christine Smith

Who, first at HarperCollins and then at SCM,
has published most of my books and to whom
I owe a great deal. With thanks.

Peter Vardy
Easter 2016

A website to accompany this book, with additional information
and resources can be found at www.puzzleofchristianity.org

Contents

ONE

United and Divided

Jesus of Nazareth, Jesus the Christ, is at the centre of Christianity. This, at least, is clear but beyond this, defining the essence of Christianity is full of difficulties. It is like trying to capture a rainbow or the light from the sparkling drops of a waterfall as they reflect the sun. Christianity has many facets and many forms. It is the largest religion in the world with nearly 2 billion adherents and these are found in every country in the globe. Christians are united and also divided. They are united around the centrality of the person of Jesus, His unique status and the extraordinary message He came to convey, but divided in many ways on the nature of the message, on doctrine, beliefs, ethics, forms of worship and even the status of the New Testament.

It would be easy to focus on the lack of unity in Christianity – and this lack of unity certainly exists. Major Christian churches are often at loggerheads and the disagreement between Christian groups can be profound and deep. Some Protestants do not regard Catholics as Christian at all. The teaching authority of the Catholic Church, the Magisterium, has historically been hostile to Protestantism and used to deny salvation to those who were outside their church; indeed, they ruled that there was only one Church: their own. Pentecostal churches, particularly in the United States and Africa, owe much to the charisma of individual church leaders and there is limited unity beyond the centrality of the Bible and the person of Jesus. Orthodox Christians have traditionally been suspicious of Western Christianity and have sought to remain faithful to the tradition of the early Church, whilst liberal Christians in the West have often diluted traditional Christian beliefs to such an extent that not much remains.

The history of Christianity has been full of disagreements, with so-called 'heretical' groups being persecuted because of their deviance from what was accepted as orthodoxy. There was no unity in the early centuries of Christianity, with a considerable range of different interpretations and beliefs. Forging unity and then seeking to maintain this has also been a challenge and it has particularly occupied the main Christian churches. There has been violence, torture and persecution as well as fierce attacks over what may seem to be small points of doctrine. It would be easy to reject the whole of Christianity on these grounds and many critics have done so. And yet, beneath the tensions and the sometimes violent disagreements, like the *De profundis* or the deep tone of a bass bell, there is something profound, significant and important happening – something of enormous contemporary relevance and something on which hundreds of millions of people down the centuries have been willing to stake their lives. Christianity has been responsible for some of the greatest art and the greatest acts of heroism and altruism, as well as compassion, nobility and virtue – as well as, it must be admitted, terrible persecution and suffering. Christian thinkers have generated some of the most profound philosophy as well as science and business practice. European culture has been founded on Christianity and this has been exported around the globe. Many of the internationally accepted values endorsed by the United Nations have Christian origins.

To understand Jesus of Nazareth it is important to understand the culture in which He lived. The Roman Empire 2,000 years ago covered most of central and southern Europe as well as North Africa. Its armies were dominant and its civilian administration, although reasonably fair, was harsh and unyielding, as well as viciously cruel to those who dissented. Being a Roman citizen carried great privileges and most of the inhabitants of the territories that Rome conquered longed to share in the wealth, power and prosperity of the Empire. Slaves were common and slavery was accepted.

Slaves often came from the nations conquered by Rome in battle but they could rise to positions of influence. Most, however, were desperately poor and appallingly treated. Society was clearly hierarchical with the great families of Rome at the top. Money was of central importance, as in most societies, and a certain amount of social mobility was possible, but always within fairly narrow limits. Any resistance to the Imperial power of Rome was suppressed viciously and effectively. The Roman Senate and the Emperor had ultimate power, but this was delegated to administrators and officials in the various territories of the Empire. However, these officials all recognised that they were fully accountable to Rome for keeping order, for sending taxes back to Rome and also for ensuring that Roman values and Roman religion were maintained. Rome had its own pantheon of gods, and emperors were sometimes deified. The Jews held a special position, as their religion was tolerated. Rome occupied Palestine and what had been, in the remote past, independent Jewish territory. Unlike many subservient peoples, the Jews were proud and continually dreamed of regaining their freedom. Their lands had been frequently conquered in the past but, eventually, they had always regained their independence, and at the time of Jesus there were many who dreamed that this independence would come again.

Jesus was a Jew and this culture was second nature to Him. Jews were the first monotheists – the first to worship a single God. Jews were proud of their identity. The Roman authorities left them free to practise their religion, provided they obeyed the laws of Rome and paid the very considerable taxes that were demanded of them. The Temple in Jerusalem had recently been rebuilt but Rome asserted its domination by occupying one of the corner towers. Rome had little time for Jewish religion and practices but they were tolerated, not out of sympathy but because it was the easiest way of keeping a potentially troublesome people quiet. There was a vassal king, Herod, who was allowed a limited degree of autonomy, and the Jewish priests were also allowed a certain amount of freedom to manage religious affairs.

In understanding any period in history the cultural context is important and this is undoubtedly the case when seeking to understand Jesus of Nazareth. In the case of Jesus, however, His national background was even more important than that of almost any other historical figure. To say that He was a Jew does not begin to capture what this meant; the depth of culture, theology, civilisation, expectations, disappointments, resentments and hope that lay behind this single word was massive. Jews, more than almost any other nation, are a people with a long history. They saw history as the arena in which their God, the God of the whole creation, cared for and looked after them in spite of great suffering. Jews saw themselves – and still do – as a people chosen by God, the chosen people whom God would always protect and, in the last analysis, preserve. This hope and expectation has always been borne out in spite of the most terrible persecution and oppression as well as systematic attempts at genocide. The other nations and sects of the ancient

Figure 1: A Torah scroll is the holiest book in Judaism. It is hand written by a scribe in Hebrew and contains the first five books of the Hebrew Scriptures. Every synagogue has such a scroll and Jesus would have read from one like this (see Luke 4:16–20).

Middle East have all disappeared; the Moabites and Assyrians, the Philistines and the Babylonians, the Romans and Greeks have all been swept away, to be replaced by nation states with changing boundaries and identities. However, Jewish identity has been preserved.

In order, therefore, to begin to understand the person of Jesus of Nazareth it is essential to understand something of Jewish history – or at least history as it was seen by the Jews and recorded in the Torah and the other books which Christians refer to as the Hebrew Scriptures. These Scriptures tell the story of the history of a people and their interaction with their God: of their origins, their faith, their failures, their hopes and disappointments. Modern scholars differ about the extent to which this story is historically accurate but there is no doubt that it was considered as true by Jews at the time of Jesus and, indeed, by many Jews and Christians today. In the next chapter a very brief account will be given of this history, and this is not mere background. It is not possible to understand what Christianity is until one has understood that Jesus was a Jew and He was seen as a fulfilment of the Jewish Scriptures. Jesus, Christians believe, is the highest point of God's love for, and interaction with, the world. It is no mere coincidence that He was born as a Jew. God's relation with the people of Israel goes back to the dawn of recorded time and, as history develops and God interacts with human beings and human affairs, it is Jesus who brings to fruition all the long history and expectation of the people of Israel.

TWO

From the Beginning of the Universe

Christians see the world as created by God and dependent on God. God sustains the universe in existence and, were it not for God, there would be no universe. The universe is incredibly orderly and behaves according to mathematical and physical laws. These laws are intelligible to human beings and the universe as a whole has meaning and purpose grounded in the will of God. This is one of the most important Christian beliefs and it is shared by Jews, Muslims and many others around the world. For Christians, God is loving as well as personal and wills the universe into existence as a free act of love for the whole of creation.

We now know that the universe began to exist from a singularity – the infinitely small, dense matter which suddenly expanded in the 'Big Bang' and from which the present state of the universe can be traced. The dating of the universe is generally agreed by scientists to be about 13.7 billion years ago and scientists also agree that the specific conditions which enabled the 'Big Bang' to occur had to be unbelievably precise for a universe to form at all. There are various possible ways of seeking to explain the incredible improbability of the singularity. One explanation is to say that 'it just happened'. Extraordinary and improbable things do happen and the universe is just one of those improbable things. Another is to say that there are a near-infinite number of possible universes (in other words, a multiverse) and we just happen to be in the universe that had the right conditions for stars, planets and life to form. Christians reject both of these and see the universe as a result of the purposeful intention of a loving creator God.

This idea has its roots in the earliest stories in the Hebrew Scriptures where God's creative Word is held to have uttered the universe into existence. God is also shown as responsible for the sea and dry land, for all animals, birds and fish and, above all, for the creation of men and women. Men and women are the pinnacle, the crown of creation, and God created a perfect world for them and was pleased with all that God had created. The story of the Jews, therefore, begins with creation. The Word of God is central to the creation story and indeed to the whole of the Hebrew Scriptures. It is the Word of God that creates the heavens and earth, and it is the Word of God that later comes to the great Hebrew prophets. The God of the Hebrews is beyond all human categories. The whole of the universe cannot contain God, and yet God is radically present among God's chosen people. The Word of God is therefore active and creative. It is a Word for guidance, exhortation and sometimes condemnation. The Word has power and can not only create from nothing but also intervene in and through human affairs.

There are two different creation stories written, biblical scholars generally agree, about 400 years apart and, of course, long after the events that they seek to describe. They recount, in different ways, the universe coming into being and the presence of human beings in the world.

However, these stories continue with the immediate disobedience of the two figures recorded as placed in the perfect world (the Garden of Eden) which God created – Adam and Eve. This disobedience of these two primal figures led to disruption of the world with the entrance of pain, death, evil and suffering. The Hebrew Scriptures are in no doubt about the extraordinary position that human beings occupy in the whole created universe. They are the apex of creation and are essentially different from everything else in the created order because they have rationality and also free will.

Obedience to the Word of God is a central theme in the Hebrew Scriptures and from the creation of the world the Scriptures record the tendency of humans to be self-centred and disobedient. This disobedience is not a rejection of an autocratic power figure; God creates human beings and wants what is best for them, what will lead to human fulfilment.

Figure 1: *Michelangelo's painting in the Sistine Chapel in Rome shows, on the left, Eve taking the fruit from the serpent. Notice that the body of the serpent changes into the form of a woman. On the right are Adam and Eve being banished from the Garden of Eden by an angel with a sword (Genesis 3:23–24).*

The story of Adam and Eve begins the Hebrew Scriptures and most Western Christians consider that it represents a myth – but myth can convey truth. The truth resides in the claim that God created the universe and all that is in it, and that human beings are in a special position, having free will. They constantly choose to disobey and yet God always forgives and provides a new start. A peaceful and wonderful world is portrayed and human beings were placed in it to enjoy it and to enjoy God's presence. However, for modern Christians, the issues are more complex. Most Christians accept Darwin's theory of natural selection and, whilst maintaining that God created and sustains the universe, nevertheless see human beings as evolving from lower animals. Generally, Christians do not see a tension between their faith and science, although there are some who still hold to a literal interpretation of the text and who therefore reject evolution – but these are a minority.

Following the exclusion of Adam and Eve from Eden, God also showed God's care for them by cherishing them and being with them in spite of their difficulties. This is another theme found throughout both Judaism and Christianity – that God will never forsake God's people and will be with them even though this presence may not be obvious. The story of Adam and Eve and the population of the earth continues through the story of Noah, when God is recorded as being so angry with human beings because of their selfishness and disobedience that the whole of creation was nearly destroyed but Noah and his family and the entire created order were preserved as a result of the righteousness of Noah and the mercy of God. Some Jewish rabbis have seen parallels with the subsequent righteousness of the Jews preserving the whole of creation from destruction.

Arguably, the single most important figure in the Jewish Scriptures is Abraham. He was a descendant of Noah and lived in the city of Ur in what is now Iraq. He worshipped a single God and this was unusual and unpopular in the world of his time. The legacy of Abraham was enormous. He is revered as the father not only of the Jewish nation but of all Jews; he is seen by Muslims as the first to submit to Allah and, therefore, the first Muslim; and by Christians as the 'father of faith', as his whole life is centred on obedience to, and worship of, God. The story of Abraham is at the core of the faith of any Jew and Jesus would have been no exception. The whole of Abraham's life was based on trust in God and in the promises of God, even when these promises seemed absurd. He trusted God when God promised him a son even though his wife, Sarah, was past the menopause. He trusted God in every aspect of his life, even to the extent of being willing to place obedience to God before his duty to his son and family. It was to Abraham and his descendants that God is held to have made a covenant or promise that the land of Israel in Palestine would belong to them, and Jews still look to this promise as a justification for a Jewish homeland. Abraham was the first to show clearly the single most important requirement of the God of the people of Israel: that God demanded absolute loyalty.

God had to be at the centre of the whole of the life of every devout Jew. Everything else was to be put in second place. It was failure to keep this command that Jews saw as the chief reason for the troubles that were to befall them in their history.

God entered into a covenant, effectively a binding promise, between God on one side and Abraham and his descendants on the other. Provided the children of Abraham maintained loyalty to God, then God would protect them. God would never abandon them totally, even though at times God might seem far away.

Abraham had two children: one by Sarah's slave Hagar (with whom Abraham slept at the request of Sarah when she was convinced that she was barren and could not have children) and the other by Sarah herself. The second child was named Isaac (which means 'laughter') and it was from Isaac and one of his two sons, Jacob, that all the tribes of Israel were seen as descended. Blaise Pascal referred to the 'God of Abraham, God of Isaac, God of Jacob, not of the philosophers and the scholars'. He was emphasising the personal nature of God and the relationship that God is recorded as having with these three great ancestors of the Jewish nation and which he considered continued in the Christian tradition. It is important to recognise that the people of Israel and modern Jews see themselves as descended from Abraham through Isaac and then Jacob; there is a real sense in which the people of Israel were a great extended family. Jews, therefore, were concerned with their lineal descendants – parents mattered. Jews tended to marry Jews and Jewish identity was maintained by dietary laws and by various practices, including the removal of the foreskin from the penis of baby boys (circumcision). Jewish identity has always been a key feature in maintaining the existence of the people of Israel, and these outward signs were seen as acknowledgement of this dependence.

The Hebrew Scriptures record the story of the people of Israel who were, at this early stage, merely a group of families descended from Abraham, Isaac and Jacob. The extended family prospered but, eventually, they faced starvation and famine in Palestine where the rains are often uncertain. After years of drought, they were forced to flee to the land of Egypt which, because of the river Nile, had always been an area of prosperity; the adventures and events which gave rise to this Exodus are related in detail. God's hand is always seen as working through history; at the time, isolated and seemingly unrelated events occur but behind these events is God's guiding hand. Christians sometimes refer to 'salvation history': God acting through history to bring God's purposes about. An anonymous poem called 'The Loom of Time' expresses this well:

> *Man's life is laid in the loom of time*
> *To a pattern he does not see,*
> *While the weavers work and the shuttles fly*
> *Till the dawn of eternity.*
>
> *Some shuttles are filled with silver threads*
> *And some with threads of gold,*
> *While often but the darker hues*
> *Are all that they may hold.*
>
> *But the weaver watches with a skilful eye*
> *Each shuttle fly to and fro,*
> *And sees the pattern so deftly wrought*
> *As the loom moves sure and slow.*
>
> *God surely planned the pattern:*
> *Each thread, the dark and fair,*
> *Is chosen by His master skill*
> *And placed in the web with care.*
>
> *He only knows its beauty,*
> *And guides the shuttles which hold*
> *The threads so unattractive,*
> *As well as the threads of gold.*

Not till each loom is silent,
And the shuttles cease to fly,
Shall God reveal the pattern
And explain the reason why

The dark threads were as needful
In the weaver's skilful hand
As the threads of gold and silver
For the pattern which He planned.

History is not a mere series of events; still less is it simply based on decisions made by human beings. For Jews, God's hand lies behind the whole of human history and it was God who took the fledgling people of Israel into Egypt. Once there, the group of families settled and grew prosperous, only to find with the emergence of a new ruler that they were seen as immigrants and resented. Their numbers increased, but they were made into slaves and their lot was a miserable and unhappy one. Still the Scriptures record God as being with them and that they maintained their faith, hoping against all expectation for deliverance. This eventually comes with the extraordinary story of Moses, a Jew but raised as an Egyptian. God is recorded as taking this outsider and using him as an instrument to lead the people of Israel back to the land promised to their forefather Abraham.

This is another theme constantly recorded in the Hebrew Scriptures – that God does not favour and choose the strong and powerful but often works through those who are seen as weak and who are outsiders to power structures. God does not depend on human strength and ingenuity nor does God value people on the same basis as human beings. Moses was an unlikely outsider and had to stand against the might of the Egyptian ruler, the Pharaoh, but with God on his side was able to free the people of Israel. They fled from oppression in Egypt and, in later times, persecuted Christians remembered God's hand working to save the people of Israel. Christians were to come to see themselves as 'the new Israel' and, therefore, stories of deliverance and salvation in the Hebrew Scriptures became related to Christian concerns.

Although the people of Israel successfully left Egypt, protected by the direct action of God, their lack of faith is not disguised in the Scriptures. They wandered for many years in the harsh environment of the Sinai desert and many felt initially that it would have been better to remain as slaves. God appeared to have become an absent God. Having lived in Egypt, they were used to the Egyptian gods that were visible, so they made an

Figure 2: This painting by Nicolas Poussin, The Adoration of the Golden Calf (1634), is an imaginative re-creation of the god in the image of a golden calf created by the people of Israel when they felt abandoned in the Sinai desert (Exodus 32:1–4).

idol – a golden calf. This seemed much more real and immediate than the remote God who appeared to have deserted them and left them to be wandering nomads. In other words, they lost faith; they did not realise that God's timescale was not theirs. The Hebrew Scriptures are frank in recognising the continuing disobedience of the people of Israel, but always God remains faithful. So it proved in this story, and after many years of hardship and wandering in the desert, as their numbers increased still further, they were eventually led back to the place they considered home, the land they believed to have been promised them by God through God's promise to Abraham.

It was on the way out of Egypt that God is recorded as giving the people of Israel the Ten Commandments which are the cornerstone of Jewish law, although this law is amplified by many other commands given by God over the centuries. They eventually arrived back in Palestine, only to find it peacefully settled with strong and powerful cities, and their presence was resented and opposed; the locals certainly did not recognise any rights of this strange and alien people. However, the people of Israel had been through great hardship and they maintained their unity, moulding themselves into a formidable fighting force and conquering, in a series of wars, much of the land that was to become Israel.

The new land of Israel was divided between twelve tribes, representing the twelve sons of Jacob. They were surrounded by neighbours who wished to destroy them and the identity of the people of Israel was under constant threat. Only in loyalty to God, they believed, could their identity be safeguarded, and the Hebrew stories contain myriad accounts of men and women and the whole nation being preserved by God in times of crisis when all hope seems to be at an end. Indeed, the preservation of hope and trust when all the evidence runs in the opposite direction is another feature of the Hebrew Scriptures.

There is no single piece of territory that can be described as ancient Israel – the borders were fluid and changed over time. When the people of Israel came out of Egypt they described this as an Exodus and Jews saw themselves as 'coming home' to their forefather's land. During this time they were led by a series of great leaders or Judges (one of them was a woman, Deborah; see Judges 4:4–5:31). The tribes of Israel retained their own identity, living in different areas and, initially, they avoided the cities. Yet the Judges could call them together in time of war to unite against a perceived military threat.

The prophets have a vital role to play in understanding Jewish history. They were often lonely and isolated figures, harsh and unyielding. However, they continually spoke up in the name of God, standing for justice and goodness in the face of power and corruption. Above all, they stood for the necessity for God to have a central place in the life of the Jewish state and for high moral standards as well as concern for those who were weak and vulnerable. The prophets did not speak on their own authority. The Word of God came to them and they were, effectively, the mouthpieces of God, sometimes speaking with reluctance because they often faced death or persecution from those in power. However, the reality of God's Word to them was so great that it was almost impossible to resist. The prophets, however, could also be wrong; the story of Jonah is the story of an insular prophet, obsessed with the rightness of the people of Israel and the wrongness of everyone else and convinced that God favoured only Israel. The whole book is a wonderful story to make it very clear that, whilst God is the God of Israel, God is also the God of the whole world and that good and righteous people are to be found beyond Israel's borders. Jonah is forced to recognise this, for him, uncomfortable truth. Never, except in the early days, did the people of Israel see their God as one amongst a number of local gods. They were convinced that the whole created order depended on God alone and that all other gods were merely human creations with no significance or power at all.

Initially the people of Israel were wanderers. Abraham and his descendants would have been like modern Bedouin and, even when they came with their extended families into Palestine after leaving Egypt, they were essentially a tribal and pastoral people. Settling into cities came later. There was suspicion not only of a king but of any central capital and even of a temple. Their God was an invisible God, the Lord of the whole earth, and no human-made building could contain God. What was more, the Ten Commandments had specifically forbidden any representation to be made of God so no statues or other idols were made. The people of Israel could not even utter the name of God and one of the Ten Commandments specifically condemned taking the name of God in vain. The result was that the nearest thing to a temple was a travelling 'ark' or tent which was seen as the symbol of holiness and the dwelling place of God on earth.

In these years it was felt that only God could be the Lord and Master of Israel. Religiously, therefore, the idea of having a king was treated with scepticism. However, political and military expediency made the choosing of a king necessary. Three great kings unified and, in the case of two of them, extended the national borders: first Saul, then David (the greatest king of all, who was also a musician and a poet and who ruled over the kingdom of Israel at the time of its broadest extent) and finally Solomon. It was during David's reign, many modern biblical scholars argue, that the story of Abraham was written down. The boundaries of David's kingdom coincide closely with the land promised by God to Abraham, but it was only for a very short period that Israel actually controlled these territories.

David was at one time held to be the author of many of the psalms which have been recited or sung in Christian churches down the centuries. One of the most significant directly attributed to David was Psalm 23:

> The LORD is my shepherd, I lack nothing.
> He makes me lie down in green pastures,
> he leads me beside quiet waters,
> he refreshes my soul.
> He guides me along the right paths
> for his name's sake.
> Even though I walk
> through the darkest valley,
> I will fear no evil,
> for you are with me;
> your rod and your staff,
> they comfort me.
> You prepare a table before me
> in the presence of my enemies.
> You anoint my head with oil;
> my cup overflows.
> Surely your goodness and love will follow me
> all the days of my life,
> and I will dwell in the house of the LORD
> for ever.

> (Psalm 23:1–6)

This psalm, with its message of trust in God no matter what the outward circumstances might be, represents a wonderful statement about Jewish and Christian faith in the righteousness, power, goodness and mercy of God in spite of all difficulties. However, what God required in return was obedience to God's laws and, above all, acting justly. The prophet Amos was later to express this well when, speaking on behalf of God, he said:

> *I hate, I despise your religious festivals;*
> *your assemblies are a stench to me.*
> *Even though you bring me burnt offerings*
>   *and grain offerings,*
> *I will not accept them.*
> *Though you bring choice fellowship offerings,*
> *I will have no regard for them.*
> *Away with the noise of your songs!*
> *I will not listen to the music of your harps.*
> *But let justice roll on like a river,*
> *righteousness like a never-failing stream!*
>
> (Amos 5:21–24)

Failure to act justly or to obey God's commands were seen as breaches of the covenant relationship with God and, when these happened, the people of Israel saw disasters, oppression and persecution as a direct result.

The choice of a king was not considered a matter of expediency nor did the most powerful necessarily come to power. The decision was God's and the choice often unlikely and improbable beginning with the first king, Saul, chosen by Samuel, one of God's prophets, to whom the Word of God had come. Saul was in many ways a good king but he grew increasingly self-centred and no longer placed God and God's commands at the centre of the life of the nation. He became increasingly jealous of a young boy, David, who slew in individual combat one of the most powerful champions of a neighbouring tribe with whom the people of Israel were at war – Goliath. David developed into a brave and fearless soldier and was the closest friend Saul's son, Jonathan. He was good looking, young, a fine musician and ordinary people looked to him in admiration.

Saul's anger grew and eventually open enmity broke out between King Saul and David, by now one of his strongest generals. David had to flee for his life. Eventually Saul died by the intervention of God and David took over. This whole saga is recounted in the Hebrew Scriptures in very human terms, but God's hand lies behind the whole of history and King David was to become the greatest of all the kings of Israel.

When he was young, David was a mere shepherd boy with no lineage or power base, and yet it was he who was chosen by God to succeed Saul. It is important to understand that Israel did not see themselves as simply another state who happened to worship God. God was at the centre of their whole life and self-understanding. The debate over whether or not to have a king, and even which king to choose, was always couched in theological terms. David did not feel that he was worthy to build a temple for God and this task fell to Solomon, David's son. Solomon was revered for his wisdom and wealth but lost some of his father David's kingdom, and from then on the State of Israel began to contract, splitting into two to form a northern kingdom and a southern kingdom. All the time, the Scriptures see God's hand behind these developments and God, through the prophets who spoke in God's name, directing the people and maintaining unity in the face of constant outside threats.

King Solomon had many wives and many of these were not Israelites; the problem was not multiple wives but that these wives brought with them worship of foreign gods. This practice continued and increased after Solomon's death and, under King Ahab, the worship of the God of Israel almost disappeared or, at the least, was under grave threat. There were few genuine prophets left, but there was Elijah, one of the greatest of all the prophets. King Ahab had married a foreign wife, Jezebel, who had extended the worship of foreign gods into Israel. There were over 400 priests of this new god, Baal, and the God of Israel was increasingly ignored.

Elijah had to flee for his life because the priests of the other gods wanted to destroy him. God eventually came to Elijah and told him to stand on the mountainside. First a great wind came that tore at the mountains – but the Lord was not in the wind. Then came an enormous earthquake – but the Lord was not in the earthquake. Then came a great fire – but the Lord was not in the fire. Finally, there was a still small voice asking Elijah, 'What are you doing here?' Alone, hungry, and isolated, Elijah felt that everything was hopeless. He replied:

> *I have been very zealous for the* Lord *God Almighty. The Israelites have rejected your covenant, torn down your altars, and put your prophets to death with the sword. I am the only one left, and now they are trying to kill me too.*
>
> (1 Kings 19:14)

Effectively the people of Israel had abandoned their God and Elijah was hiding in fear of being murdered. All hope seemed to have vanished, as is often the case in the long history of the people of Israel. God told Elijah to anoint two new kings, whom God names, and a new era begins. This is a pattern that runs throughout Israel's history. Israel ignores God and seems to abandon worship and obedience entirely, but a small remnant remains faithful and rekindles once more worship and praise of the one true God.

Elijah issued a challenge to the priests of Jezebel's god: Elijah and they would each take a bull and make an altar. Then the priests of Jezebel's god were to call down fire from heaven by calling on their god. This they did, dancing round the sacrifice all day and cutting themselves whilst praying – but nothing happened. Elijah mocked them, saying, *'Shout louder! . . . Surely he is a god! Perhaps he is deep in thought, or busy, or travelling. Maybe he is sleeping and must be awakened'* (1 Kings 18:27), but still there was no response. Finally, Elijah came forward to the altar he had built. He had water poured over his sacrifice and then called to the God of Abraham, Isaac and Jacob. Fire descended from heaven and the sacrifice was consumed. Elijah had all the priests of the foreign god put to death. Jezebel was furious and vowed to kill Elijah. However, it was Jezebel who died and her body was fed to the dogs. The worship of one God was reintroduced across Israel.

After the death of Solomon there were a series of ineffective kings and Israel, now divided into two kingdoms, gradually became weaker and weaker. Warfare with neighbouring tribes or countries, as well as warfare between different leaders, was almost constant and the people of Israel saw themselves depending on their God for their protection. The weakness of Israel compared to the increasingly powerful neighbours that surrounded them was to culminate in possibly the most catastrophic event in Israel's history – the destruction of Jerusalem by the Babylonians. Jeremiah was another one of the greatest prophets in Israel's history. He called the people of Israel back to loyalty to God and to placing God at the centre of their lives, but the people did not listen. Like many of the prophets, he was ignored and scorned and felt his own life under threat. God's Word, however, was commanding. He had to prophesy in front of the king, and the prophecy was uncomfortable, speaking truth to power is always likely to lead to opposition! He foretold the destruction of Jerusalem, the enslavement of the people of Israel and the death of the king. Not surprisingly, hardly anyone believed him. Jeremiah had no doubt that the prophecy would come true but he also had hope for the future. He bought a field to show his confidence that, one day, the people of Israel would be able to return after the destruction that he had foretold as imminent.

The Hebrew Scriptures see the Babylonians as agents of God punishing the people of Israel for their wickedness. The Israelites lost everything. Their identity was founded on three things: Temple, King and Land. All these were destroyed: the King was killed, the Temple was pulled down and the leading figures among the people of Israel were taken off into captivity. It should have been the end of the Israelites: one more little nation vanquished by a regional power and disappearing from the pages of history. That they did not do so was due to their faith in God and also the memory of their previous exile in Egypt. They maintained their identity in Babylon by seeing themselves as being in exile from their homeland. They showed loyalty and service to the Babylonian state but insisted on maintaining their religious identity, not intermarrying and above all maintaining their faith that God would deliver them and bring them back to their homeland. What was even more important was that they came to a startling new understanding of their relationship with God; being faithful to God did not depend on having a temple, or a king, or occupying a particular piece of land. It depended, rather, on inner loyalty to the covenant established between God and the people of Israel. They would not eat pork or work on the Sabbath (the seventh day of the week in the Jewish calendar, which God had commanded as a rest day); they would circumcise their male children; and they would obey the Torah (the first five books of what Christians regard as the Hebrew Scriptures). Above all they would not worship other gods, and the Hebrew Scriptures tell stories of the incredible bravery of people going to hideous deaths rather than break God's commands. The startling and new idea that it was loyalty to the covenant with God, and to God's commands, that was of central importance rather than worship in a particular building eventually made it possible for Jewish communities to flourish in any society, maintaining their identity and religious practices and yet otherwise being loyal to the state.

Eventually, after many years in Babylon, the Israelites were allowed to return and immediately started building the walls around Jerusalem and also rebuilding the Temple. In spite of their realisation whilst in Babylon that land and Temple were not essential, these ideas were, and are, deeply rooted in the Jewish psyche and returning to their homeland was a powerful symbol. In the centuries that followed, the armies of a number of empires swept over the small land of Palestine, and Israel did not regain full independence although still the dream remained. The conquering armies tried many ways to stamp out and destroy Jewish practices, identity and worship but none of them succeeded. Jewish armies were raised and destroyed and the inexorable forces of the mightiest armies of the world crushed whatever military power Israel managed to assemble. In the process tens of thousands of young men from Israel died convinced that they were fighting for their God and that God would deliver them. All these empires had conquered, destroyed and absorbed many local peoples but the identity of the people of Israel remained intact. The latest empire to control Palestine was that of Rome and it was, therefore, under the control of the Roman imperial power when Jesus was growing up.

In the time of Jesus there were Zealots who dreamed of freedom from Rome and establishing a new, independent kingdom of Israel. They looked back to the great glory days of King David and believed that God would be on their side in an attempt to drive out the Roman occupying power. It was a foolish dream but similar foolish dreams had come to fruition before and many Jews, either secretly or not, thought back to the old days. They resented the presence of the Romans as a heathen occupying power and thought that a great leader might emerge, a new Messiah, a 'son of David' (their greatest king and military leader) or saviour of the people who would be a mighty warrior and would lead the people of Israel to independence in their own country.

Jesus, then, grew up with all these folk memories, with knowledge of the history of Israel, within a society confident in its superiority as a people chosen by God but also oppressed and powerless on the periphery of a great empire. It may seem strange to start a book on understanding Christianity with so much attention to the history of the Jewish people, but Jesus was a Jew and all Jesus' initial followers were Jews. The Hebrew Scriptures and the story of 'salvation history' – God working God's purposes out throughout the history of the Jewish people, culminating in the incarnation of Jesus – are central to any real understanding of the nature of Christianity. Jesus is held to be the hinge of history, the fulcrum point on which world history turns, since Christians believe that it is in Jesus that God fully reveals God's self to human beings, it is in Jesus that all people are opened to the love and forgiveness of God, and it is in Jesus that God becomes incarnate and comes to earth in human form.

The Life of Jesus

Recounting the 'Life of Jesus' is far from straightforward and takes us to the heart of the difficulty in trying to give an account of 'What is Christianity?' today. There are four Gospels in the Christian New Testament (the word 'gospel' means good news). They are named Matthew, Mark, Luke and John and for more than 1,500 years Christians believed that these were the names of the authors of the different Gospels. Today, as we shall discover, this is seen to be highly problematic.

The Gospels include various accounts; there are accounts of Jesus' birth; a few stories of events immediately following His birth; records of His ministry and death; and one description of an event when He would have been about twelve years old. However, Christians are divided as to the status to give to these narratives. Some would insist that they are literally true (even though there are differences between them) and others would see them as conveying central truths about Jesus but also making significant theological points, whilst still others maintain that there is very little that we can know for certain about Jesus' life. There is a wide diversity of views.

Whilst there may be disagreement among Christians about the details of Jesus' life, there is almost no doubt at all among historians that He existed. The evidence in favour of the life of Jesus of Nazareth is actually much stronger than for most historical figures. The evidence of His message is also very strong – but the details of His life are subject to more disagreement.

Christians used to see the four Gospel books as written by four separate figures but, as will become clear later (see Chapter 10), the Gospels of Matthew and Luke contain all of Mark's Gospel and also have other material in common. Matthew, Mark and Luke are referred to as the 'Synoptic Gospels'. The Gospel of John is rather different and is generally considered to have been written later (see pp. 130–2). The Synoptic Gospels were written as historical accounts of the life, death and resurrection of Jesus Christ. Events are described, sayings are recorded and Jesus' teachings are shared with the world. The authors of the Synoptic Gospels wanted to show that Jesus was the Messiah of Jewish expectation and to show how He lived among people on earth. They wanted to show that Jesus fulfilled all the prophecies in the Hebrew Scriptures. The nature of these prophecies is disputed among scholars but there is no doubt that the people of Israel expected a deliverer to be sent. The general expectation was of a great warrior who would drive out the occupying power and restore the independence of Israel as well as the Davidic kingdom. The Messiah that the Gospels portray was very different indeed from this and they show that Jesus challenged Jewish expectations. The Messiah was not to be a great warrior but God Himself who came from heaven to show human beings how to live, to deliver them from sin and to establish a new 'kingdom of God' in the world that was not based on military might or an independent Jewish state but was instead a kingdom of love and commitment to God founded in the hearts and minds of Jesus' followers.

The Gospel of John is in a different category. It shows the divinity of Jesus and, in particular, that Jesus represented the coming of God as a human being into the world (God becoming incarnate). Jesus is shown as the culmination of a divine plan for the whole of creation. The Gospel of John is regarded by most scholars as much more theological and possibly, therefore, less historical. Almost all scholars agree that it was written much later than the other three Gospels, perhaps around AD 90–120 (Jesus died about AD 33). However, there are dissenting voices to this view and some, such as the late J. A. T. Robinson, argued for a much earlier dating. The general assumption is that a more theological gospel would be dated later, but this is not necessarily the case. Some of the earliest Christian documents are letters or epistles written by the apostle Paul, and these are also highly theological. However, the general academic consensus is for a later dating.

Because of disagreements about the historicity of the accounts of Jesus' life, giving a summary of it is not at all easy. There is no single view in Christianity about Jesus' life. All we have are the accounts in the Gospels and the stories passed down and accepted by Christians over the centuries. How historically accurate they are is almost impossible to determine. This might seem to imply that nothing can be known with any degree of confidence about Jesus, but this is not the case. In the next chapter, when Jesus' message is outlined, this will become clear. For the moment, however, some account needs to be given of Jesus' life and this will be done by reference to the stories in the Gospels.

In the Hebrew Scriptures, Isaiah 9:6–7 records that God will send someone who would reign on the throne of David and would be a 'Mighty God' and 'Everlasting Father'. Christians see this as pointing to the life of Jesus.

The Gospels record Jesus as being born of a young girl called Mary who was engaged to a man named Joseph. Joseph was of the tribe of Benjamin and could trace his descent back to King David (something that Matthew's Gospel spells out in detail). However, Joseph is not recorded in the Gospels as the natural father of Jesus. Luke's Gospel records an angel telling Mary that God had chosen her to bear a son even though she had not slept with a man (this event is called the Annunciation). This

Figure 1: This picture by Henry Tanner (1898) is of the Annunciation. Mary is shown sitting on a bed and the angel appears not as a human form but as a pillar of light.

was before she and Joseph had got married, while Mary was still a virgin. The father of Jesus is seen not to be a human being but God. Jesus, Christians believe, is the Son of God. (Although this phrase was also used of the great kings of Israel such as David, for Christians it means much more than this: that God became human in Jesus.) Christians tend to praise Mary because of her faithful obedience to the command of God and see her as the crucial female example of obedience and loving service to God as well as the ideal mother. It is significant that in Islam Mary is also revered as the mother of Jesus and that Mary was also a virgin. God, in Islam, is held to have conceived Jesus in Mary's womb rather like God created Adam at the beginning of the creation story. There is much in common between Christians and Muslims in the reverence they accord to Mary, but Muslims would claim that Jesus is one of the leading prophets and not, as Christians claim, the incarnation of God's Word.

The engaged couple, Mary and Joseph, were travelling to Bethlehem in response to a requirement by the Roman governor that everyone should return to their ancestral town to complete a census, when Mary went into labour. The inns were all full and, according to Luke, the birth took place in a stable (although in the Eastern Orthodox Christian tradition the birth is held to have taken place in a cave). This is portrayed as an extraordinary and pivotal event, with shepherds in the hills being visited by an angel to tell them of the birth, while Matthew's Gospel has wise philosophers or astrologers from the East following an extraordinary star which led them to the house where the infant Jesus lay. Even King Herod, the vassal king who governed Israel under the Romans, was recorded as having a dream that 'the king of the Jews' had been born. Fearing for his crown, Herod sent out an order that all babies under two years old should be killed to ensure that no future king survived. Matthew's Gospel records Jesus' parents, having been warned in a dream about the danger, fleeing to Egypt and then coming back out of Egypt. This enabled Christians to argue that Jesus should be seen as the new Moses who had been prophesied to come out of Egypt to deliver his people from slavery (Deuteronomy 18:15–18).

There is no record of Jesus' childhood except for one short scene (Luke 2:41–51) when His parents took Him to the Temple in Jerusalem. Surrounded by the huge crowds, He became lost and Mary and Joseph searched for Him. They eventually found Him talking to the wisest rabbis and impressing them with His depth of understanding. The young boy Jesus, when confronted by His concerned parents, expressed surprise and asked them why they did not expect Him to be about His Father's business (clearly indicating that His father was not Joseph but God).

A tradition grew up among the early Christian Church that Mary remained a virgin and never slept with Joseph even after the birth of Jesus. There is no textual evidence for this and it was a belief intended to show Mary's purity. The Gospels record Jesus having brothers but mainstream Christians who support the perpetual virginity of Mary say that this refers to spiritual brothers, or else they were children of Joseph from a former marriage, and that Mary had no children apart from Jesus.

Jesus' actual ministry lasted either one or three years (the Gospels differ). What is clear is that He gathered a disparate group of close friends, followers or disciples around Him. They were outsiders to the world of power and influence – a tax collector, fishermen – ordinary people whom He called to give up everything and to follow Him, which they did willingly. He was clearly a charismatic person and His message of God's love and forgiveness had huge appeal. Jesus' ministry started with His baptism in the River Jordan (which meant immersion in the waters of the river as a symbol of being cleansed from sin and a new beginning) by an extraordinary man who was about the same age as Jesus. John the Baptist had spent years in the desert wilderness fasting and living very simply and calling for a renewal of commitment to God, demanding that people give up their complacent lives and live in a different way. He also prophesied the coming of the Messiah or Saviour. Jesus went to John for baptism and, in one of the most significant moments recorded in the Gospels, John recognises Jesus and declines to baptise Him because he considers that it is Jesus who should baptise him, not the other way round. John understands that this is the person about whom he has been prophesying and does not consider himself worthy to carry out the baptism. Jesus insists and, in a key moment, the heavens are recorded as opening; a dove descends on Jesus whilst God's voice proclaims, *'This is my Son, whom I love; with him I am well pleased'* (Matthew 3:17). The dove would have reminded readers of the Gospels of the dove sent out from the Ark by Noah to find dry land when the whole of the known world was engulfed in flood water. In Christian theology, the dove has come to symbolise both peace and the Holy Spirit which God sent down on Jesus at His baptism, just as believers are later meant to receive the same Spirit at their baptism. The role of the Holy Spirit and its significance will be made clear later.

Baptism was not just a crucial event in Jesus' life; it was also a central command by Jesus recorded in the Gospels. He sent His disciples out to live simply among people, to preach the good news that He came to bring (the word 'gospel', as we have seen, means good news) and also to baptise people. Matthew's Gospel records Jesus as saying: *'Therefore go and make disciples of all nations, baptising them in the name of the Father and of the Son and of the Holy Spirit'* (Matthew 28:19). The practice of baptism therefore became central for all Christians; this is the moment when the Spirit of God is believed to fall on the baptised person and make the individual fully part of the Christian community. The Christian practice of baptism varies. Many churches have infant baptism when the child is baptised as a baby and welcomed into the Church. Vows to renounce evil and to commit to God are taken on behalf of the baby by the parents and 'godparents' (these are two or three people who promise to help take care of the spiritual upbringing of the child, although in many parts of the world this spiritual side of the godparents' role has become peripheral). Some Christians, however, hold that baptism should be delayed until a person can make the promises to renounce evil and to hold fast to Christ for themselves, whilst others practise 'full immersion' baptism; instead of a few drops of water being sprinkled on the person to be baptised, they are immersed completely in water in the way that Jesus would probably have been baptised in the River Jordan. For most Christians, baptism is the mark of the formal entry of a person into the Christian community.

Figure 2: This picture is full of symbolism. Jesus stands where the river Jordan ends, symbolising the end of the old covenant and the beginning of the new. He is baptised by John. On the left three figures represent the Trinity, the middle of which (God the Son) looks apprehensively at the scene; He knows it will end in His death (a sepulchre is in the distance). Behind, this a man strips off, ready to be baptised. His colouring is the same as Jesus', indicating all Christians share in Jesus' baptism. The overhanging tree represents the love of the Father, the dove represents the Holy Spirit and Jesus Himself represents the Son. The prickly trees in the background represent the Pharisees who pass disapprovingly in the middle distance.

The Gospels record Jesus going into the desert wilderness to be alone and to pray. For instance: *'Very early in the morning, while it was still dark, Jesus got up, left the house and went off to a solitary place, where he prayed'* (Mark 1:35).

During one of these times of solitary prayer and contemplation He faced severe temptations and tests. The possibility of taking alternative paths in life was very real and these temptations came to Him with great force and attractiveness. He is shown as being tempted by the devil and, again, Christians differ as to how this is to be understood, some believing the story should be taken literally and others holding that it is a metaphor for Jesus wrestling with real internal temptations. The existence of the devil, an angel who disobeyed God and rose in rebellion against God, is taken for granted in the New Testament and by many Christians who see the world as a battleground between God and the devil. However, all agree that the devil is subject to God and will eventually be defeated by God. Indeed Jesus Himself, in resisting temptation and dying for all human beings, is seen to have defeated the power of the devil even though his influence still continues and needs to be resisted. What is clear is that Jesus' commitment to God from the youngest age was overwhelming and He was able to resist temptation and, Christians have traditionally held, was able to remain free from sin.

Jesus then embarked on His ministry which, as we have seen, lasted one to three years. He had no settled home, did not marry and depended on the generosity of women and others who supported Him and His followers. Women played a vital part in His ministry and were some of His closest friends. Jesus remained all His life within a fairly narrow area of Palestine, teaching and talking to people and showing them, through stories or parables, the nature of God's love and of God's coming kingdom even if, as we shall see, this love and this promised kingdom were very different from those people's expectations.

Initially it appears that Jesus preached only to Jews and saw His message as concerning only them, but He came to realise that the message He had to bring was universal. There is an important point here that divides Christians. Some Christians, influenced particularly by the Gospel of John, see Jesus as always being aware of His divine nature and always preaching both to Jews and Gentiles. However, many mainstream Christians see Jesus' teaching as developing over time and Him coming to realise that God's message was for all human beings and not simply the Jews.

One of the most extraordinary and well attested aspects of Jesus' life was that He mixed with everyone; and for a Jew this was really surprising. Devout, God-fearing Jews kept themselves to themselves. They had nothing to do with the Romans unless this was strictly necessary; they did not mix with Samaritans (the group of Jews descended from those who remained behind in Israel after the Babylonian captivity and who were despised by mainstream Jews); they looked down on those who collected taxes for the Romans; they despised those who did not keep to the strict purity rules laid down in the Hebrew Scriptures; they tended not to talk to or mix with women outside their families and certainly would not be touched by them; they considered that women were impure during their periods and should keep to their houses; and they condemned and despised those who committed ethical failings such as adultery. Jesus, by contrast, kept company with all kinds of people; he talked to Romans and Samaritans; women were His constant companions; a devout woman massaged His feet and wiped away her tears from them with her hair (a very intimate thing to do); a former tax collector was one of His closest friends; and He was most critical of all of those who thought themselves holy and 'good'. He seemed to find God more readily in those who were outcasts from respectable society than in the wealthy and those whom others considered to be righteous and good. It was not surprising that He became both exceedingly popular with ordinary people and exceedingly unpopular with the priests and those in power and authority.

In many ways Jesus was a scandalous figure, an outsider who challenged the complacency of the supposedly religious society in which He lived and who had little time for those who were pleased with themselves because they had 'kept the rules' and were convinced that this made them righteous in God's eyes. He was, at one level, a simple person because His message could be understood by everyone, whatever their background, but He was also expressing the most profound theological truths with a simplicity that no one has ever achieved before or since. Nevertheless, many Jews today would see the essential nature of Jesus' teaching as being entirely in accordance with the best rabbinic teaching tradition.

In the next chapter we will look at the message that Jesus came to bring although, in many ways, Jesus' life and message are inseparable. He preached about the love of God and the need for forgiveness and drew huge crowds. He ate in different people's houses, attended weddings and was in the middle of life in first-century Palestine. His reputation and fame grew as well as His ability to perform the most extraordinary miracles: healing people of many diseases including leprosy; restoring sight to people who were blind; enabling people who were paralysed to walk; curing a woman with a permanent period; turning water into wine; walking on water; and raising someone from the dead. Jesus never performed miracles to prove His power but always out of compassion and, in a number of cases, told the people who had been cured to say nothing about what had been done (Christians hold that the Hebrew Scriptures prophesied that the Messiah would perform miracles; see Isaiah 35:4–6). Nevertheless, as His fame spread He was constantly surrounded by thousands of people who wanted to listen to Him, and He felt physically tired and drained. He also knew that His growing reputation, as well as His message, was unacceptable to the Jewish authorities. His attacks on the priests and those in positions of wealth and influence were popular amongst ordinary people but were unacceptable to those He spoke out against who, it must be said, had a hard task maintaining Jewish religious freedom in the face of the might of the occupying power of Rome.

Shortly before His death, Jesus went to Jerusalem to the Temple with thousands of people around Him shouting His name. It was a triumphal procession with people cutting down palms from the trees along the route to lay in front of Him. He rode on a donkey which, for a pious Jew, had a symbolism drawn from the Hebrew Scriptures (Zechariah 9:9) and was an effective way of proclaiming that He was the promised Messiah, as it had been prophesied that this was what the Messiah would do. Jesus knew what He was doing and knew that He had gone too far and that the Temple authorities had to take action. He had become a major cult figure and this threatened the stability of the relationship that the leading Jews had established with the Romans. Whatever Jesus Himself may have taught, He was now perceived as a dangerous rabble-rouser by those in authority, a threat to the established social order and therefore, potentially, a threat to the very existence of the Jewish Temple and the freedom Jews had to worship. If support for Jesus got out of hand, the Romans might crack down and all the hard-won, albeit limited, freedoms that the Jews possessed might be taken away. Their fears were not groundless. Less than forty years later, in AD 70, the Romans utterly destroyed Jerusalem and the Temple, and there was to be no Jewish state until 1948.

Jesus had a last meal with His twelve closest friends in Jerusalem and performed an extraordinary action in washing the feet of His disciples. This would have been a task that a servant of a wealthy man might perform for an important visitor, yet Jesus, the acclaimed prophet and hero of the hour, did this to His disciples. It was an inversion of every normal expectation and challenged, once again, their perceptions of what it meant to be a leader amongst a people dedicated to the service of God.

The Gospels record that, during the last meal with His disciples, one of these friends, Judas, decided to betray Him. It may have been because Judas was disappointed in Jesus and had expected another sort of leader, perhaps one who would lead the people of Israel to military victory over the Romans, or it may have been self-interest. Judas betrayed Jesus to the Temple authorities in return for thirty pieces of silver. The authorities arrested Jesus and placed Him on trial. He was too much of a threat to civil order to be allowed to live, but the Temple leadership did not have the authority to put him to death; this punishment was reserved for the Romans. The High Priest and his followers, therefore, are recorded as taking Him to the Roman procurator, Pontius Pilate, who, after a show trial in which he came to the conclusion that Jesus was innocent, sentenced Him to death. Pilate seems to have acted against his better instincts, but anyone who might purport to be a king would be unacceptable to the Roman Emperor and, therefore, sentencing an insignificant Jew to death probably seemed a politically expedient act. Even then, Pilate tried to let Jesus go free, as it was the custom to allow one prisoner to go free at the time of the main Jewish holiday. Pilate appealed to the crowd, asking them whether they would prefer him to free a robber and thief named Barabbas, or Jesus. Given the popularity of Jesus the week before, and the crowds that surrounded Him, Pilate might well have expected Jesus to be the automatic choice, but the High Priests had got the crowd on their side and their choice fell on Barabbas. Jesus was, therefore, taken off to be crucified.

Figure 3: The crucifixion was a degrading, agonising and humiliating punishment, but Christians see it as their key symbol, representing Jesus sacrificing Himself out of love for all human beings.

Crucifixion was an appalling punishment used routinely by the Romans. The condemned person had to carry their own cross and was then nailed to it (with nails through the wrists and ankles, although medieval art portrays the nails as going through the hands and feet). The cross was then lifted up and it could take up to twenty-four hours for a person to die. The pain was excruciating. Death usually came from asphyxiation, as the person could no longer breathe. In Jesus' case, however, it was necessary that He should die within three hours as the Jewish holy day, the Sabbath, was about to start, so a soldier put a spear into His side to hasten His death. His mother, Mary, was at the foot of the cross as Jesus died, with one of His closest friends, John. After His death, Jesus' body was taken down from the cross and He was placed in a tomb owned by a wealthy follower of His – Joseph of Arimathea.

There is another crucial claim associated with the crucifixion of Jesus which is made by Christians, and that is that human beings are in a state of sin, whether because of the sin of Adam and Eve, which affected the whole of humanity, or by individual sin. This sin distorts and undermines what it means to be a human being and deprives people of the chance to fulfil human potential. What is more, given that God is just, this sin requires punishment. Christians believe that God, through the person of Jesus, takes this sin on Himself; God suffers for every human being and, in so doing, releases

Figure 4: *The statue of Christ the Redeemer towers over Rio de Janeiro in Brazil. The outstretched arms represent the redemption of humankind through the crucifixion.*

people from the effects of sin. It is for this reason that Christians call Jesus both their Saviour, because He saves them from the effects of sin, and also their Redeemer, because He redeems people from their sin and atones for the errors both of every individual and also of humankind as a whole. Protestant Christians often refer to Jesus as their personal Saviour, and this is because they see Jesus suffering and dying on the cross out of love for every human being and taking on Himself the effects of their sin. Jesus makes the ultimate sacrifice out of love for His friends (as Christians feel themselves to be).

The symbol of Christianity became the cross, which was extraordinary as, for the Roman world, crucifixion was seen as the ultimate symbol of degradation. Yet for Christians, it is the triumph of good over evil, of forgiveness over sin, of love over hatred, of life over death. The cross is where the power of God's love is shown most clearly.

Three days after being crucified, Jesus rose from the dead. This, of course, is one of the most important Christian claims and is central to Christian belief, so it needs to be dealt with in more detail in the chapter following the next one, which deals with Jesus' teaching.

FOUR

The Message of Jesus

There is something artificial about separating the message of Jesus from the life of Jesus: the two are so closely related. For the people amongst whom Jesus lived, His life and actions were as important an expression of His message as His teachings. Given that Christians consider that Jesus is God's Word made flesh, it follows that Jesus' life and teaching are equally important. This was particularly the case as He often taught in parables. Parables are stories that are intended to be revelatory. They reveal insights and convey truths but they also reveal something about the people who interpret the parables. Parables seldom have a single meaning.

Jesus stands firmly in the Jewish tradition and many Jews today would be happy to see Jesus as a great rabbi or teacher who affirmed what was central in Judaism. However, there are also key differences. Two of the most important are:

1) Jesus did not see Himself as just another rabbi or teacher. He was clear that He was in a unique relationship with God, which Jews found very hard to accept. He referred to Himself as 'the Son of Man', but the Gospels indicate that this is a way of emphasising the human side of his nature without in any way undermining His unique status as the incarnate Word of God.

2) Jesus was unequivocal in believing in a life after death, and many of His Jewish contemporaries were far less clear about this. In fact, whether there was a life after death was a major point of dispute between two of the most influential groups

of Jews – the Pharisees and the Sadducees. The idea of a life after death had come to prominence in Judaism reasonably late, probably around three centuries before Jesus. Some contemporary scholars see Jewish thinking as having been influenced by the deaths of tens of thousands of young men during what became known as the Maccabean rebellion, which was one of many attempts to achieve independence for Israel after the Babylonian captivity. Given the fidelity of God to God's chosen people, it was felt that the suffering of so many young men could best be explained by a life after death. However, many Jews did not take this position; Judaism has always been a religion anchored firmly in this world rather than the next and concentration on post-mortem survival has always been somewhat peripheral. Jesus, however, proclaimed a life after death and, more than this, emphasised the father-hood of God and God's love for all human beings. The word 'all' here is significant, as it became clear to Jesus during His ministry that life after death and fellowship with God were open to all human beings and not just the Jews. This was a crucial new insight. It is not clear that Jesus always realised this; stories such as Jesus talking to the Samaritan woman (John 4:4–26), or His healing of the servant of a Roman centurion (Luke 7:1–10), seem to indicate that He came to a gradual realisation of the universality of God's love. This was, however, an insight that was already present in some strands of Judaism. For instance, the prophet Jonah was forced to recognise that God was the God of the whole of creation, not just of the chosen people of Israel. Again, Christians will differ here; some will hold that Jesus had perfect knowledge throughout His ministry, so the idea that He 'came to recognise' something would be rejected.

On one occasion Jesus was approached with a very simple question, but one with profound consequences. Matthew and Luke's Gospels record different occasions for the question. In the Gospel of Luke, it is asked by a lawyer (Luke 10:25) and in Matthew by a rich young ruler (Matthew 19:16). The question was universal: 'What must I do to inherit eternal life?' The questioners were probably expecting a simple answer. In Luke's Gospel, Jesus turns the question round and asks the questioner what is written in the Jewish law. The lawyer's reply is succinct:

> *'Love the Lord your God with all your heart and with all your soul and with all your strength and with all your mind';* and, *'Love your neighbour as yourself.'*
>
> (Luke 10:27)

Jesus agrees and tells the lawyer to go away and do this. The first part of the quotation is the Jewish *Shema* which every devout Jew would have recognised, and the second is the Great Commandment or Golden Rule. It seems so simple! The lawyer, being a lawyer, then asks, 'Who is my neighbour?' and Jesus tells the parable of the good Samaritan:

> *'A man was going down from Jerusalem to Jericho, when he was attacked by robbers. They stripped him of his clothes, beat him and went away, leaving him half-dead. A priest happened to be going down the same road, and when he saw the man, he passed by on the other side. So too, a Levite, when he came to the place and saw him, passed by on the other side. But a Samaritan, as he travelled, came where the man was; and when he saw him, he took pity on him. He went to him and bandaged his wounds, pouring on oil and wine. Then he put the man on his own donkey, brought him to an inn and took care of him. The next day he took out two denarii and gave them to the innkeeper. "Look after him,"* he said, *"and when I return, I will reimburse you for any extra expense you may have."*
>
> *'Which of these three do you think was a neighbour to the man who fell into the hands of robbers?'*

> *The expert in the law replied, 'The one who had mercy on him.'*
>
> *Jesus told him, 'Go and do likewise.'*
>
> (Luke 10:30–37)

It is worth noting that the expert on the law replied, '*The one who had mercy on him.*' He could not bring himself to utter the name of the Samaritans, so despised were they by devout Jews, and yet the Samaritan is the hero of Jesus' story. The significance of this is profound. Firstly, Jesus is speaking to a devout Jew who would have regarded Samaritans as pariahs, so making a Samaritan the central figure in the story would be profoundly disturbing. Secondly, the characters who ignored the needs of the injured man were a priest and a Levite. The tribe of Levi was the tribe from whom the priestly class were normally drawn, so, effectively, Jesus is saying that two of the types of people who, in Jewish society, were regarded as most holy and righteous were, in fact, not so. It was the outsider, the Samaritan, who recognised the need of the injured Jewish person. Jesus' message is clear: one's neighbour is anyone who is in need, irrespective of race, skin colour or religious belief. This message was to be central as Christianity became the largest religion in the world. Christianity was not just another Jewish sect; it was a universal religion. Its roots lay in Judaism, but its message of the love of God and its demand to love other human beings was universal.

Jesus emphasised this continually. He frequently taught in stories or parables which are appealing but have multiple meanings and great depth – and can often be uncomfortable. In one of these stories Jesus spoke of the criteria that God would use to decide who would go to heaven and who would go to hell after death. The story challenged his audience but it maintained the same theme that runs through all his teaching:

> *When the Son of Man comes in his glory, and all the angels with him, he will sit on his glorious throne. All the nations*

will be gathered before him, and he will separate the people one from another as a shepherd separates the sheep from the goats. He will put the sheep on his right and the goats on his left.

Then the King will say to those on his right, 'Come, you who are blessed by my Father; take your inheritance, the kingdom prepared for you since the creation of the world. For I was hungry and you gave me something to eat, I was thirsty and you gave me something to drink, I was a stranger and you invited me in, I needed clothes and you clothed me, I was ill and you looked after me, I was in prison and you came to visit me.'

Then the righteous will answer him, 'Lord, when did we see you hungry and feed you, or thirsty and give you something to drink? When did we see you a stranger and invite you in, or needing clothes and clothe you? When did we see you ill or in prison and go to visit you?'

The King will reply, 'Truly I tell you, whatever you did for one of the least of these brothers and sisters of mine, you did for me.'

Then he will say to those on his left, 'Depart from me, you who are cursed, into the eternal fire prepared for the devil and his angels. For I was hungry and you gave me nothing to eat, I was thirsty and you gave me nothing to drink, I was a stranger and you did not invite me in, I needed clothes and you did not clothe me, I was ill and in prison and you did not look after me.'

They also will answer, 'Lord, when did we see you hungry or thirsty or a stranger or needing clothes or ill or in prison, and did not help you?'

He will reply, 'Truly I tell you, whatever you did not do for one of the least of these, you did not do for me.'

Then they will go away to eternal punishment, but the righteous to eternal life.

(Matthew 25:31–46)

This message was (and is) challenging because Jesus is saying that the people who will be welcomed into God's kingdom are the people who visit those in prison or those who are sick, the people who feed the hungry or give water to the thirsty; and the people who are destined for hell are those who fail to do this. What is more, when someone does these positive things to any other human being it is as though they are being done to Jesus Himself, and when someone in need is ignored, it is Jesus who is ignored. This again emphasises the Christian claim that God is intimately involved in the world and that love of any other human being is directly related to love of God.

The message of the universal love of God was not easy for the early Christians to accept and, after Jesus' death, there were many of his original followers who still wanted to see Christianity as merely the development of orthodox Judaism. They considered, therefore, that following Jesus meant becoming a Jew and taking on all the rigorous food laws and religious laws that the people of Israel considered normal. It also meant that males had to be circumcised. This position would have restricted the growth of early Christianity as it would, effectively, have become a Jewish sect. It took divine intervention and the activity of one of the most significant of the apostles – St Paul – to demonstrate that these laws were not necessary.

So the first and most important command which Jesus affirmed was the absolute centrality of the love of God. Secondly came unconditional love of neighbour. The first command every Jew would recognise and accept, but Jesus

Figure 1: *Statue of the Archangel Michael defeating the devil (Coventry Cathedral). Christians hold that it is the power of love that can defeat the forces of evil and that this love was shown most clearly in Jesus' life, teaching and death.*

taught that the second should be taken literally: that is, it did not apply to Jews alone. It also questioned whether those who were thought to be holy were really so.

For Jesus, the love of God for every human being was essential. God was the Father of all human beings and should be addressed in the intimate way that a child addresses a father. God was a God of love, wanting above all what was best for individual human beings. God would always welcome back those who failed, those who did wrong. Jesus told many parables to illustrate this, including the parables of the Prodigal Son, the Lost Coin and the Lost Sheep. For Jesus, God almost cared more for those who were lost than those who were faithful. The person who was a failure and marginalised had more need of God than the person who was always faithful.

It is an issue of trust. Christian teaching is that the Christian should trust their whole life to God and should be willing to accept and believe in God's love and forgiveness. God's love is unconditional; it does not come as a result of a person being virtuous or good. God's love is there, whatever happens, like a parent who will always love a child, no matter what the child does, and simply wants the child to return. In the Parable of the Prodigal Son, Jesus tells the story of a rich man who had two sons, one of whom was obedient, stayed at home and worked hard. The other, however, demanded from the father that the eventual inheritance he could expect should be given to him. He then left home and spent all his father's money on a dissolute life. He ended up destitute and sleeping among the animals. In despair, he decided to go back to his father, recognising that it would be better to be one of his father's lowest servants than to go on living as he had been doing. When he returned, the father ran to greet him, put on him the choicest clothes and laid on a great feast for him. This was not because he had done anything good – he had not; but simply because he had returned home. The other son resented this because he had spent all his life being loyal and working hard, yet his father had never laid on a similar feast for him. Jesus explained that God loves those who have failed, those who have ignored God and yet come back, almost more than those who never need forgiveness. It is not, however, easy to accept being loved unconditionally and many reject God because they simply cannot accept that God loves them as they are. Trust in this love is, therefore, a central element of Christian belief.

Figure 2: Rembrandt's painting of the Prodigal Son (c. 1669) shows the father welcoming back his penitent son. One of the hands of the father is male, the other female. The poverty of the returning son is shown in his clothes and also in him only having one shoe. Jesus referred to God as Abba (Mark 14:36) – a very intimate term similar to 'Daddy' today. God is seen as the Father of all who wants nothing more than to welcome people back, however far they may have strayed in terms of selfishness and love-lessness.

What is more, Jesus taught that Christians should refuse to judge others. Only God could truly see into the heart of another human being. Only God could judge justly. If any Christian judged others, then he or she would be judged harshly by God. If Christians forgave others, they would be forgiven by God. One man asked Jesus how many times he should forgive his brother – seven times? Jesus said, *'I tell you, not seven times, but seventy-seven times'* (Matthew 18:22). In other words, Christians should act towards each other as God acted towards them and should be willing to forgive again and again – and yet again.

Jesus was absolutely clear that the way Christians behaved towards other human beings would determine the way God behaved towards them. God would judge a person by the innermost nature of their heart and not by appearances. Jesus therefore condemned those who would make a display of their religious observances. If people were fasting, He said that they should disguise the fact; if people gave to charity, they should do so anonymously. If the real motive for doing good was in order to be recognised by other people, then the good actions were actually just self-centred (Matthew 6:1–4). Jesus said that people should do acts of kindness without others knowing; God sees into the hearts of everyone and will reward those who do good and punish those who do evil. Jesus was clear that God knows everything: not even a sparrow dies without God knowing about it. Humans are worth more than many sparrows and all human actions are seen by God and judged accordingly (Matthew 10:29–30).

Jesus was, however, clear that God's love was a demanding love. God had to be placed at the centre of a person's life and the love of God had to be shown in action. There was no room for complacency, and the idea of trusting in the love of God and ignoring the need for practical action runs contrary to Jesus' message. Jesus specifically warned of a rich man who decided to take life easy and enjoy his wealth: that very night his soul 'was demanded from him' (Luke 12:16–21). In other words he died and had to face God and account for his life. Anyone who ignores those in need, or the demand for practical action to relieve suffering, effectively ignores God. Words without action are empty.

The one category of people that Jesus did condemn was those who deliberately ignored God or pretended to be devoting their lives to God when they were not. He utterly condemned the priests and religious leaders who were so proud of their own reputation as holy and good people but, inside, were self-centred and corrupt. His language about these people was anything but temperate (Matthew 12:34–37). The one incident that the Gospels record when Jesus seemed to have lost His temper was when He went into the Temple in Jerusalem and found it filled with merchants selling things and people who changed money. He was angry that they had turned what should have been a house of prayer to God into, as He termed it, a den of robbers. He took out a whip and physically attacked the merchants. His anger was greater because He is recorded as calling the Temple 'my Father's house' (John 2:13–17) referring, of course, to the Christian claim that Jesus was the Son of God and not the son of any human father. Instead of a place of holiness and devotion to God, the Temple had become something very different. The extent, therefore, to which Jesus would have been seen as a scandalous and uncomfortable figure by those with money and power is hard to over-emphasise.

For Jesus, prayer should be at the centre of a person's life. Prayer was like talking to a close friend and Christians should bring all their concerns to God. His disciples asked Him to teach them to pray, and the Gospels record what has become the most famous prayer for Christians, called 'The Lord's Prayer':

> *Our Father in heaven,*
> *hallowed be your name,*
> *your kingdom come,*
> *your will be done,*
> *on earth as it is in heaven.*
> *Give us today our daily bread.*
> *And forgive us our debts,*
> *as we also have forgiven our debtors.*
> *And lead us not into temptation,*
> *but deliver us from the evil one.*

(Matthew 6:9–13)

The word 'Amen' is generally added at the end of Christian prayers and means 'so be it'. It is used at the end of all prayers, even prayers said by the priest or leader of worship, and links those participating with the prayer. It is important to note that Christians ask to be forgiven by God in the same way they forgive others; in other words, if they do not forgive others, God will not forgive them.

If God is truly at the centre of a person's life, then all the things that normally preoccupy people will assume lesser importance. When Jesus' called His first disciples He called them to leave everything behind: friends, family and possessions. Disciples are required to put God centre stage in their lives and, if this is done, then money, reputation, sex, appearance and all those things that most people value so highly will be seen in their proper perspective. This does not mean that they are irrelevant, just that once a person seeks to devote their life to God, these other things can only ever be of peripheral importance. It is not possible to serve both God and worldly desires and interests.

Jesus preached the coming of the kingdom of heaven, but this was not what the people amongst whom He was living expected. He did not preach a new Davidic kingdom which would throw out the Romans and establish Jerusalem as the seat of a new Jewish government. The kingdom that Jesus proclaimed was a kingdom in people's hearts. This was in some ways a radical and new idea, although the basis for it lay in the Hebrew Scriptures and the teaching of the prophets. Bringing people to see this new understanding of God's kingdom was not easy; it was not the message that people wanted to hear.

Jesus realised that His message would not be readily received. He likened it to a farmer who was scattering seed: some of it fell on stony ground and withered almost as soon as it germinated; other seed fell on poor ground and sprang up but had no roots and died; whilst still other seed fell on good ground (Matthew 13:3–9). Similarly, the message of Christianity would not be well received by many; some would either ignore it or else take it on board with enthusiasm, but abandon it as soon as doubts or difficulties came along. Jesus never expected that His message would be accepted by everyone, nor that it would be popular. He said that following Him would involve pain and suffering, misunderstanding and rejection, and it would be hard (Matthew 10:17–18, 38–39). On one occasion He said that it was easier for a camel to go through the eye of a needle than for a rich man to enter the kingdom of heaven (this is a reference to a very narrow gate into the walled city of Jerusalem which a loaded camel would have been unable to enter) (Mark 10:23–25). Someone with wealth and possessions will find that his or her heart is anchored in these and it will be almost impossible to centre life on God. Jesus said if money or power or reputation is really important to a person, then this is where their heart will be.

Jesus found the greatest faith in people who were on the outside of conventional society: a poor widow who had almost no money but gave a few coins which, for her, represented a great deal; a

Roman centurion who trusted Jesus' power to heal and accepted that, when Jesus spoke, his servant would be healed even though the servant was a long distance away; a woman caught in adultery who trusted Jesus even though everyone else condemned her; another woman who wept for her sins; blind beggars, lepers who were despised and outcasts – these were Jesus' followers initially.

The rabbis and teachers of Jesus' time had built up a set of rules that regulated every aspect of the life of a devout Jew, and for many of these people keeping the rules had become an end in itself. The Pharisees in particular considered that devotion to God could be measured by the extent to which one kept the rules. Jesus cut through this and taught that what mattered was the change within the heart of a person, not whether they kept the rules. For instance, He and His disciples were criticised because, when crossing a cornfield on the Jewish holy day (the Sabbath) they ate a few ears of corn. This broke the rules, as picking corn was considered to be work and work was not allowed on the Sabbath. Jesus' critics said that Jesus' failure to condemn His disciples meant that He was not a devout Jew (Luke 6:1–5). On another occasion, He failed to wash before a meal and He was criticised because this was one of the strict rules that a Jew had to follow. He talked to people who were regarded as sinners and outcasts, something that no pious Jew would do. He touched a leper, which was condemned by the Jewish law. He healed a person on the Jewish holy day and this was also condemned (Luke 6:6–11). The teachers of His time were continually trying to trap Him and to show that He was not really a faithful Jew at all, still less a prophet. On one occasion they brought to Him a woman who had been caught in the act of adultery. The punishment according to the Jewish law was clear: she had to be stoned to death. His critics thought that they had him in a trap – either He had to forgive her and show that He rejected the Jewish law and was not a genuine prophet at all, or He had to condemn her and all His talk of forgiveness would be undermined. Jesus' response was simple. He said that whoever had never committed a sin should throw the first stone. Clearly no one was in this position, so they all went away and left Him with the woman. Jesus did not condemn her; He merely said gently, *'Go now and leave your life of sin'* (John 8:3–11). Gentleness and yet a firm devotion to God was at the heart of all Jesus did, and this message shone through in a way that the teaching of the priests and law-givers of the time did not.

Whereas most Jews of the time were angry with the Romans, Jesus treated those Romans He met with compassion and understanding. On one occasion an attempt was made to trick Him by asking whether Jews should pay taxes to Rome (Luke 20:20–26). Again, whichever answer He gave would seem to land Him in trouble. If He said that taxes should be paid, then He would not be seen as a devout Jew, as Jews bitterly resented the Roman taxes, so He would become unpopular. If He said that taxes should not be paid, then He would have been arrested by the Roman authorities. It seemed He could not win. His answer was simple. He asked for a coin to be shown to Him and then asked whose head was on it. 'Caesar's,' was the answer; He simply said, *'Then give back to Caesar what is Caesar's, and to God what is God's.'* In other words, what mattered was not the issue of taxes but where the hearts of people really were. Many were so preoccupied with money and material things that God had been altogether forgotten.

Jesus was in no doubt that the way a person lived would determine what happened after death, and He was also in no doubt that there was a separation between heaven and hell. The punishments in hell were severe. In one case Jesus told the story of a rich man who went to hell and a poor man, Lazarus, who used to sit at the gate of the rich man and beg, and who after death went to heaven (Luke 16:19–31). The rich man pleaded for mercy or, at least, that Lazarus could be sent to his living relatives to warn them. Jesus said that no move was possible from hell to heaven and that sending someone who had died to the living relatives would not achieve anything. If they did not believe the Jewish prophets, they would not even believe if someone rose from the dead (a poignant look forward to His own resurrection).

We have already seen that at the baptism of Jesus the Holy Spirit descended on Him in the form of a dove. The role of the Holy Spirit is vital in Christianity; it is seen as the Spirit of God in God's self which strengthens, comforts and, in some cases, guides Christians. Jesus said to His disciples that when He died He would not leave them alone, as the Holy Spirit would remain with them. The Holy Spirit, Jesus and God in God's self are one in Christianity; this gives rise to one of the most important of all Christian doctrines. This is that God is Trinitarian. God is one, but God is also Three. Father, Son and Holy Spirit are the three persons of the undivided Trinity with no separation between them. It cannot be emphasised strongly enough that this does *not* mean that there are three gods, as some critics were to later maintain. Christianity is firmly committed to both the unity of God and to God's essentially Trinitarian nature. This is, Christians accept, a mystery, but it is a mystery that is at the heart of Christian faith. The Trinitarian doctrine means that when the Holy Spirit comes to a Christian this is the same as God in God's self. Fifty days after Jesus' death, at what has become called Pentecost, the Holy Spirit came directly to Jesus' followers when they were gathered together. The presence of the Holy Spirit provides, therefore, the guarantee that God is with them always in a very personal way.

Figure 3: Andrei Rublev's extraordinary icon of the Old Testament Trinity, depicting the three visitors who came to Abraham (Genesis 18:1–15), shows God as three persons – Father, Son and Holy Spirit – sitting at a table with a fourth place set for the viewer. The chalice (the cup used for wine in Catholic and many other Christian services) symbolises the Eucharist or Mass in which Christians participate. The figures are not looking at each other but form a circle to include the viewer.

Towards the end of His ministry, Jesus sent His followers out with a command to spread the good news (the Gospel) which He had come to deliver. He is recorded as saying:

Therefore go and make disciples of all nations, baptising them in the name of the Father and of the Son and of the Holy Spirit, and teaching them to obey everything I have commanded you. And surely I am with you always, to the very end of the age.
(Matthew 28:19–20)

As we saw in the last chapter, just before He died Jesus shared a meal with His twelve closest friends. This has become known as the Last Supper. At this meal Jesus took bread and broke it and shared the pieces amongst His disciples; however, He also said words that were to have a decisive impact on future Christian practice: *'This is my body given for you; do this in remembrance of me'* (Luke 22:19). Then He took wine and when He had given thanks He again shared this with His disciples, saying, *'This cup is the new covenant in my blood, which is poured out for you'* (Luke 22:20). These words form the basis for what Christians variously call the Eucharist, the Mass, or the Lord's Supper. Different Christians have varying understanding of how these words of Jesus are to be interpreted. Catholic Christians take the words literally and have long argued that, at the Mass, when the priest consecrates the bread and wine, there is a 'change of substance' and it becomes the body and blood of Christ, although the believer continues to experience it as bread and wine. This gives rise to the Catholic practice of the consecrated bread or wafer being adored by the believer, and of the priest consecrating the bread and wine (which only a priest can do) and then this being distributed to the faithful by a lay person. Catholics call bread that has been consecrated and kept in this way 'the reserved sacrament' and it is kept close to the altar in a tabernacle with a candle burning beside it. Other Christians, such as Anglicans, maintain that Jesus is 'really present' at the Eucharist but they do not specify in what way (see p. 118). Many Protestant Christians see the bread and wine as symbolically representing Jesus' presence (some Protestants use fruit juice instead of wine because of the alcoholic nature of wine). There are, therefore, differences in understanding. Nevertheless, almost all Christians are united in the importance of taking seriously Jesus' words at the Last Supper.

Jesus had twelve close friends or disciples who accompanied Him throughout His ministry. Three of these were particularly close to Him – Peter, James and John. James and John were brothers whilst Peter was a former fisherman, an impetuous man who would often speak first and think later. Jesus prophesied that the kingdom of heaven was coming and that He, His disciples and all who followed Him would share in this kingdom. Gradually the disciples came to realise that this was not an earthly kingdom but a heavenly one and, naturally enough, the question arose as to who would be the leaders and closest to Jesus in His new kingdom. The mother of James and John came to Jesus and asked if her sons could sit one on His left and one on His right when He came into His new kingdom (Matthew 20:20–23). In asking this, she showed a lack of understanding as to the nature of the coming kingdom. Unlike earthly kingdoms, the new heavenly kingdom would be one of love and service where those who sought to be first would be least important and those who were humble and thought nothing of themselves would be first. It was an inversion of all the values underlying worldly power and achievement. Jesus pointed out that the path to the new kingdom lay through service to others, suffering and death – hardly an attractive prospect. He also made clear that Christians would necessarily suffer in this world, just as He would have to suffer. Jesus, therefore, inverted all the normal ideas of power often associated with God. For Jesus, God's power was shown most clearly in compassion, suffering and love. It was the power of weakness, not of might. This was emphasised in the picture of Jesus dying on the cross: dying like a common criminal, alone, despised and rejected by human beings. Yet, Christians hold, this is God in God's self dying on the cross. God becomes human and suffers as a human and does so out of love.

Peter was impulsive but had a genuinely good heart. He felt himself totally committed to Jesus and would have done anything for Him. However, the Gospels are realistic. When Jesus was about to face arrest and His coming death, and Peter vehemently declared his love and undying loyalty, Jesus gently told him that, before the cock crowed to indicate that the night was over, Peter would deny

Him three times. After Jesus' arrest Peter followed Jesus to the High Priest's house where He was taken, but Peter was recognised and was accused of being one of Jesus' disciples. Peter denied it in the strongest terms (John 18:15–27). This happened twice more and, after the third denial, the cock crew. Peter felt bitterly ashamed and angry with himself. This close friend of Jesus was weak and fully capable of failure, yet this was the man whom Jesus chose to lead the Church that would carry on His work after His death. This is part of a theme running through both the Hebrew and Christian Scriptures: that God chooses those who are outsiders and who are despised in worldly terms, not the powerful and successful.

One of the controversial passages in the Gospels specifically concerns Peter. Peter was formerly called Simon and is renamed Peter by Jesus. The Greek word *petros* means 'stone' or 'rock' and Jesus uses a play on words to say, *'you are Peter, and on this rock* [petros] *I will build my church'* (Matthew 16:18). Peter is given the keys of the kingdom of heaven and is told that the forces of evil will not prevail against the Church. Catholics hold that all authority is given by Jesus to the Church thus founded and that Peter and his successors are placed at its head: *'whatever you bind on earth will be bound in heaven, and whatever you loose on earth will be loosed in heaven'* (Matthew 16:19). This is central to the Catholic understanding that Peter was the first leader of the Christian Church – the first Pope – and that successors to Peter would have authority over the Church on earth and in heaven. Still today the papal seal has the symbol of crossed keys, indicating that the keys of the kingdom belong to the Pope and Catholic priests can release or forgive people for sins committed on earth.

Figure 4: *The papal crest of Pope Francis, showing the crossed keys of St Peter which appear on every papal crest. The letters 'IHS' are the first three letters of the Greek word for 'Christ'. The motto below the crest reads 'miserando atque eligendo' ('by showing mercy and by choosing').*

Protestants tend to play this passage down or even consider that it may have been inserted before the Gospels were produced in their final form and are, therefore, less willing to give authority to the Church. This is an issue to which we will need to return.

Jesus' death was not, however, simply the death of another innocent human life. It is also seen as a sacrifice. The idea of a sacrifice is not one that is widely accepted in the modern world. A sacrifice occurs when a person gives up something of value which they treasure for a higher cause. Sometimes a person is held to have sacrificed their life in a battle by allowing themselves to be killed to save the lives of comrades. In all religions, sacrifice has been an important idea, ranging from the willingness of an individual to sacrifice their own self-interest to help others, to the sacrifice of something they value in order to achieve self-discipline. Jesus, Christians hold, sacrificed His own life out of love to bring people back to God: to eliminate the cumulative centuries of sin and disobedience and to allow a new start.

The real power of God, Christians hold, is shown on the cross in Jesus dying, alone and abandoned, out of love for all human beings. So Jesus lays down His life, willingly and by His own choice, for His friends. What is more, He specifically says that His friends are all those who listen to what He taught and take His words seriously: who try to love God and love their neighbours with all their heart and mind and soul (John 15:10–15). Christians, therefore, see Jesus laying down His own life and suffering an agonising and terrible death in order to bring people to God, to redeem them from the cumulative effects of sin. It is for this reason that Christians refer to Jesus as their Saviour, the one who saves them from the effects of sin and disobedience and brings them home to God their Father. Jesus is not just the Saviour of all Christians. Jesus died for His friends and, in so doing, atoned for their sins. The punishment that is justly due to all human beings who have failed and who have sinned is cancelled because of Jesus' acts of suffering. Jesus, when He dies, pays the price of sin for all believers. The fairness of the universe is maintained.

FIVE

The Resurrection and the
Initial Spread of Christianity

The New Testament consists of the four Gospels, a number of letters written by St Paul and others, a final book called Revelation and the Acts of the Apostles. The Acts of the Apostles (often referred to simply as 'Acts') is generally agreed to have been written or compiled by the author of Luke's Gospel and is a second part of this work. It contains some of the earliest records of what happened immediately after Jesus' death.

In Chapter Three we saw that Jesus was crucified by the Romans. After His death, His body was placed in a cave hewn out of rock, with a large stone rolled across its entrance. His death is commemorated on the day that Christians call 'Good Friday' (pp. 205–7) at about three o'clock in the afternoon and His body would have been placed in the tomb the same day. In the heat of Palestine, it was essential that bodies were buried quickly. Jesus' friends and disciples were in despair and also full of fear that the Jewish authorities might hunt them down next. They were dispirited and demoralised. Their friend and leader, for whom they had given up everything, was dead and all His promises seemed to have come to nothing.

On the Sunday morning, either one or two women (the accounts differ) went down to the tomb. These were Jesus' closest friends and they went there to mourn. They found that the huge stone had been rolled away and that the tomb was empty – the body had gone. The grave clothes, in which Jesus' body would have been wrapped, were neatly placed in a corner. One Gospel account records that two angels were in the tomb (John 20:11–13). The fear and consternation felt by the women are not hard to imagine. One of them saw someone she took to be a gardener and, thinking that he had taken Jesus' body somewhere else, she asked him where the body had gone. The supposed gardener simply uttered her name, 'Mary,' and she instantly recognised that it was Jesus (John 20:14–18). She ran to throw her arms round Him in amazement and joy, but He said no: He had not yet ascended to His Father and her Father, to His God and her God. Mary was instructed to go and tell the disciples what had happened. In another Gospel account it is Peter who comes down after Mary and therefore sees what has happened (Luke 24:9–12).

Mary Magdalene is a pivotal figure in the Gospel accounts who, with others, supported Jesus financially and was with Him constantly throughout His ministry:

After this, Jesus travelled about from one town and village to another, proclaiming the good news of the kingdom of God. The Twelve were with him, and also some women who had been cured of evil spirits and diseases: Mary (called Magdalene) from whom seven demons had come out; Joanna the wife of Chuza, the manager of Herod's household; Susanna; and many others. These women were helping to support them out of their own means.

(Luke 8:1–3)

Figure 1: *This painting by Titian shows Jesus still with a few grave clothes after his resurrection. Mary Magdalene is trying to touch Him and Jesus is pulling away. Mary is shown here with ginger hair, and this has significance (see pp. 231–2).*

In some disputed texts, written soon after Jesus' death, Mary is recorded as one of the apostles. However, Christians from the fourth century AD onwards began to associate Mary Magdalene with another Mary, a prostitute who washed Jesus' feet and was forgiven by him (see p. 31). What cannot be questioned is that Mary Magdalene played a central role immediately after Jesus' resurrection. In Eastern Christianity she is described as 'equal to the apostles' and the Orthodox Church maintains that she was a virtuous woman all her life. In Western Christianity she is sometimes described as 'the apostle to the apostles', as it was she who brought news of Jesus' resurrection to His disciples.

The news that Jesus had risen from the dead and had been seen by Mary and Peter was greeted with amazement and some incredulity by the disciples, and one of them, Thomas, simply could not believe it. He said, understandably, that he would not accept it as true unless he could see Jesus for himself and place his finger in the hole in Jesus' side where the soldier's spear had pierced it, and also in the holes in His hands. When Jesus did appear to Thomas and he finally believed, Jesus said that those who believed without seeing the physical evidence had greater faith and were more blessed (John 20:24–29). Jesus appeared to the disciples in a locked room (they were hiding and in fear of arrest) on other occasions. On one occasion, as two of the disciples were walking to a nearby town called Emmaus, Jesus walked with them without them recognising Him. It was only in the evening, when He shared their meal and broke bread with them, that they recognised Him (Luke 24:13–35). One of the most famous appearances of Jesus was to St Paul (Acts 9:1–19), although in this case Paul heard a voice rather than seeing Jesus.

Christians record several stages after Jesus' death. In the first stage Jesus appears to various disciples and followers with the same body that He had when He died; the marks of the nails were in His hands and feet and the spear mark could be seen in His side. The next stage began when He ascended to God (this is referred to as the Ascension). After this, Jesus does not appear in bodily form, but the Holy Spirit comes to the new Christian followers.

If one event is more crucial than any other to Christian belief, it is the resurrection. The apostle Paul wrote:

And if Christ has not been raised, your faith is futile; you are still in your sins. Then those also who have fallen asleep in Christ are lost. If only for this life we have hope in Christ, we are of all people most to be pitied.

(1 Corinthians 15:17–19)

Jesus was a remarkable and extraordinary human being (as well, Christians claim, as being God incarnate) but the event that singles Him out from every other remarkable teacher is the resurrection. It is reasonable, therefore, to ask what evidence there is for the resurrection. Clearly, we have the recorded testimony of those to whom He appeared after His death, but what other evidence is there?

One of the most remarkable and extraordinary phenomena in history is the extent to which Jesus' followers – a small, frightened group who were in hiding for fear of the Jewish Temple authorities who had just, with the co-operation of the Romans, slain the disciples' leader – changed to a group who went out with total confidence and joy, preaching 'Christ crucified'. They no longer had any fear at all and, indeed, some were put to death, meeting their death calmly in the total conviction that death was not the end. This was a crucial mark of the early Christians: they faced death without any fear. This transformation is very hard indeed to explain in terms of a psychological delusion or mass paranoia. The best and simplest explanation, Christians hold, is that the stories of the resurrection are true. No other explanation can so persuasively account for the total alteration that took place in the frightened disciples, particularly as this was not an expectation shared by most Jews and it would have been greeted with incredulity by non-Jews.

Jesus made clear that, in rising from the dead, he had defeated the power of death: *'I am the resurrection and the life. The one who believes in me will live, even though they die; and whoever lives by believing in me will never die'* (John 11:25–26). Death was no longer the end and the power of death to bring fear and a sense of meaninglessness to the lives of individuals was destroyed. Death was now to be seen as merely a door to a richer and more perfect life with God in heaven. Christians, therefore, did not fear death, as it marked the entry into eternal life. Christians also came to believe that Jesus had defeated the powers of hell. Hell was a place of permanent exile from God, and a tradition grew in Christianity that Jesus descended to hell before rising from the dead. By so doing, Jesus released those who had died from the power of hell, so both death and hell were no more to be feared. This did not mean that Christians did not believe in hell – they did. However, hell was a place of freely chosen exile from God and, given the permanent possibility of forgiveness by God, the door was always open in this life to return to God, just as a penitent son returns to his father.

The resurrection is at the heart of Christianity, as is the identity of Jesus. He asked His close friends at one point in His ministry: *'Who do people say I am?'* They replied that popular opinion differed: some said He was Elijah who had come back again; some said one of the great prophets. Jesus then asked, *'Who do you say I am?'* and the impulsive Peter replied, *'You are the Messiah'* (Mark 8:27–29). In many ways this is the key issue. Who is Jesus? If He was just a great teacher and a great Jewish rabbi, then Christianity is false. If He was an extraordinary prophet – one of a long list of prophets – then Christianity is false. Christians affirm that Jesus is the Christ, the chosen one of God, God's Word, God incarnate come to redeem the world by His sacrifice. If this is true, then the resurrection is not improbable at all.

Before Jesus ascended to God the Father, He promised His disciples that He would not leave them alone and comfortless but would send the Holy Spirit or Paraclete (Counsellor) to them. Christians are firm in their belief that God is one, yet God is three persons in one. Thus the three persons of the Trinity are God the Father, God the Son (Jesus) and God the Holy Spirit. Since the Three are nevertheless One, when Christians talk of the Holy Spirit being with them, this is equivalent to saying God or Jesus is with them. After Jesus ascended, the disciples were praying together when a tremendous wind tore through the house and a tongue of fire rested on the head of each of the disciples. They were then able to speak in many different languages and they could be understood by people who had come to Jerusalem from many different nations. This event is celebrated in the third most important of the Christian festivals, which is called Pentecost. This occurs fifty days after Easter day (the day when the resurrection of Jesus is celebrated). An important part of the worldwide Christian community today are the Pentecostal churches, which proclaim the coming of God's Spirit and, in particular, the Spirit of prophecy given to various church leaders (see pp. 217–8).

Christianity spread initially among Jews and it must be remembered that there were Jewish communities and often synagogues in all the major centres of the ancient world. However, after Christianity was opened to non-Jews (see p. 61) there was explosive growth among people of all races. Often the early Christians were women or slaves who responded to Jesus' central message of God's love and forgiveness.

Initially the Christian message was spread by word of mouth and small groups of believers started to meet in each other's houses. However, there was little in the way of central organisation and each community was autonomous. The New Testament was not in existence at this stage and verbal reports of Jesus' message, death and resurrection were all that was available. It was inevitable that diversity of beliefs and practices should emerge.

No other single character was more influential in the early years of Christianity than St Paul. He was originally a devout Jew and, before his conversion, was a bitter opponent of Christianity who was authorised by the Jewish leaders to use all means to stamp out what was seen as a new and heretical sect. After his conversion, he became fearless in preaching. Although he had not known Jesus personally, he considered that he was an apostle just as much as the apostles commissioned by Jesus during His life, as he felt that he had had a personal commission from Jesus. Most of Paul's preaching was to non-Jews and when the leaders of the Christian community in Jerusalem heard of this, they opposed what he was doing. The issue was one that was bound to arise; Jesus was a Jew, all his initial followers were Jews, and so now the question was whether all Christians had to be subject to the Jewish law (including strict dietary laws as well as the circumcision of males). The apostles in Jerusalem, under Peter, initially felt that this was necessary but Paul did not. When, therefore, the Jerusalem leaders challenged Paul about this, he travelled to Jerusalem to resolve the issue. We have a record of the meeting in the Acts of the Apostles (15:1–21). Some of the leaders were committed to opposing Paul and insisting that Christians had first to become Jews, but Peter challenged this as a result of a vision he had received from God. In the vision, Peter saw an immense tray of food descending from heaven including various foods forbidden to a pious Jew. God told Peter to eat, but Peter refused, saying that he would not eat food regarded by Jews as unclean. God replied, rebuking Peter and saying that he should not call unclean what God had cleansed (Acts 10:9–16). Peter, therefore, became convinced that Paul was right, and so Paul was allowed to continue to preach to the Gentiles, and there was no requirement for the early Christians to become Jews. This was a crucial turning point since, if this had not happened, Christianity might have remained an obscure Jewish sect rather than spreading across the world.

Paul was responsible more than anyone else for the spread of Christianity. He travelled through much of the known world in an epic series of journeys, almost all on foot or by boat, and wherever he went he left communities of new Christians. However, once Paul had left these communities, they were directionless and things began to go wrong. Different opinions began to take hold about doctrine and the way the Christian life should be lived. For instance, in one community, instead of the new Christians commemorating the Last Supper as a solemn meal to remember Jesus, it became a huge feast with the wealthy showing off their wealth (1 Corinthians 11:17–34). Paul had to write firm letters setting these new Christian communities straight and pointing out their errors. He was also constantly calling the young Christian churches back to being faithful to the fundamental Christian message:

Now, brothers and sisters, I want to remind you of the gospel I preached to you, which you received and on which you have taken your stand.

(1 Corinthians 15:1)

I am astonished that you are so quickly deserting the one who called you to live in the grace of Christ and are turning to a different gospel – which is really no gospel at all. Evidently some people are throwing you into confusion and are trying to pervert the gospel of Christ.

(Galatians 1:6–7)

Therefore, from the earliest years of the Christian Church there have been deviations of belief and the need to ensure that the fundamental claims of Christianity are preserved. What is, perhaps, most surprising is not the divergences but the extent to which a fundamental unity of belief is maintained.

St Paul's influence has been profound, not only in enabling Christianity to spread amongst non-Jews, but also because of the numerous letters ('epistles') he wrote to many of the churches that he founded or visited. He had profound insights into Christianity, its challenges, the hope it provided and the centrality of the figure of Jesus and of love. Nowhere is this expressed better than in his letter to the Corinthians:

If I speak in the tongues of men or of angels, but do not have love, I am only a resounding gong or a clanging cymbal. If I have the gift of prophecy and can fathom all mysteries and all knowledge, and if I have a faith that can move mountains, but do not have love, I am nothing. If I give all I possess to the poor and give over my body to hardship that I may boast, but do not have love, I gain nothing.

Love is patient, love is kind. It does not envy, it does not boast, it is not proud. It does not dishonour others, it is not self-seeking, it is not easily angered, it keeps no record of wrongs.

Love does not delight in evil but rejoices with the truth. It always protects, always trusts, always hopes, always perseveres.

Love never fails. But where there are prophecies, they will cease; where there are tongues, they will be stilled; where there is knowledge, it will pass away. For we know in part and we prophesy in part, but when completeness comes, what is in part disappears. When I was a child, I talked like a child, I thought like a child, I reasoned like a child. When I became a man, I put the ways of childhood behind me. For now we see only a reflection as in a mirror; then we shall see face to face. Now I know in part; then I shall know fully, even as I am fully known.

And now these three remain: faith, hope and love. But the greatest of these is love.

(1 Corinthians 13:1–13)

Extracts from Paul's letters are frequently read in Christian churches around the world and his influence cannot be overstated, although he was also clear that he was not speaking in his own name but in the name of the risen Lord Jesus. St Paul preached fearlessly wherever he went, often adapting his preaching to the local situation. So when he came to Athens, where people believed in many gods, he started speaking by saying that he had seen an altar dedicated, 'To the unknown God'. He therefore set out to proclaim the unknown god as revealed by Jesus (Acts 17:16–33). Often his preaching made people angry, particularly orthodox Jews. On a number of occasions his life was threatened. As he travelled, so his fame spread and so did the influence of the Christian Gospel. Paul became known as a troublemaker, simply because controversy and opposition followed him around. He was therefore placed under arrest.

Paul, however, was a Roman citizen, and this carried many privileges. Rome was the master of the known world and a Roman citizen was immune from trial by local jurisdictions. All a Roman had to do was to say, 'I appeal to Rome' and local courts could no longer try him; he had to be taken to Rome for trial. This happened to St Paul in Jerusalem (Acts 21–22) and he duly appealed to Rome. He was therefore sent on the long and slow journey to Rome, accompanied by a soldier escort. As he travelled, so he continued to preach. He eventually came to Rome where he was placed in prison pending trial. The conditions were quite civilised and he was able to receive visitors. The Christian message had already spread as far as Rome and there were Christian followers in Rome who hastened to visit Paul, and he preached to them. Numbers grew even faster and so did Paul's reputation.

Jerusalem was the initial centre of the Christian Church. It was in Jerusalem that the original disciples of Jesus lived, and as long as Christianity was seen as a Jewish sect, this made sense. However, once Christianity became open to people of all races, then Jerusalem was no longer the natural centre. With its enormous population and its position of influence, Rome eventually became the new centre, particularly as St Peter is reported to have travelled to Rome and to have died there. What is more, Jerusalem was totally destroyed by the Roman armies in AD 70: the Temple was demolished, the city walls were pulled down and the city was almost razed to the ground. Jerusalem, therefore, could no longer be seen as the centre of Christianity. Tradition has it that Paul died in Rome, eventually sentenced to death by an emperor nervous of the growing appeal of Christianity, but martyrdom was something that was welcomed by the early Christians and the numbers of believers grew even more rapidly.

Little is known of the development of Christianity in the sixty years after Jesus' death, apart from the letters of Paul and a few others, but what is clear is that its growth was explosive and Christians were soon to be found in all corners of the Roman Empire. However,

Figure 2: Roman religion included the cult of the Emperor. Some of the emperors were declared gods after their death. This statue shows the Emperor Augustus (27 BC–AD 14).

Christianity was seen as a new sect and was viewed with great suspicion. Christians believed in a single God whereas Romans and Greeks believed in many gods. What was more, Roman emperors sometimes declared themselves to be gods and demanded that everyone should offer sacrifices at altars dedicated to them. This, of course, Christians could not accept. What was worse, stories grew up associating Christians with terrible practices such as eating human flesh. It is, perhaps, easy to understand why this would be the case, since at the Lord's Supper Jesus' own words were used, commanding His followers to eat His flesh and drink His blood in the form of bread and wine. This became a central part of Christian worship in future generations when Christians shared bread and wine in memory of Jesus (there are complex issues here to which reference will be made later). These stories, and the extent to which Christians were seen as some sort of secret society, began to attract the attention of the authorities and, under some emperors, Christians were persecuted.

There were many contributory factors. The values of Christians ran completely counter to the values of Roman society. Christians also rejected the glorification of power and money, and the cult of masculine strength and imperial domination that was normal in the Empire. They preached compassion and the equality of all people – including women and slaves. They preached love, fidelity in marriage and a negative attitude to sexual promiscuity. All these ideas made them in some way alien to normal Roman society, and aliens tend to be viewed with suspicion by the authorities.

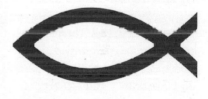

Figure 3: One of the earliest Christian symbols was the Ichthus. This is a simple outline of a fish and is found at ancient Christian sites. It was sometimes used as a way for persecuted first-century Christians to communicate. Apart from the links to various Gospel stories about Jesus and fish (several of His disciples were fishermen), the Greek letters (ἰχθύς) are also an acronym which translates into a statement of faith: Ιησους Χριστος Θεος Υιος Σωτηρ – 'Jesus Christ, God's Son, Saviour'.

Combined with the explosive growth of Christianity in the early years was a growing (if varied) persecution. Christians were tortured and killed and, increasingly, were used as fodder in the great arenas of the Roman Empire where gladiators fought to the death and wild beasts entertained the mob by killing people. The Christians, instead of resisting and providing entertainment, sang hymns as they waited to be killed. Their lack of fear added to their strangeness when compared with the rest of society. Christians had no fear; they were convinced that God was supporting them and that the God of love would care for them. Death was nothing; it was but a doorway to eternal life. Unlike some suicide martyrs today, however, the lives of the early Christians were filled with love and a commitment to compassion for those who were weak and even for those who were putting them to death – for whom they prayed. Some early Christian communities shared all their possessions and pooled their resources.

It is really quite extraordinary. Christianity started its explosive growth in a society with great inequality, where courage and strength were glorified, where bravery in battle was seen as the highest virtue, where the favourite public entertainment was to see human beings killed in a brutal manner and where sexual permissiveness was rampant. Against this background Christianity offered love

Figure 4: The Colosseum in Rome – one of many such arenas across the Roman Empire where Christians were persecuted and fed to wild animals. Their response was to sing hymns and not to be frightened of death.

of an unseen God, total trust in God, a spirit of peace and love for all human beings regardless of their race or social class, fidelity to one partner in marriage and no material rewards at all: simply the assurance that the love of God the Christian experienced in this life would continue after death and that death itself was a triviality: merely the gateway to everlasting life. It could not have been a more counter-cultural message, yet within three centuries this tiny 'new' religion focusing on a man crucified as a common criminal in a remote Roman province had become the official religion of the Emperor of Rome. People who followed Jesus found a peace and a joy that they had never before experienced. They trusted each other and this trust was a liberation and a new experience. They refused to judge others and instead sought to help them in any way they could. The response was persecution and ridicule and the might of the greatest empire the world had ever known turning on Christianity and using every means to suppress it. All that happened was that it grew even faster.

In these early formative years (about AD 40–120) the earliest Christian doctrines and ideas began to develop. We have already seen that many biblical scholars consider that John's Gospel must be the latest Gospel to be written as it is more theological than the Synoptic Gospels. This may well be true (although the shortest Gospel, that of Mark, is also highly sophisticated, albeit in a different way), but what is less certain is that theological sophistication depends necessarily on date. St Paul had a very developed and sophisticated theology yet all scholars acknowledge that Paul's letters are the earliest records of Jesus' life, message and death.

Central Christian ideas and doctrines were established within seventy years of Jesus' death. One of the earliest records is a letter written about AD 115 by Ignatius of Antioch to the Smyrnaeans in which he starts by praising the firmness of their faith and then goes on to say:

> *Jesus Christ is truly of the family of David with respect to human descent but Son of God with respect to the divine will and power, truly born of a virgin, baptised by John . . . truly nailed [to the cross] in the flesh for us under Pontius Pilate and Herod the Tetrarch in order that we may raise a banner for the ages through his resurrection for his saints and faithful people, whether among Jews or Gentiles, in the one body of the Church.*
> (Michael W. Holmes [editor and translator],
> *The Apostolic Fathers*, 2007)

It is clear, therefore, that from an early date some central Christian ideas were agreed and that the authority of a central Church was recognised.

There is, it must be admitted, a trend in recent years among some academic theologians and biblical scholars to 'explain away' anything in the Gospels that actually presents Jesus as the person Christians believe He was – God incarnate, come to earth out of love for human beings, who died on the cross and was resurrected. If this basic claim is rejected, then the theological insights or miracles recorded in the New Testament can easily be seen as a human construct reflecting on prior events. Yet Christians claim that, in the incarnation, the heavenly and earthy realms intersect. There is no longer a division between heaven and earth. The old boundaries are destroyed and undermined. The miracle stories are no more than one would expect if God came to earth as a mere human being – fully human but still fully God. This God consented (as John's Gospel claims) to take flesh and to live among human beings, sharing their condition and weakness, sharing in their troubles, suffering and joy. God in God's self became incarnate and consented to be crucified on the cross to redeem human beings from the cumulative effects of sin and pain, and to restore once more the relationship of love between God and human beings which had always been intended since the creation of the world.

After the death of Peter and Paul, and with Rome now established as the recognised centre of a growing number of Christian communities, the need became clear for some sort of organisation and some clarity about the nature of Christian beliefs and practice. It is in these first decades after the death and resurrection of Jesus that the early Christian Church was formed and began to lay the groundwork for the growing Christian understanding of God, of Jesus and of human beings in relation to God. The process was to take several centuries and it is to this that we must now turn, as these events are essential to understanding Christianity today.

SIX

The Development of the Early Church

As the numbers of Christians grew at an explosive rate in the four centuries after Jesus' death, there were many fierce debates about the nature of Christian doctrine and about which ideas were to be considered as 'orthodox' or true and which were to be considered as 'heretical' or false. The basic Christian story was interpreted in many different ways by groups who had particular ideas or interpretations. The lack of a clear central authority in the early years made this problem worse; each major city had its own bishop and these bishops came together very occasionally to agree on orthodoxy. Communication was, of course, slow. It was not until AD 324 that Christianity became recognised as the official religion of the Roman Empire. Even though Rome was acknowledged as the centre, the autonomy and authority of local bishops were consider-able in the early centuries. Often local churches had been founded by significant individuals such as St Paul, amongst many others. One good example of this is the Coptic Church.

Coptic Christians are largely found in Egypt and see St Mark as the founder of their church in Alexandria. Some closely asso-ciate St Mark with St Peter and see much of the text of St Mark's Gospel as being influenced by

Figure 1: Coptic crosses are often elab-orate. They may contain a circle to represent God's eternal love. The three points at the end of each arm of the cross may represent the Trinity. The twelve points are sometimes said to represent the twelve apostles.

Peter. What is certain is that Mark travelled throughout much of the Roman world with St Paul. The influence of Mark's Gospel on the Coptic Church is particularly strong even today. Coptic Christianity may well be one of the earliest of the Christian churches and has maintained an almost unbroken line since the early years. Coptic Christians have faced great persecution over the centuries, particularly when North Africa was conquered by the Muslim armies, and they particularly look to Jesus' saying that just as He was persecuted, so would His followers be (John 15:20). Coptic Christians today form a very small percentage of the Egyptian population but their influence over the centuries has been profound. They were one of the first churches to argue that Jesus was both fully God and fully man (the theological term for this is 'one hypostasis in one nature') and, as we shall see, this was to profoundly influence the rest of Christianity.

The main heresies or challenges to early Christian beliefs are listed below. The word 'heresy' means a departure from orthodox Christian beliefs. Heresy was a particular feature of the early Church but, also, of the later Catholic Church, which saw the authority of the Church founded by Jesus as being paramount and held that the Holy Spirit preserved the Church from making fundamental errors of doctrine. Anyone, therefore, who rejected the teaching of the Church or sought to amend or alter it in its fundamentals, was regarded as a heretic. This does not, of course, necessarily mean that the so-called heretics were wrong – just that they were considered to be wrong by a major part of the Christian community. It is, perhaps, helpful to be clear on the main heresies, as these help to illuminate the Christian doctrines that arose.

Marcionism

This was one of the earliest heresies and was one of the first to be condemned by the Church in Rome in AD 144. Within about a hundred years, therefore, of Jesus' death we have a clear Church organisation in Rome capable of taking a stand on an issue of doctrine. Marcion argued that the fierce and vengeful God of the Hebrew Scriptures was very different from the God of love of the Christian Scriptures. He therefore maintained a dualist position with two forces in the universe: one good and one evil. The Christian God revealed by Jesus was opposed to the Hebrew God who was seen as evil. For the Marcionists, love was the key to all Christian teaching and Marcion's supporters tended to be strongly anti-Jewish because of their rejection of the God of the Hebrew Scriptures. They also rejected the main Gospels with the exception of the Gospel of Luke, which they revised (it was called the Gospel of Marcion; some modern scholars reverse this order and maintain that the present Gospel of Luke is based on Marcion's Gospel). Release from this world comes from the God of love revealed by Jesus who calls Christians to put the world firmly into second place, to develop their spiritual nature and to let love guide them in all their dealings with the world.

Mainstream Christianity rejected Marcionism, as it was firmly committed to continuity between the Hebrew and Christian Scriptures. Certainly it did not reject the importance of love, but it saw Jesus as fulfilling and completing God's revelation through the Hebrew prophets and in no sense being opposed to their teaching.

Gnosticism

Marcionists were Gnostics but the term 'Gnostic' covers a wide movement of ideas which pre-dated Christianity and continued into the Middle Ages. In many cases it was associated with the idea of secret knowledge which was only available to initiates. There are many different Gnostic positions but they all tend to deny that the world is good and, therefore, tend to be negative about most of the features of the world, often including marriage, sex and the enjoyment of food. They generally see the world as a battleground between the forces of evil and the forces of light or goodness. Human beings are essentially spiritual creatures, creatures of light who are imprisoned in earth-bound, material bodies. The task of human beings is, therefore, to avoid being corrupted by the material world and to seek to develop their spiritual potentialities so that, after death, they will be reunited with the light from which they originally came.

The early Gnostics saw all matter as being evil and, therefore, they held that when Jesus died it was only His spirit that ascended to God and not His body. One of the important parts of the early Christian creeds specifically rejected this, and all Christians today affirm the central importance of the claim that Jesus' body was physically resurrected.

The negative attitude to the world was an important feature of some parts of early Christianity and, if adopted, could easily have led Christians to deny the importance of the world – but they did not do so. Traditionally, Christianity has always affirmed that the world is good and is the creation of a good and loving God. The evil and suffering that entered the world were never God's plan or intention and were due to the actions of free beings created by God to love God and each other. Nevertheless, the influence of Gnosticism has continued as a minority position among some who claim to be Christians. Possibly the most important single instance of Gnosticism resurfacing was amongst the Cathars in south-west France in the twelfth century, and we will return to them later.

Arianism

Arianism was one of the most important and influential Christian movements. Arius (*c.* AD 256–336) argued against the view that Jesus, God the Son, has always existed along with God the Father. He was drawing on a previous heresy called Monarchianism. Monarchians held that Jesus was an ordinary human being into whom God the Father had placed a divine spark. They were some-times called 'adoptionists', as they maintained that Jesus was the adopted Son of God and not, therefore, part of God's essence.

Arius did not originate the theological position that carries his name. His was a view that had been held for a long time before he put it forward but it became identified with him because the controversy came to a head around his person. Arius argued that God the Father has always existed but that the Son was not pre-existent with the Father but was created by the Father. This was a most important issue; it nearly divided the Church and, in the fourth century, it was far from clear which position would be regarded as orthodox. The supporters of Arius were very strong; his position seemed to make much sense, as Jesus Himself seemed to regard God as superior to Him. He specifically said that no one should be called good except God the Father of all and that He was ascending after His death to His Father and the Father of everyone. The baptism of Jesus, when the Holy Spirit descended on Him, could therefore easily be regarded as supporting Arius' position. This in no way denied the supreme

Figure 2: This extraordinary and beautiful mosaic is from the 'Dome of the Arians' in Ravenna, Italy. There are twelve figures surrounding the central figure of Jesus, who is being baptised. In very early images such as this, Jesus is shown as being half immersed in water (in later centuries this practice declined; see the image on p. 29) and is baptised with a small amount of water poured over the head. God the Father is to the left of the picture and the Holy Spirit, in the shape of a dove, is above. Effectively this is the moment when Jesus became adopted as God's Son – hence representing the Arian position.

sovereignty of God the Father, nor did it deny that Jesus was the Son of God or that the Holy Spirit intimately connected the two.

Like all the history of heresies in the early Church, the position was complicated. Arius was a priest in Egypt and he attacked his bishop, Alexander of Alexandria (note the reference to Coptic Christianity above), as being a heretic for holding that the Son had always existed with the Father. Alexander gathered 100 bishops from Egypt and Libya together in a Council and they condemned Arius, in spite of him having considerable support. They declared him to be a heretic and he was excommunicated (effectively excluded from the Christian Church). Arius' support came in particular from the East of the Roman Empire. Bishops from the East gathered together and condemned the Council called by Alexander and reinstated Arius. The Emperor Constantine, the first Christian Emperor, tried to resolve the problem but actually made matters worse. In AD 325 he called together the great Council of Nicaea, the largest gathering of Christian bishops that had ever met, with 300 in attendance. The primary aim of the Council was to resolve this theological issue. The resulting statement, now called 'The Nicene Creed', was meant to condemn the Arians. However, the Arians could accept most of the wording of this creed, albeit by reinterpreting the way words were used, so the position was not really clarified. Things got more complicated because in AD 327 Arius was reinstated and one of his closest allies, Eusebius, became one of the Emperor's nearest advisors. Effectively the Emperor had changed his mind. This is an example of the political trends that have affected the development of Christian doctrine. Christians have always been committed to the idea of truth but it is important to recognise that the development of ideas in the early Church was affected by political intrigues.

Arius died in AD 336 and there followed a confused period of about sixty years, including a time when a pagan emperor came onto the Roman imperial throne. It was not until AD 379, when the Emperor Theodosius took the throne in what was then the eastern part of the Roman Empire, that things settled down. Theodosius was a firm opponent of the Arian position and he deposed the bishops who supported this. In AD 381 he called together a great Council of Christian bishops in Constantinople (now called Istanbul). The Creed that was produced then – essentially the Nicene Creed with some amendments to make it clear that the Arian position was heretical – represented the final refutation of the Arian heresy. From then on almost all Christians have accepted that Jesus pre-existed with God and was not created as subservient to God. It must be accepted that Theodosius forced through his position and that the intellectual basis for the Arian claim has considerable merit – nevertheless, it became a heresy.

Nestorianism

Nestorians claimed that Jesus was two separate persons – a human being and also a divine being – believing that Jesus had two totally distinct natures and rejecting the claim that Mary was 'the Mother of God', as this would mean that God was brought into existence at the time of His birth and would, effectively, be younger than Mary. The divine Jesus, the Nestorians held, was pre-existent but the human Jesus came into existence as the child of Mary.

Nestorius was initially a monk but he was also a brilliant teacher and was invited by the Eastern Emperor, Theodosius II, to become Patriarch of Constantinople. (Constantinople was the centre of Eastern Christianity and the seat of power of the Eastern Roman Emperor, so the Patriarch of Constantinople was the second most senior position in the Christian Church, the Bishop of Rome being the most senior of all.) The Nestorians argued that Mary should be described as *Christokos* or 'Mother of Christ' not *Theotokos* or Mother of God. Nestorianism was partly a reaction to Arianism, as it wanted to hold onto the view that Jesus' divine nature pre-existed with God from the beginning of time, but by separating Jesus' human and divine natures it made a breach in the understanding of Jesus as both fully God and fully man that was unacceptable. Therefore, the position was eventually declared to be heretical.

Pelagianism

Pelagianism was different from the other heresies set out above because, whereas these were concerned with the status of the Trinity, Pelagianism was concerned with the nature of human beings. Pelagius was a British monk who first came to Rome in about AD 380. He argued that human beings are born innocent; in other words, they are free from any stain of Original Sin. He therefore rejected the ideas of St Augustine. The doctrine of Original Sin was important as it held that all human beings were affected by the sin of Adam and Eve in the Garden of Eden. Jesus, therefore, had to accept the sin of all human beings on Himself. He was the Saviour of all people as, without Jesus' sacrifice and death on the cross, they would be condemned due to the effects of Original Sin. Pelagius rejected this and held that every human baby is innocent at birth and that it is up to the will of each individual to decide to act in a morally good or evil way. This was a profound attack on two principal Christian ideas.

Firstly, Pelagianism rejected the idea of Original Sin, which entered the world with the disobedience of Adam and Eve in the Garden of Eden. It therefore rejected Jesus' role as Saviour. This was important enough in itself, but the second issue was even more important. If human beings are free from sin at birth and can then decide for themselves whether to be good or evil, then there is no need for the grace of God which, early Christians insisted, was necessary to help people to live a virtuous life. St Augustine held that in the absence of grace no one could be virtuous. Only the Christian was eligible for Divine Grace, so only Christians could do good acts since, necessarily, a good act required the grace of God. Non-Christians, therefore, could not do good acts; it was essential to first become a Christian. Two people might each do what we, today, would regard as a good act but only the person motivated by love of God and strengthened by the grace of God would actually be doing a good act. Pelagius rejected this. He held that anyone was capable of being either good or evil and that grace was not required. This means that the Greek philosophers or believers in other gods could do good acts just as much as the Christian. This would have represented a profound attack on the nature of the Church as, in order for someone to be good, Christianity was not essential and, therefore, the need to be baptised and to join the Christian Church was diminished.

Pelagius was not initially condemned and, indeed, a council of bishops in AD 415 specifically said his writings were not heretical. Pope Innocent I proclaimed that Pelagius was not a heretic, but he was succeeded by Pope Zozimus in AD 417 who, while initially refusing to condemn Pelagius, finally did so. He formally condemned Pelagianism as a heresy in AD 418.

The issue centrally revolves around free will. Are human beings born free and capable of making their own decisions? If so, Pelagius was right. If, however, it is held that Original Sin (the sin resulting from the disobedience of Adam and Eve in the Garden of Eden) has corrupted individuals so that they have lost their freedom, then Pelagius was wrong, as Jesus' role as Saviour was vital in freeing people from the stain of Original Sin.

From the years of debate about Christian doctrine emerged the Christian creeds – the formal statements of traditional Christian belief. The best known is the Nicene Creed which, as we have seen, was drafted in AD 325 and amended at the Council of Constantinople in AD 381. The origin of the Creed is much older and some hold that it goes back to the time of the first Christian apostles, but many modern scholars have doubts about this and consider that the origin may be about a hundred years after Jesus' death, and the Creed would then have been modified in succeeding years in response to the challenges which have been outlined above. It seems likely that, from the early years, Christians recited the Creed as a formal statement of their common belief. The revised version of the Nicene Creed is as follows:

> *We believe in one God, the Father Almighty, Maker of heaven and earth, and of all things visible and invisible. And in one Lord Jesus Christ, the only-begotten Son of God, begotten of the Father*

before all worlds, Light of Light, very God of very God, begotten, not made, being of one substance with the Father; by whom all things were made; who for us men, and for our salvation, came down from heaven, and was incarnate by the Holy Ghost of the Virgin Mary, and was made man; he was crucified for us under Pontius Pilate, and suffered, and was buried, and the third day he rose again, according to the Scriptures, and ascended into heaven, and sits on the right hand of the Father; from thence he shall come again, with glory, to judge the quick and the dead; whose kingdom shall have no end. And in the Holy Ghost, the Lord and Giver of life, who proceeds from the Father, who with the Father and the Son together is worshipped and glorified, who spoke through the prophets. In one holy catholic and apostolic Church; we acknowledge one baptism for the remission of sins; we look for the resurrection of the dead, and the life of the world to come.

This Creed summarises the key Christian beliefs that the Church has affirmed through the centuries. Its main features are:

- Belief in one God. The statement 'we believe' is significant – the Creed was designed to be used as a communal part of worship and represented a statement of shared belief. This is still the case today in most Christian churches.
- God is the maker of 'all things' – the Lord and creator, therefore, of the whole universe, including spiritual realities. The Christian God is not a local God – God is the creator of the cosmos.
- Jesus is the only Son of God but is 'begotten not made' and is of 'one substance' with the Father. This is a complex inter-relationship of ideas. Jesus is born as a human being but pre-existed His birth. Jesus is not created directly by God but born of Mary; yet Jesus also pre-exists with God. The second person of the Divine Trinity is no different from God the Father (which is what 'of one substance' means) and existed with the Father 'before all worlds' – in other words, before the universe

came into existence. However, the second person of the Trinity takes flesh and becomes human when Jesus is born.

- Jesus came to earth (was incarnate) to save human beings from the effects of sin. Because of this, He is considered by Christians to be the Saviour of the world. This led later Protestant Christians to emphasise Jesus' role as the personal Saviour of every Christian and so the personal relationship with the risen Lord Jesus became important.
- The Creed firmly anchors belief in history. Jesus was born of the Virgin Mary. Mary was held to be a virgin and her conception was caused by the action of the Holy Spirit (see pp. 25–6). Also, Jesus was crucified under Pontius Pilate – a clearly named, historical Roman figure. This grounds Christian belief as being directly related to the historical events of Jesus' birth and death.
- Jesus died on the cross and rose from the dead and ascended into heaven. The crucifixion and resurrection are at the heart of Christian faith.
- The Holy Spirit (or Holy Ghost) is the third person of the Divine Trinity and proceeds from the Father. This latter phrase is important and was to cause a major division in the Christian Church later (see pp. 85–6). The Holy Spirit is the same as God's Word which created the universe and which spoke through the Hebrew prophets (thus emphasising the continuity of the God of the Hebrew Scriptures with the God worshipped by Christians).
- Belief in one 'catholic' Church. The word 'catholic' means universal, so this is just a way of affirming belief in one universal Church of Christians. Note the use of the small 'c' in 'catholic' – it is not a phrase specifically related to the Roman Catholic Church.
- There is a single baptism which marks the entry of an individual into the Christian Church and baptism marks a point where sins are forgiven – it represents a 'new birth', a new start. This goes back to Jesus saying that his followers needed to be 'born again'. Some within the Church call themselves 'born again' Christians, as they have new life guided, strengthened and inspired by the Holy Spirit of God.

Almost all Christians consider acceptance of the Nicene Creed as being an essential prerequisite of being a Christian. Some groups, such as Jehovah's Witnesses and the Church of Jesus Christ of Latter Day Saints, reject the Nicene Creed, and some evangelical Christians who give priority to the Bible do not accept it simply because it is not contained in the Bible. However, most mainstream Christian churches do accept it and it comes closest, therefore, to a clear summary of mainstream Christian belief.

Deciding on a single creed took almost 300 years and debates about Christian theology and doctrine continued, but it was remarkable that the unity of the Church was maintained and, by the fifth century, there was broad agreement about the essentials of Christian belief. This did not last, however, and divisions about doctrine continued to plague the history of Christianity.

In spite of these divisions and discords, the spread of Christianity continued. For most Christians, Christianity was not about doctrinal differences but rather living out a relationship of love with the God revealed perfectly by Jesus of Nazareth. It was about turning away from worldly priorities and caring for, and showing compassion to, every human being irrespective of creed, race, religion or social status. It was about putting obedience to the one God into first place and refusing to allow any idols (or other priorities) to get in the way of this obedience and this relationship. Christianity started among the poor – women, slaves and people who were not considered respectable – but its influence spread and within three centuries of Jesus' death it had become established as the official religion of the Roman Empire. Doctrinal differences, therefore, were of secondary importance compared with living the Christian life and trying to bring others to experience the love and forgiveness of God.

SEVEN

Unity, Growth, Division and Discord

Christianity became the official religion of the Roman Empire in AD 324 but the Empire itself was in decline, with constant attacks on almost all fronts culminating in the sack of Rome in AD 410. The Christian Church faced severe threats after this event and the near collapse of the Roman Empire. Romulus Augustus, the last Western Roman Emperor, was deposed in AD 476 and thus began what has been referred to as 'the Dark Ages'. The Roman Empire had been in retreat for some time and, after 476, the authority of Constantinople, the centre of Eastern Christianity, became even more important. The greatness of Rome and its mastery of the entire known world was gone, although the Christian Church continued to expand, with missionaries being sent out across Europe and further afield with great success. Monasteries were founded, often based on the example of the early Christian individuals who went off into the desert to find God in solitude and prayer. No one was more influential in the movement than St Benedict (c. AD 480–537), who established the idea of a rule-based monastic life and whose 'Rule of St Benedict' still guides the lives of tens of thousands of Christian monks in Benedictine and related communities around the world today.

Benedict came from a wealthy Roman family and was well educated. He knew all about the attractions available to a wealthy young man, including love, but he rejected all these in order to take seriously the Christian message and to seek to live his whole life drawing closer to God. He left Rome to seek a place to be away from the bustle of the city and lived as a hermit for several years. He became well known for his piety, gentleness and holiness and when, some years later, the abbot of a local Christian monastery died, the monks asked Benedict to become their abbot. He took up their offer but relations broke down and, according to the stories that have been passed down, the monks tried without success to poison him. He left the monastery and went back to the valley where he had previously lived. He built twelve small monasteries, each under the guidance of an abbot, and he became abbot of one of these. From such modest beginnings Benedict began to found schools to educate children. Possibly his greatest achievement was the 'Rule of St Benedict' which describes how to live a life centred on Christ and built on service to others. The Rule governs almost every aspect of life and is as relevant today to those seeking the monastic path as it was when Benedict first wrote it. It calls monks to obedience, to prayer, to service to visitors, to work to support the monastery but, above all, to humility. It was a message that many in the wealthy cities of Europe would have rejected in the sixth century, as many would today, but it is also a message with a timeless appeal.

People responded to the Christian message and, across Europe, kings, courtiers and ordinary people rejected the old idea of idols and instead accepted the Christian concept of worshipping a single God. It was an extraordinary transformation. The old power of Rome was declining rapidly and its imperial authority was becoming a thing of the past, but out of this collapse in influence came a new authority based on Christian teaching and worship of God that gave people hope in times that were otherwise violent and dark.

There were a variety of tradi-

Figure 1: *Celtic stone crosses such as this are still to be found in Ireland, Scotland, Wales and Cornwall.*

tions across the Roman world with different forms of Christianity, although unity was maintained by the central authority in Rome, based on an agreed version of the Bible (the Vulgate), the Creeds and the liturgy. One of the most distinctive and enduring variants was Celtic Christianity, although many historians today doubt there was any defined body of practice or belief that could be described as 'Celtic'. In Wales, Cornwall, Ireland and parts of the rest of Britain, there developed an approach to Christianity that was in some ways distinctive and is worthy of note with a strong emphasis on the natural world, a far more influential role for women, and a central part for art and music. In the sixth and seventh centuries control from Rome was less tight providing space for local variations of Christianity to develop. St Patrick and St Columba were certainly influential figures in Ireland and Britain. However, Celtic Christianity never denied the supremacy of the Pope and saw itself as part of the one, united Christian Church. Some popular books seek to show Celtic and Roman Christianity as opposed but there is little evidence for this; at most, Celtic Christianity marked a local variation on the united Christian vision and the united Christian Church centred on Rome. It was common at the Reformation (see Chapter 8), when the Church of England broke from Rome, for some writers to appeal back to an ancient British version of Christianity, but the evidence for this is limited. What is certain is that in Britain and Ireland there were variations in Christianity; for instance, both Britain and Ireland were still very much tribal societies and slightly different 'Christianities' emerged based on tribal loyalties. Monasteries were founded and there was a real sense of religious commitment and enthusiasm amongst the Celts. Some abbots and leaders of churches were married and their positions were often passed onto their sons. There is some limited evidence of women having a more prominent role. There was no parish system and, therefore, local monasteries, hermits or holy men, as well as wandering preachers, were the greatest influence.

What is known is that in AD 596, Pope Gregory I sent St Augustine to convert the Anglo-Saxons and to establish himself as bishop over much of southern England. This was an attempt to exert control over the local churches and Augustine's efforts were not well received by the existing bishops. They effectively refused to accept his authority. Augustine wanted the already established Christian Church not only to submit to him but also to change the date they had been using for Easter, to join with him in a mission to the Anglo-Saxons and to bring their method of baptising people into line with the Roman practice. All these demands were rejected. That there were tensions between the local churches and the Roman Church is unquestioned, but much of the mythology concerning Celtic Christianity is based on limited evidence and the few facts we have may, perhaps, say more about those who, in the Middle Ages and today, write about Celtic Christianity than help us understand what actually took place. Nevertheless, the importance of Celtic Christianity as an idea today shows a deep yearning within the Christian community for a simpler, more feminine and nature-based Christianity than is found in many of the traditional churches and, in this respect, the Celtic vision (even if it derives from a later date) remains significant.

The Christian Church remained centred on Rome but there were now two great powers in the Christian world – one was Rome and the other was Constantinople. Christian leaders in the East, which was ruled by the Emperors in Constantinople, always acknowledged the precedence of Rome, but this was to change as Roman power dwindled. In particular, in AD 867 the Patriarch of Constantinople seized on a variation in the Nicene Creed accepted by the Western Church and used this as a pretext to claim that the whole Church centred on Rome had entered into heresy.

In order to understand the significance of this, as otherwise it will seem trivial, it is essential to understand that the united Christian Church, including all the bishops from the known world, had come to an agreement on the wording of the Nicene Creed (see pp. 74–5; 77–8). Certainly, there had been strong disagreements and, as we saw in the last chapter, many passionate advocates of alternative positions but, in the final analysis, agreement was reached. What was more, this agreement was by the united Christian Church. Any departure from this agreement by a particular group was seen as heretical. Effectively the Church, after much agonising and debate, had agreed a formula of words which everyone accepted. Change could not be made without everyone agreeing.

The Patriarch of Constantinople focused on the fact that the Western Church, centred on Rome, had made a change to the Creed without the universal agreement that was essential. The change appeared small, but it was the principle that mattered. The Western Church had departed from the agreed formulation and, therefore, had departed from the unity that had been so hard won.

The change started very early. The Nicene Creed had been amended and finally agreed at the great Council of Constantinople in AD 381 (see p. 75). However, within fifty years, the Western Church had made an alteration. The change originated in what is now France but spread and became widely accepted in the West. The Nicene Creed included the words, *'I believe . . . in the Holy Ghost, the Lord and Giver of life, who proceeds from the Father'*. The words *'proceeds from the Father'* were inserted in AD 381, although they were not there in the original AD 324 Creed and were taken from the Gospel of John (15:26). The Western Church added the words *'. . . and the Son'* so that the Creed was revised to read: *'I believe . . . in the Holy Ghost, the Lord and Giver of life, who proceeds from the Father and the Son'*. The position appeared perfectly reasonable. The Arians had held that the Father pre-existed the Son and created the Son, but if this was rejected (as it had been) then it seemed reasonable to hold that the Holy Spirit proceeds from both Father and Son together. However, this is to miss the point. The Eastern Church was adamant that *no* change could be made in the agreed formulation of Christian belief without acceptance by *all* the Christian bishops at a universal council. The Western Church had made such a change and was, therefore, guilty of heresy.

There were political overtones here as well. Rome was weak and the Eastern Church was asserting its strength, but it held that it had a good basis for doing so. In AD 867 the leader of the Western

Church, Pope Nicholas I, was excommunicated by the Patriarch of Constantinople. Tensions between West and East increased and culminated in the greatest split in the history of Christianity.

Various attempts had been made to resolve the conflict and, on both sides, there was real reluctance for a split. It must be remembered that communications at the time were very slow. Legates had to be sent to speak in the name of their masters and sometimes these legates exceeded their powers. This may well have happened in Constantinople. Three legates were sent by Pope Leo IX with powers to negotiate a settlement but also the power to act in the Pope's name. They went to the Patriarch of Constantinople but they were rude and almost certainly exceeded their authority. Pope Leo died on 19 April 1054 and, with his death, the authority of the legates he had sent ceased. However, the legates took no notice and continued to act effectively on their own authority, and on 16 July they acted decisively. They entered the wonderful church of the Hagia Sophia ('holy wisdom') in Constantinople during the Divine Liturgy on a Saturday afternoon and placed a Papal Bull of Excommunication on the altar. This excommunicated the whole of the Eastern Church. It was an extraordinary event.

The Patriarch of Constantinople was popular and considered to be a holy man. He had great support and he, in turn, excommunicated the Western Church. The split was complete and is still with us. In Eastern Europe, the Orthodox Church is dominant and centred, at least in principle, on Constantinople (now Istanbul), although the Russian and Greek Orthodox Churches are today the most important. The Eastern Church considered that it acted on principle and would argue that the Western Church has continued to impose new teachings without the authority of the united Church. Examples would include the declaration by the First Vatican Council in 1870 that the Pope is infallible when promulgating certain doctrines – something never accepted by the Orthodox. In practice this power has only been used once since then, when Pope Pius XII declared that all Catholic Christians had to accept, as a matter of faith, that Mary was assumed directly into heaven; but, again, it was the principle that mattered (although Pius IX's 1854 declaration about the Immaculate Conception is also considered infallible, even though it pre-dated the Council).

The Orthodox Church emphasises the autonomy of individual bishops and patriarchs. The Patriarch of Constantinople is considered to be *primus inter pares* (or first among equals) among patriarchs of the Eastern Church. He is not considered to have authority over other patriarchs. Many Orthodox theologians would have no difficulty in accepting that the Pope is effectively the supreme patriarch, but would deny him authority over the rest of the Church and would demand that the Western Church revert to obedience to the teachings of the early Church as put forward in the Council of Nicaea. The importance of this split and its depth cannot be over-emphasised.

The Orthodox Church developed a profound spirituality and, in particular, a strong commitment to the writings of the early Church Fathers. Whereas St Augustine was decisively important in forming the thought of the West, in the Eastern Church there were a wide range of early Church Fathers who were revered and who were seen as paradigms in helping people to find God. The tradition of icon painting developed in the eleventh century in Constantinople and was exported to Russia as Christianity came to dominate there. Icons are not merely paintings; they are meditative aids, traditionally produced by monks, and every brush stroke represents a prayer to God. They

Figure 2: This icon is not about St George killing a dragon. It depicts a saint fighting and conquering his own internal desires and appetites. The 'dragon' acquiesces in its own 'death' and the icon is remarkably peaceful. Icons such as this are aids to prayer and meditation.

are ways of helping people to contemplate the extent to which the transcendent world of God and the angels interpenetrates the 'normal' world. The universe is seen as essentially a hierarchy with God, the angels and the saints at one level and the everyday world at another. These are not, however, separate realms; the transcendent world interpenetrates every aspect of the supposedly normal world, and the strength of God and the saints can be available to the committed Christian who, through prayer and fasting, seeks to come closer to God and to be obedient to God.

The Western Christian Church continued to develop in power and influence. Islam posed a real challenge in the ninth and tenth centuries. The Islamic armies had conquered the whole of North Africa and invaded Spain, conquering almost the whole of the country. They were gradually driven back by Christian forces before the twelfth century. Europe now entered a time of conflict between nation states but also of relative stability. In the West, the authority of the Church in Rome was undoubted. Almost everyone was a Christian and the power and authority of the Church rivalled or exceeded that of nation states. People, priests and bishops were obedient to the king and queen of the country in which they lived but also to the Pope in Rome. This tension created great problems, with Popes intervening in political disputes and claiming rights for the Church that effectively made it independent of the authority of kings, for instance, by claiming that Church lands and income should not be taxed and that only Church courts could put members of the clergy on trial. Bishops and monasteries became powerful and wealthy, with individual bishops sometimes controlling their own armies and having a lifestyle closer to that of an earthly prince than a servant of God. Indeed, some bishops were referred to as 'prince bishops' and their political power in some cases rivalled that of the great feudal dukes and earls.

Between the political intrigues, the battles between nation states and the increasing power and authority of the Western Church centred on Rome, the ordinary life of Christians continued. The message that Jesus preached of love and forgiveness, of resurrection and hope, continued to be preached and was widely accepted. As the Church grew powerful there were, as in any human institution, those who were corrupt and who sought power for their own ends. But these were constantly challenged by those who recalled the Church and Christians to fidelity to the gentle but demanding message preached by Jesus.

A good example of this was an extraordinary man born in AD 1181 – Francis di Bernardone. Francis came from the city of Assisi at a time when the modern Italy did not exist. There were city states which fought each other on a regular basis. Francis came from a wealthy family of cloth merchants. In many ways he was like any other rich young man. He enjoyed parties and bright clothing, but there was another side to his character. He was selling cloth in the market of Assisi on behalf of his father when a beggar came and asked for alms. Francis emptied his pockets and gave the beggar everything he had, much to the amusement of his friends and the anger of his father.

In 1201, at the age of twenty, he went off, like other young men from his city, to fight against the neighbouring city of Perugia. He was captured and kept a prisoner for a year, returning to Assisi in 1203. He resumed his carefree life but the serious side of his character was becoming more important to him. In 1204 he had a serious illness and this led him to begin to recognise more clearly the importance of the spiritual side of life. In 1205 he enlisted to fight for a neighbouring army but he had a profound spiritual experience and felt more and more uncomfortable with the wild life led by his friends. He gave up his life as a soldier, returned to Assisi and began a life dedicated to prayer and seeking God, as well as looking after the most terribly afflicted lepers. He went on a pilgrimage to Rome and had a profound religious experience in the Church of San Damiano when he felt Jesus speaking to him from a cross, saying, 'Francis, Francis, go and repair my house which, as you can see, is falling into ruins.' Francis thought this meant that he should repair the church in which he was praying, so he sold his horse and dedicated himself to helping the priest to rebuild the little church.

Figure 3: The Cross of St Damiano includes other figures around the central image of Christ, including Mary, mother of Jesus, John the Evangelist and Mary Magdalene. At the top of the cross Jesus is shown ascending into heaven, with the hand of God the Father extended in blessing.

A few years later, in February 1208, Francis had an experience which changed his life. The sermon for the day was preached on the verse in Matthew's Gospel (10:9) in which Jesus tells His disciples that they should go out into the world, preach the coming of God's kingdom, call people to repent of their sins and take nothing with them, not even a staff or stick. Francis felt he had received a great revelation and decided to take this seriously. He devoted himself to a life of radical poverty and service. This was to be the basis of his life, and his gentleness and love of everyone he met – no matter how mean, diseased and despicable – were to transform the Church.

Francis of Assisi (for so he was to become known) decided to dedicate his whole life to God and to those who were poor and had nothing. He was not an academic or a scholar, but he knew his Bible well and took seriously Jesus' command to care for those in prison, those who were poor and outsiders. This was his task – to care for all those whom society derided and rejected: lepers, robbers, prisoners and other outcasts. What was more, his absolute commitment to poverty was disturbing to a Church which had become committed to wealth and power, and for which a hierarchy of power seemed to be normal. The example of Francis influenced others and men came to join him, attracted by his gentleness and his commitment to God and the service of others.

As we have seen, the Church at the time of Francis was powerful. Monasteries were rich, bishops built palaces for themselves and all too often the simple Christian message was ignored. Francis realised that the vision he had received in St Damiano calling on him to 'rebuild the house' of Jesus referred not, as he thought at the time, to the little church in which he prayed but to the rebuilding of the very fabric of the Church as a whole. In a way Francis was a revolutionary, challenging all that the Church stood for in terms of power, influence and money, but he was also a faithful servant of the Church. He went to the Pope in Rome in 1209 with his first followers and he must have cut a disturbing figure amidst the wealth and pomp of the papal court. He asked permission from the Pope to form a religious order and, although initially reluctant, the Pope gave his assent on 16 April 1209. Francis and his hundreds of thousands of subsequent followers have always been loyal servants of the Church but have also constantly returned the Church to Jesus' simple message of love and service to suffering humanity.

Francis chose not to be ordained as a priest and his followers were called 'friars minor' as they did not initially accept the office of priest, still less of bishop. They were absolutely committed to poverty and service in a radical manner. In the same year as he went to Rome, Francis was preaching in his home city of Assisi and one of the congregation was a young woman called Clare. After the sermon she realised her vocation and, with Francis' blessing, established a women's religious order which became known as the 'Poor Clares', following in the spirit of St Francis.

In 1219 the Christian Crusaders were fighting Muslims in Egypt. Francis went to Egypt with a few of his followers. He tried to persuade the Crusaders not to fight, but they mocked him, even though he warned them that if they continued to do so they would suffer great losses. The Crusaders attacked the Muslim forces and were defeated, and the Sultan who led the opposing forces declared a truce. St Francis crossed the battle lines to see the Sultan. Most people must have thought he was mad, crossing the lines of fierce battle to go to the enemy who were demonised by most of the Christian community. Indeed, the Christians saw themselves as fighting the Muslims in Jesus' name. However, the Sultan received Francis courteously and, so the story goes, Francis challenged the Muslim courtiers to a test of faith through fire. He said he would be willing to be the first to enter a raging fire if the Sultan would embrace Christianity, should Francis come out unharmed. The Sultan refused but was so impressed that he gave Francis safe passage back to the Christian lines and asked Francis to pray that the Sultan might be given the wisdom to discern where true faith lay. Profoundly affected, Francis said that his followers should thenceforth regard Muslims as friends and brothers rather than as enemies. A few years later, he prayed for the safety of the Sultan when another crusade was planned.

It was Francis who first produced a nativity scene, which is so familiar to Christians today, with the baby Jesus in a manger surrounded by animals, Mary and Joseph, and others. Francis' simplicity, gentleness and goodness transformed the lives of everyone he met and he has left an indelible legacy.

Figure 4: *The first crib, using live animals, was produced by St Francis. Modern cribs feature Mary and Joseph, shepherds and wise men who came to worship the baby Jesus.*

Tensions, however, continued to arise within Christianity and dissenting groups became vocal. One such group was the Cathars in south-west France. The Cathars were dualists; they saw the world as evil and they believed that their task was to return to the source of all being, the light that was within every person. They accepted the world but considered themselves to be strangers in it, as Jesus had said would be the case for His followers. They lived lives of simplicity and love and their influence grew very rapidly. They rejected some of the fundamental doctrines of institutional Christianity, particularly the power and authority of the Church centred on Rome. The Pope and the authorities in Rome considered this to be a threat and in 1208 called for a crusade to suppress the Cathars.

The word 'crusade' is generally associated with Christian armies attempting to take control of Jerusalem from the Muslims, but this crusade was Christians against Christians. It was the attempt to obliterate and to eliminate what was seen as a powerful and appealing heretical movement. At the time, France as we know it today did not exist and south-west France south of Toulouse was effectively independent. The crusading forces swept down and destroyed Carcassonne, Béziers, Toulouse and much of the surrounding area. Tens of thousands were killed and what was seen as a false belief was suppressed in a brutal manner. The whole of the town of Béziers was burnt, with every man, woman and child being killed, even though only a few citizens of the town were Cathars. The last Cathar was burned in a tiny village in the mountains west of Lézignan called Villerouge Termenès. It was at this time that the Inquisition was formed to enforce compliance with orthodox beliefs. Heretics were brutally tortured and burnt to death (the Church authorities carried out the torture but passed the victim over to the civil authorities to burn the person alive). It was one of the worst blemishes on the record of the Christian Church. Christianity has not always been a force for good and the suppression of the Cathars was a particularly bloody and ignoble part of history.

Francis of Assisi was only one of many influential individuals in this period; another was St Dominic (1170–1221) who formed 'the Order of Preachers' (or Dominicans) in 1216. Dominic brought together a group of like-minded men who wanted to preach the

Gospel message. At this time only priests were allowed to preach (one of the criticisms by the established Church against the Cathars was that lay people were allowed to preach) and Dominic wanted to form an Order of Preachers (hence the abbreviation OP, *Ordo Praedicatorum*) who would proclaim the message of Jesus set out by the Church. However, preaching the orthodoxy of the Church soon led Dominic's Order into conflict with those who did not accept Church teaching, and the Dominicans were to become some of the most influential of the Inquisitors who wished to impose orthodoxy on Europe through the Inquisition. People were encouraged to accuse their neighbours if they were suspected of heresy and many people falsely accused others out of fear that, if they did not, they themselves would be accused.

The whole of Europe was Christian in the thirteenth century and the power of the Church affected every aspect of life. Rome was as powerful as any king and, indeed, more powerful than most. The Church controlled every aspect of life and also controlled the gates of heaven and hell. At the time hell was seen as a physical place where those who were damned were tortured in the most extreme way, and this torture went on for ever. Graphic paintings showed devils driving those in hell into fires of unimaginable ferocity. Fear of hell was a central idea motivating people to be good and to support the Church. Salvation was only to be obtained through the offices of the Church and its priests. Without penance and forgiveness, without being baptised and receiving the sacraments, the gates of hell stood wide open. Today few Christians think in these terms, although the existence of hell as a physical place is still affirmed by many (by no means all) Christians (see pp. 155–8).

The Church had long taught that, after death, souls went to heaven or hell, but there was a third possibility which applied to most Christians; this was that souls would go to an interim place called purgatory where the sins they had committed in life would be purged. St Thomas Aquinas held that the fires of purgatory would be more terrible and painful than anything endured in life. Everyone who went to purgatory would eventually get to heaven but a

Christian could spend thousands of years in purgatory being punished or cleansed from the sins they had committed. The Church could, however, grant absolution from these sins and reduction of the time in purgatory. This could be achieved in various ways, but they involved penance, rejecting sin and doing good works, which could include paying money to the Church. This gave rise to the practice of selling indulgences. In other words, in return for payments to the Church, the Church would grant release from a period of suffering in purgatory. The impact of this on faithful people is easy to imagine. If one imagines oneself in this medieval world with death approaching, then to pay money to the Church could ensure freedom from, or reduction of, punishment after death. The Church and bishops became even richer, the power and influence of the Church increased: but not in the way St Francis wanted. The Church was seen by some to have become identified with the interests of those in power and no longer to stand for the values and the message of love and gentleness that Jesus came to preach.

Both the Franciscans and the Dominicans were initially dedicated to 'apostolic poverty'; in other words, living simply and owning nothing, in the way that Jesus seemed to have lived. The Church authorities, with their great wealth, found this to be threatening, as it was a position that was popular with many ordinary people who were becoming critical of the wealth of the Church. In 1323, the then Pope, therefore, declared it a formal heresy ('erroneous and heretical') for anyone to claim that Jesus and His disciples had no possessions and were poor. This directly contradicted a totally opposing resolution adopted by the Franciscans in 1322 but, of course, obedience to Rome took precedence. The Franciscans and others, as a result of this, began acquiring property and wealth in a somewhat similar way to other religious orders.

Against the wealth and power of the Church a group of Christians protested, and for this reason they became called Protestants. Ordinary people increasingly began to be able to read the Bible for themselves, so they were able to compare the message of Jesus recorded in the Bible with the power, wealth and influence of the

Church. An increasing number of people began to feel that the message in the Gospels was not the same as that proclaimed by the Church, and they began to question. This was combined with general improvements in education, an increase in prosperity which brought an expansion of the middle classes and the beginning of a role for scientific enquiry. This challenged the previously unquestioned power of the Church and the truth that the Church was held to convey. Copernicus had challenged the accepted wisdom of the Church which held, following Aristotle, that the earth was the centre of the universe and all the stars and planets revolved in circular orbits round the earth. Galileo took this challenge further. There were, therefore, a whole series of interconnected events which meant that Church authority began to be doubted. Out of this period of rapid social and intellectual change came the Reformation.

EIGHT

Reformation and Counter-Reformation

One of the most important arguments between Christians concerns which is to be given priority:

1) The Church, or
2) The Bible.

This issue underlies many misunderstandings between Christians and still provokes great argument. Very broadly (and all these issues are complex and cannot easily be simplified), Catholic and Orthodox Christians give precedence to the Church, which they see as being founded by Jesus to carry on His work in His name and which is placed on earth to bring people to God, whereas Protestants see the Bible as primary, the individual's relationship with God as central and the Church as secondary. As one might expect with a debate that has continued for nearly 2,000 years, the issues are not straightforward.

Protestants see the Bible as crucial and consider that it is inspired directly by God. The Bible is, therefore, the key text for the Christian and each Christian should be able to read the Bible for himself or herself and develop his or her own relationship with God. The Church is secondary to the primacy of the biblical record. Whilst the Church is important, it is nevertheless to be judged against the word of the Bible. This was the great Protestant theologian Martin Luther's position when he rejected the teaching of the Catholic Church, of which he was a member, and demanded that if anyone wanted to refute his arguments, this should be done by 'the plain word of Scripture alone'. Many Christians find this position persuasive; however, the alternative position is just as convincing.

Those who see the role of the Church as being primary will say that it is the Church that put the Bible together. There were many early accounts of Jesus' life; as the number of Christians grew, so too did the number of stories about Him and His life. Some of these were considered to be true, and others were seen as legends or stories told after His death by those who never actually knew Him. It became important, therefore, to separate those stories which could be regarded as reliable and authoritative from those that were less reliable. This process took about 200 years after Jesus' death. It was not until then that the 'canon' of the New Testament was broadly agreed. The canon comprises those books and letters about Jesus which the Church considered authoritative and reliable. Catholics, therefore, see the New Testament as a collection of vitally important early records about Jesus, assembled by the Church.

The debate between these positions is ongoing. Until about 1965 (the time of the Second Vatican Council), the Bible tended to be regarded by Catholics as not being of the same central importance as it was among Protestants. In the 'modernist crisis' (which will be explained on pp. 139–40) some Catholic commentators on the Bible were condemned by the Church. This meant that in the early years of the twentieth century, there were few Catholic biblical scholars and academic study of the Bible was discouraged in Catholic circles. This is no longer the case today, and Catholic and Protestant academics together study the Bible and seek to understand its sources and origins.

One of the greatest Christian theologians and philosophers of the last 2,000 years was St Thomas Aquinas (1225–74). A member of the Dominican religious order, he taught at the University of Paris at a time when this university was the foremost in the Western world. Aquinas taught at a crucial period in history (the mid thirteenth century), as the works of Aristotle had been lost in the West and had only recently been imported from Islamic centres of learning. Aquinas, therefore, was one of the early Christian thinkers who had access to the full works of Aristotle. His great genius was to produce a synthesis of Greek philosophy with Christianity.

Aquinas separates Natural and Revealed Theology. Natural Theology is the understanding of God that can be known by human reason. It includes arguments for the existence of God and basic knowledge about the nature of God and God's attributes. Revealed Theology is based on divine revelation in the Bible or is derived from the Church. For Aquinas, nothing in Revealed Theology is held to contradict Natural Theology, but Revealed Theology amplifies what can be known by reason. Revealed Theology includes the doctrine of God's creation of the world, the nature of the Trinity and the incarnation of Christ. Aquinas' work was to have a profound effect on the Catholic tradition.

The greatest divide in Christianity happened, as we have seen, in 1054 with the split between the West and the East. Even more serious, however, in terms of the long-term fragmentation of Christianity was the Reformation. Many factors came together at the same time which provided fertile ground for the Reformation to take hold, but the translation of the Bible into local languages from Latin, the invention of the printing press which meant that Bibles were freely available to ordinary people, and new developments in scientific enquiry were major contributors. However, there were also broader social changes, with the development of an enlarged middle class as well as more widely available education, which enabled the old authorities to be challenged and people to develop a new sense of freedom. These merely provided the right circumstances for the Bible to do its work. The Bible, read by ordinary people, now became, for many, the yardstick for defining what Christianity was about. Underlying this was a rejection of the position taken by Aquinas that philosophy and theology were handmaids. The reformers thought that reliance on Greek philosophy had distorted Christianity and they sought to bring people back to obedience to the Bible alone as the perfect revelation of God.

Whilst almost every commentator will acknowledge the importance of the above factors to the Reformation, there is another one that is often ignored; and that is the importance of the Franciscan movement. As we saw in the previous chapter, Francis of Assisi was not an academic. He took the Bible seriously and sought to live a Christian life based on this. His followers were poor and initially embraced poverty; they challenged the wealth of the other great religious orders. Their love for all human beings, their commitment to the teaching of Jesus and to following Him closely had a profound influence. In many ways the Franciscan movement (see pp. 190–1) was to be a precursor to the Protestant Reformation. Whilst the Franciscans were faithful Catholics, they provided an example of a simple lifestyle and the need to place the Bible at centre stage, and these were to be features of the Reformation. The key difference between the Franciscans and the reformers was that the Franciscans did not deviate from their loyalty to the Catholic Church and the Pope in the way that the reformers did; they always worked within the structures of the Church.

There were various key figures who contributed to the Reformation and gave expression to the new understanding of Christianity to which it gave rise, but none were more important than Wycliffe, Hus, Luther and Calvin.

John Wycliffe (*c.* 1324–84)

Wycliffe was an English theologian at Oxford University. He was strongly influenced by the great Franciscan writer, William of Ockham. Wycliffe was a brilliant biblical scholar and was one of the first to translate much of the Bible from Latin into English. He argued that the Bible should be supreme in the life of a Christian. He believed that, in secular matters, the king should be supreme over the Pope and questioned the power and influence of the Church. Wycliffe argued that the huge Church lands should be taken away and administered by civilians. He wanted the monasteries to be abolished, as they did not feature in the Bible, and he argued that the vast landholdings of the monks should be given to the people.

Not surprisingly, this view was strongly resisted by the clergy and the monks; and Wycliffe was accused of heresy. However, his views were popular with ordinary people, who in many cases viewed the power and money of the Church in negative terms. Wycliffe was also influenced by the Franciscans who devoted their lives to poverty and the proclamation of the Gospel.

Wycliffe's message was spread across England by so-called 'poor priests' who went out two by two. They lived a life of poverty, were not in religious orders and they preached the Gospel to the people. They wore dark-red robes and carried a staff. Pope Gregory XI condemned them, calling them 'Lollards', which was meant as an insult but became a badge of honour. (The name 'Lollards' probably has Dutch origins and refers to 'mumblers' or those without academic training in theology.) They preached what they saw as God's law, which they held was the only basis for Christianity and was firmly based on the Bible. One contemporary commentator said that towards the end of Wycliffe's life, every second person in England was a Lollard.

Wycliffe's approach was very popular with ordinary people. He challenged his opponents on the basis of the text of the Bible and argued that the Bible was God's revealed word and, therefore, should be the only authority. This was to be a fundamental principle of the Protestant Reformation – that the Bible should take precedence over the teaching of the Church. Wycliffe challenged the power of the Pope in increasingly strident terms and came to regard the Pope as the source of evil. He rejected the power and hierarchy of the Church and saw them as leading people away from the message of Jesus. Wycliffe argued that there was no need for a Pope in Rome. The Christian community might need a leader, but this should be someone who most closely followed Jesus and His message. God, as Trinity, was present everywhere and it was God who was the real leader of the Church, not the Pope.

In spite of the impact that Wycliffe made in his lifetime, his influence declined in England after his death. The power of the Church remained strong, and it was in Europe that Wycliffe's greatest legacy remained – particularly through the work of the Bohemian reformer Jan Hus.

Jan Hus (c. 1371–1415)

Hus was twelve years old when Wycliffe died. King Richard II of England married Anne of Bohemia and they travelled to Bohemia and took Wycliffe's ideas with them. Hus adopted these ideas and set out to reform the Church in Bohemia on the lines set out by Wycliffe. Hus argued that indulgences were not biblical and were a means of the Catholic Church increasing its wealth. He also rejected the ability of the Pope or bishops to call for people to take up arms (the Crusades were obviously in his mind). The correct response was to follow the teaching of Jesus and to pray for enemies rather than to fight them; again, the legacy of St Francis may be seen here (see pp. 91–2). In 1412, three of Hus's followers who had condemned the practice of the Church selling indulgences were beheaded, and tensions rose further between the many followers of Hus and the Church. Hus was excommunicated (i.e. excluded from the Church) in 1411. Public riots in support of him took place and the government attempted to support Hus, as he was very popular, but the power of the Church prevailed. He was put on trial (having first been promised safe passage, but the Church then reneged on this commitment). He was not allowed a legal defence and was condemned, humiliated, degraded and then burnt at the stake on 6 July 1415. This is still celebrated as a public holiday in the Czech Republic. His last words were reputed to be: 'God is my witness that I have never taught that of which I have by false witnesses been accused. In the truth of the Gospel which I have written, taught, and preached, I will die today with gladness.'

His followers split into two groups: the Hussites (there is still an active Hussite Church in the Czech Republic) and the Taborites. The latter were more extreme and rejected the Roman Catholic

Church because, they argued, it was not founded on the Bible. The Taborites were to found a group called the Moravian Church (or the Unity of Brethren) in 1457, and this group expanded into Germany and formed one of the first Protestant church communities. The Moravian Church sent out more missionaries than any other Protestant group and it was missionaries from the Moravian Brethren who were later to convert John Wesley.

Martin Luther (1483–1546)

Many who have not studied the history of Christianity see Martin Luther as the founder of Protestantism. Although the influence of Luther cannot be exaggerated, as we have seen above, there were major figures before Luther who anticipated much of what he was to teach.

Luther became an Augustinian monk in 1505. He was thus firmly in the Catholic tradition and had studied St Thomas Aquinas and William of Ockham as well as other key figures. Luther had an ambivalent attitude to the philosophy of Aristotle and also St Thomas Aquinas because, whilst he valued their rigour, he did not believe that reason could bring a person to God. He felt that, in monastic life, he was going through the motions of faith, but faith did not really 'strike home' to him as something he personally appropriated. This was not because of lack of dedication; accounts of his life portray him as seeking to dedicate himself to God through fasting, prayer and study, but somehow all this effort did not seem to bring him any sense of a personal relationship with God. To an extent, his monastic life did not seem 'real'. Luther was ordained as a priest in 1507 and in 1508 he became a lecturer on the Bible at the University of Wittenberg in Germany.

In 1517, twelve years after Luther entered the monastery, the Pope sent an emissary, Johann Tetzel, to Germany to sell indulgences. The Pope badly needed money to rebuild the magnificent Basilica of St Peter in Rome and Tetzel was charged with raising this money. The

Catholic Church argued that whilst faith in God was important, this alone could not save a person from hell – faith had to be manifested in charitable works. Further, the Church had been given authority by Jesus to decide who went to heaven and to hell (*'If you forgive anyone's sins, their sins are forgiven; if you do not forgive them, they are not forgiven'* – John 20:23), but, more importantly, it had been given authority to let people off time in purgatory (see pp. 94-5; 156). Anyone who went to purgatory would eventually achieve the Beatific Vision of God but, in the meantime, their suffering would be prolonged and terrible. The Church taught that paying money to the Church was a charitable act by which time in purgatory could be reduced or eliminated. If a person was wealthy and dying it was very appealing to donate money to the Church to get time off purgatory. As Johann Tetzel is meant to have said: 'As soon as the coin in the coffer rings, the soul from purgatory springs.' Luther strongly objected to this and said that forgiveness belonged to God alone. This was the beginning of his attack on the authority of the Pope and the Church.

On 31 October 1517 Luther decided to write to his local bishop, arguing against the practice of selling indulgences. Enclosed with his letter was a document that was to become famous, called 'Disputation of Martin Luther on the Power and Efficacy of Indulgences'. This came to be known as 'the Ninety-five Theses'. The language of this document was quite direct and it is not surprising that the Church should have seen it as an attack. For instance, in Thesis 86 Luther asks: *'Why does the Pope, whose wealth today is greater than the wealth of the richest Crassus, build the basilica of St Peter with money from poor believers rather than with his own money?'* Luther, however, was not content with simply having written a letter; he also placed a copy of his Ninety-five Theses on the door of his local church, thus publicly making clear his position. This was the normal way of publicising news at the time; today's equivalent would be publishing something on the Web. People read what Luther had written and it was copied and distributed widely. Within two years copies of the Ninety-five Theses had reached England, France and Italy.

Luther argued that Jesus Christ came to earth to save human beings from their sins. No actions were needed by human beings in order for their sins to be forgiven. Jesus died on the cross to release people from their sins as a free action of love by God. Nothing more was required for salvation; faith alone was all that was needed. Each individual had to accept Jesus as their personal Saviour, and provided they genuinely repented and trusted wholly in God, then faith alone was all that was necessary. The grace and love of God would pardon all sins. Luther himself found this tremendously liberating and, for the first time, he had a personal experience of feeling released from the burden of sin. For Luther, the Bible was fundamental and any Christian doctrines not firmly anchored in it were to be rejected.

Luther's Thesis 62 says: *'The true treasure of the Church is the most holy gospel of the glory and grace of God.'* Luther and other Protestant reformers wished to return Christians and the Church to what they saw as the original Gospel message, and they rejected all the teachings of the Catholic Church which could not be shown to be based on the 'plain word of Scripture'. The importance of the Gospels and the New Testament to Protestant Christians cannot be over-estimated. However, Luther and his followers also accepted much of the teaching of the early Christian Church. In what has become called his 'small catechism' he said that his followers should recite the Apostles' Creed and the Lord's Prayer (see p. 46) every morning. What is more, Lutheran eucharistic services also include the Nicene Creed (see pp. 77–8), so the continuity between established Catholic and Orthodox Christianity and what became the Lutheran Church is considerable. Lutherans also retained bishops and the centrality of the Eucharist, so that there is much more in common today between Catholicism and Lutheranism than many people realise.

The great contrast between Luther and the Catholic Church is often expressed by saying that Luther emphasised faith and not works. The implication of this is that the Catholic Church held that the Christian achieved salvation by doing good works (including giving money), whereas for Luther it was entirely a matter of the grace of God saving a sinner. Everyone was a failure, everyone was in sin and only the grace and love of God could achieve salvation. In fact, this is a crude picture; the Catholic Church has always emphasised the importance of faith and God's grace in bringing people to salvation, and Luther always considered that faith would lead to good works.

Luther was an attractive and charismatic figure but he had a dark side as well, shown most clearly in his negative attitude to the Jews. There have always been elements in Christianity hostile to the Jews, seeing them as responsible for the death of Jesus. Jews have, throughout Christian history, been persecuted, forced to convert to Christianity or to emigrate; they have had their possessions expropriated or, in some cases, been put to death. It was not the Nazis who originated the practice of Jews being forced to wear a yellow star, but rather the Christian Church. Martin Luther was strongly anti-Semitic and it is, perhaps, not altogether surprising that in Germany, a largely Lutheran country, anti-Semitism reached its height. There is no serious Christian theologian today who would share Luther's violent anti-Semitism but it must be recognised that it marks yet another dark page in Christian history.

Central to the division between Catholicism and Protestantism was the question of how Christians got to heaven. All Christians committed sins and the issue was how these sins were to be forgiven. Catholics insisted on the need for penitence and forgiveness. In order to be forgiven, penance was necessary and sins were forgiven by God acting through the agency of the Catholic priest during confession, in which the believer told the priest of his or her sins. Some form of penance was laid down (such as saying certain prayers or sometimes going on a lengthy pilgrimage) and the priest then pronounced absolution (or forgiveness) for the sins on behalf of God. Sins could also be forgiven by making a pilgrimage to Rome at certain times, or by one person praying for another, or by the sinner making an offering to the Church – this could take the form of money – and people could even be forgiven after death if suitable offerings were made. Understandably, the Church gained great wealth as a result of such donations. Protestants rejected this and said that Jesus, by dying on the cross, had atoned for the sins of all Christians; all that was necessary was for the Christian to believe in Jesus as his or her personal Saviour. It is for this reason that Protestant Christians constantly praise Jesus as God because, through His death, Jesus opened the kingdom of heaven to all those who believe in Him. Faith alone was all that was required. However, it is important to recognise that genuine faith is empty without this being translated into works and actions of love.

The Catholic Church took time to respond but, in 1521, Luther was put on trial for heresy. He was asked at his trial whether his works were, indeed, his and whether he stood by what he had written. His reply to the second question, delivered the next day, has become famous. He said: *'Unless I shall be convinced by the testimonies of the Scriptures or by clear reason . . . I neither can nor will make any retraction, since it is neither safe nor honourable to act against conscience.'* He is also meant to have said, *'Here I stand. I can do no other. God help me. Amen.'* Luther was convicted and sentenced to death. What is more, no one was allowed to provide him with food or shelter. Luther had powerful supporters, however, and politics were involved, so he was enabled to escape and lived in disguise whilst, meanwhile, his ideas circulated.

In Judaism and Islam, the revelation of God is seen to come through the written text of the Torah or the Qur'an. Luther was following in this tradition and claiming that the written text of the Christian Bible should be ultimately authoritative for Christians. But, of course, this raises all the issues about the status of the Bible and how it is to be interpreted, and these issues still affect Christianity today.

One of the most important statements of faith in the Lutheran tradition is the Augsburg Confession (1530) which sets out Luther's position clearly. It starts by referring to the many divisions existing between Christians and says that it aims to:

*unite the divided parties in agreement on one Christian truth,
to put aside whatever may not have been rightly treated or
interpreted by either side, to leave us all to embrace and adhere
to a single, true religion and to live together in unity and in
one fellowship and church, even as we are all enlisted under
one Christ.*

Within seven years of the Augsburg Confession, this balanced and
temperate language was replaced by strident condemnation of
Catholicism. Luther's wish for unity had scant hope of success and
Europe became riven by terrible wars which set Protestant states
against Catholic states.

John Calvin (1509–64)

John Calvin was one of the foremost Reformation thinkers. He was
not as much of an innovator as his predecessors but he systematised
Reformation thought. He was born in France but spent most of his
life in Switzerland, and the legacy of Calvinism is particularly strong
in Switzerland, where it almost became the state religion. Calvin's
thought, as with the rest of the reformers, emphasised the priority
of the Bible and was negative towards the power and authority
claimed by the Catholic Church and the Pope. The figure of Jesus
was absolutely central to the reformers and anything that got in the
way of the individual Christian's relationship with Jesus was rejected.
This led Calvin to be very negative towards the veneration of saints,
the celebration of saints' days and even the rosary (a rosary is a
string of beads used by some Catholics as an aid to prayer). One
of the most important areas of theology rejected by Calvin was the
Catholic approach to venerating Mary. She has always been held in
very high esteem in the Catholic Church and statues of her are
common in most Catholic churches. The 'Blessed Virgin Mary' is
seen as a key figure by Catholics, and most Catholics would consider
that prayers and devotion to the Virgin Mary are an important part

of Christianity. Calvin rejected this totally and he argued that devotion to Mary took people away from the centrality of Jesus. It would be a mistake, however, to regard Calvin as being negative about Mary – he was not. He rejected the centrality of Mary and the veneration of her, but still considered her a remarkable example for Christians of faithfulness and humility. He also considered that she was a perpetual virgin (i.e. she never slept with her husband) and argued that she was rightfully called the mother of God.

Calvinism is in some ways an austere form of Christianity. There is little in the way of painting and statues in Calvinist churches, Jesus and the Bible are central and the awareness of human sin and failure is very strong indeed. It could hardly be regarded as a joyful approach to religion. Everything depends on the saving power of Jesus. One of the areas with which Calvin wrestled was the complex problem of God's omniscience and human freedom. If God knows everything – past, present and future – then how can human beings be free? This issue has perplexed Muslims, Christians and Jews. Most Christian thinkers have sought to reconcile freedom and God's omniscience, but Calvin was uncompromising, arguing that since God was omniscient, and since God's will was sovereign, human beings could not be free. This led him to affirm the doctrine of predestination. This is important as, instead of people being free to decide the sort of lives they would live and being judged as a result, Calvinists assert that God predestines or chooses some people to go to heaven and some to go to hell, and there is nothing that the individual can do about this – except to pray for the grace of God so that he or she may be one of the chosen ones. In saying this, Calvin was not being as innovative as some commentators assume, as a similar position can be inferred from the writings of Martin Luther and other reformers, and even St Augustine seems to get very close to this position, but it was Calvin who formulated the doctrine most clearly.

Engaging with this history may seem irrelevant to Christianity today, but it is essential for an understanding of the multifaceted nature of modern Christianity. Perhaps more important is a constant theme throughout this book that there are continual grassroots movements to return an institutionalised Christianity to something that more closely reflects the teaching of Jesus. Institutions and Christianity do not mix well and ordinary people recognise this. Today, the cynicism about Christianity amongst many people in the West is actually a reaction against established churches rather than Christianity itself. However, grassroots movements tend to be opposed by institutions and attempts are generally made to suppress them; this certainly happened with the Protestant Reformation.

The Counter-Reformation

The Catholic Church's reaction to the Reformation movement across Europe was understandably hostile, but intellectually there was no clear response until the Counter-Reformation. Various Catholic initiatives emerged to counter the Protestant Reformation; perhaps the most important single group was the Society of Jesus, founded in 1540 by a Spaniard, Ignatius of Loyola (1491–1556). The Jesuits were, and are, a missionary order of priests and brothers who took the usual three vows of poverty, chastity and obedience but, in addition, members of the Society took a vow of obedience to the Pope, representing their commitment to loyalty to the Catholic Church in the face of Protestants who rejected its authority. The Jesuits came to be considered the academic elite in the Catholic Church and they have a formidable record of achievements in missionary and educational work around the world. The animosity between the early Jesuits – who were concerned to stamp out what the Church saw as heresy and to maintain orthodoxy – and the Protestants was considerable. However, in the centuries since their formation, and inspired by the life of Jesus and the example of St Ignatius, tens of thousands of Jesuits have dedicated their lives to service, to education and to love of those committed to their charge. Many members of the Society represent wonderful examples of what a Christian life should be like, living simply and committed to the good of others and seeking to bring them to God. We see here, therefore, the contrast that so often occurs within all religion: the combination of terrible abuse with the heights of sanctity, love and self-sacrifice. The energy provided by the Jesuits did much to re-energise the Catholic Church and to move it onto the offensive to combat the rise of Protestantism, as well as to spread Christianity across the world. Jesuits also embraced science, and many great scientists (including a particularly large number of astronomers) have been Jesuits.

Most significant, however, in the Counter-Reformation was the Council of Trent which was held between 1545 and 1563. This great Council, a gathering of Catholic bishops, issued clear condemnations of many Protestant claims and provided clear and robust replies to many of the Protestant challenges. One of the most important features of the Council of Trent was the emphasis placed on the writings of St Thomas Aquinas, whose works were placed on the high altar alongside the Bible. It was the Council of Trent that, above everything else, affirmed the importance of Aquinas in the intellectual life of the Catholic Church. Three centuries later, in 1879, Pope Leo XIII recommended to all Catholics the works of St Thomas Aquinas and the Catechism produced by the Council of Trent. It is, perhaps, significant that whilst the great Councils of the early Church are recognised by almost every Christian denomination as authoritative, the Council of Trent was only a council of Catholics and, therefore, its deliberations are not recognised by most non-Catholics and, in particular, by the Eastern Orthodox Church.

Importantly, the Council declared that only the Catholic Church could interpret the Bible correctly, and any individual who claimed to make his or her own interpretation which was at variance with the teaching of the Church was condemned as heretical. The Bible and the teaching of the Church were given equal weight, but since the Bible could only be correctly interpreted by the Church, the authority of the Catholic Church was in fact reinforced. This position was to apply for at least the next 400 years and effectively defined the division between Catholic and Protestant. Put simplistically, if anyone today says, 'The Church teaches . . .' it is almost certain that he or she will be a Catholic, whereas someone who defends a position by saying, 'The Bible says . . .' will almost certainly be a Protestant.

The other highly significant position taken by the Council related to the sacraments. Seven sacraments were defined and these were held to be essential to the life of a Catholic Christian. These sacraments were:

1) *Baptism* – through which someone enters the Church. They are sprinkled with water that has been blessed, the sign of the cross is made on their forehead and they are anointed with chrism, and their parents and godparents confirm on behalf of the baby, that they believe in Christ and renounce the devil.
2) *Confirmation* – in which someone confirms the vows taken at baptism, since baptism is generally conferred on babies before they can understand.
3) *Eucharist* – the celebration (the Mass) at which the faithful share bread and wine in obedience to Jesus' final command to His disciples at the last meal before His death, to 'do this in memory of me'.
4) *Matrimony* – this is for life and represents a binding contract that cannot not be broken. (If the marriage is subsequently considered always to have been invalid, it might be annulled by the Church.)
5) *Holy Orders* – by which a layman is made a priest.
6) *Confession* (now called Reconciliation) – in which the believer confesses his or her sins to a priest and receives forgiveness and reconciliation.
7) *Extreme Unction* – given to a dying person in preparation for death (now called Anointing of the Sick – given to those who are seriously ill and not just to the dying).

Sacraments are outward displays of a spiritual reality which are administered by a priest (baptism is an exception, as this can be administered by a lay person in case of need). Baptism is universal; there is therefore no such thing as 'Catholic baptism' and Catholics recognise baptism in other churches. The sacraments – particularly Eucharist and Reconciliation – are absolutely essential in the life of a committed Catholic. Faithful Catholics are expected to attend Mass once a week on a Sunday and also on key holy days in the year.

Figure 1: In Catholic churches some Communion wafers, which have been consecrated by a priest during the Mass, may be 'reserved' for use on some future occasion, such as taking Communion to a sick person. Since this is believed to be truly the body of Jesus, some Catholics will pray in devotion before the Blessed Sacrament.

At the Mass, the faithful receive bread and wine which are consecrated by the priest and represent Jesus' body and blood. The word 'represent' here is, however, ambiguous. At the Council of Trent, the doctrine of transubstantiation was affirmed, although it had been widely accepted amongst Catholic for several centuries. Catholic theologians wished to emphasise that Jesus was really present at the Mass, and when someone ate consecrated bread and wine they were really eating and drinking the body and blood of Jesus Himself. This goes back to the Last Supper which Jesus shared with His disciples. He broke bread, gave it to His disciples and said: *'This is my body given for you; do this in remembrance of me.'* Then He took wine and passed it around His disciples, saying: *'This cup is the new covenant in my blood, which is poured out for you'* (Luke 22:19–20). When the faithful Catholic receives the consecrated bread and wine at the Mass, these are not, according to the Catholic tradition, a symbolic reminder of the Last Supper; the believer is really eating and drinking Jesus' body and blood. At first sight this seems an extraordinary claim (and, as we have seen, it gave rise to charges from the Romans that Christians were cannibals). The Catholic Church explains this by the doctrine of transubstantiation, which holds that when a Catholic priest consecrates the bread and wine at Mass, these really become the body and blood of Christ but, by a miracle, they still seem to be bread and wine. The appearance and taste do not change but the underlying reality does. There are thus held to be two miracles taking place: in the first the bread and wine is changed into Jesus' actual body and blood and, in the second, the appearance of the flesh and blood is concealed and it appears to be bread and wine. Protestants, of course, were to completely reject this doctrine as, they held, it was unbiblical. Whereas most Protestants still take part in what is variously called the Mass, Eucharist or Last Supper, they hold that the bread and wine are symbolic representations of Jesus.

More recently some Catholic theologians have attempted to restate the understanding of the presence of Christ at the Mass. In particular, two approaches are worthy of note: transfinalisation and transignification. Although not the first to put forward these ideas, the theologians Edward Schillebeeckx and Karl Rahner both explored transignification and transfinalisation as ways of understanding the Eucharist. Both argue that that Christ is really present in the consecrated bread and wine and that a change of reality occurs, but to put it very simply, transfinalisation means that at the consecration the *purpose* of the bread and wine is altered, whereas transignification refers to the bread and wine undergoing a change of *meaning*. For Schillebeeckx, this meaning is to be found in the interpersonal relationship between Christ and the believer.

In the Eucharist Christ offers Himself as a gift. Schillebeeckx argues that:

> *We ought to be concerned with an interpersonal relationship between Christ and us, an interpersonal relationship in which Christ gives himself to man by means of bread and wine which, by the very gift, have undergone a transfinalisation and an ontological and therefore radical transignification.*

The Catholic Church rejected both of these ideas as inconsistent with Church teaching on transubstantiation, as both undermine the claim that the substance, the essence of the bread and wine, is changed into flesh and blood.

The Church of England and the Episcopalian churches

Many people, when asked about the founding of the Church of England, will refer to King Henry VIII's split with Rome, due to his wish to remarry, as the beginning of the Church of England, but this is to be simplistic and to betray a misunderstanding. Members of the Church of England do not consider that a new Church came into existence with the split from Rome. Instead they maintain that there is continuity between the Church before and after the split. The first Christian missionaries reached Britain within a hundred years or so of Jesus' death and bishops from Britain were known to be at some of the great Councils of the Church in the fourth century.

King Henry VIII (1491–1547) broke with Rome and proclaimed himself to be head of the Church of England in 1534. The date is significant, as it was eleven years before both the death of Luther and the commencement of the Council of Trent. Rome was feeling sensitive to the advance of the Protestant cause across much of Europe. Because King Henry VIII had not produced a male heir, and because this was considered so vitally important to maintain the stability of the Tudor dynasty, he wished to divorce his wife, Catherine of Aragon, to marry Anne Boleyn. The Pope refused to sanction the divorce and so Henry felt he had no alternative but to repudiate the authority of Rome in order to secure the succession by getting a male heir. By splitting with Rome, Henry made himself head of the Church of England. He then appointed the bishops in England and the bishops were required to owe loyalty to him rather than to the Pope. Prior to this, Church taxes were paid direct to Rome and the revenues of the great monasteries, which owned huge tracts of English land, were exempt from state taxes. Rome controlled the appointment of bishops and the power of Rome was omnipresent. King Henry, in rejecting Roman authority, achieved various things:

1) He was able to divorce his wife and marry an attractive younger woman with whom he had fallen in love and whom, he was convinced, would give him a male heir.
2) He secured huge sums of money as he took assets (mostly land) away from the monastic orders, and funds that previously flowed to Rome now flowed to him.
3) His authority in his own kingdom became largely unquestioned as Rome could no longer intervene in order to subvert or challenge his rule.
4) Loyalty to the king as supreme sovereign and head of the Church of England was unquestioned – at least among those who did not continue to hold to the Catholic faith.

It would be a mistake to think that it was only Henry's wish for a new wife that caused the split with Rome. England had, since before the time of Wycliffe, been influenced by Protestant thought and many in England welcomed the split. After Henry's death, his son Edward VI (or, rather, the boy-king's Council who acted in his name) continued Henry's affirmation that the king was the head of the Church. However, Catholicism was restored when Edward's sister, Mary (1516–58), came to the throne. She was given the nickname 'bloody Mary' as she burnt nearly 300 Protestants as well as forcing thousands more to flee into exile. Henry's youngest daughter, Elizabeth I (1533–1603), came to the throne after Mary's death and she re-established the Church of England and in turn, persecuted Catholics.

The Church of England would argue that it was probably founded by St Augustine in the sixth century (see pp. 83–4) and that there is an unbroken link between the ancient Church and the modern one. Although influenced by figures such as Wycliffe and Luther, and although rejecting the supreme authority of the Pope (and therefore 'reformed'), the Church of England continued to have bishops, the sacraments and almost all the teachings of the Roman Church and was therefore 'catholic' (notice the small 'c', as 'catholic' here stands for the universal Christian Church, of which members of the Church of England see themselves as being a full part).

The Church of England also argues that it maintained the Apostolic Succession. In the Catholic and Orthodox Churches, it is held that Jesus commissioned the twelve apostles, and these apostles in due course consecrated bishops, and these bishops consecrated priests. Every priest, therefore, is in a direct line of succession to the apostles and, in principle, could trace back their priestly orders to the original apostles. The Church of England strongly upholds this tradition and maintains that its priests are validly ordained as priests in the one, 'catholic' (which means universal) Church.

When King Henry broke with Rome, life in the ordinary parishes of England continued in very much the same way as in the past, and most priests and bishops (there were, of course, exceptions) accepted the new position that the king was the head of the Church. Those priests had been ordained by Catholic bishops and were thus validly ordained. The bishops, similarly, had been validly consecrated as Catholic bishops. When these same bishops accepted the new Church of England and ordained priests and consecrated bishops they were, therefore, maintaining the unbroken line which went back to St Peter. This position is rejected by the Roman Catholic Church which maintains that the Apostolic Succession was broken, as there was a 'defective intention' by the bishops who became part of the Church of England and, therefore, the ordinations they performed were invalid. On this basis, in the Catholic Church's eyes, the Church of England's priests are not actually priests at all as they were not validly ordained.

The Church of England also affirms the centrality of bishops, something that many mainstream Protestant churches reject (not all – Lutherans also have bishops). Hence Anglicans in the United States are referred to as 'Episcopalians' as they affirm the importance of bishops (the Latin word *episcopus* means 'bishop' or 'overseer').

The Church of England accepts all the major Christian creeds and the teachings of the early Church Fathers. The 1662 Anglican Book of Common Prayer, which is one of the most important traditional statements of Anglican doctrine, says that the Apostles' Creed must be recited at most morning and evening services and the Nicene Creed at eucharistic services. The Church of England, therefore, sees itself as being entirely faithful to mainstream Christian teaching from the time of the early Church and, therefore, considers itself to be a reformed church but also part of the universal catholic Church.

There were, nevertheless, some significant areas where the Church of England departed from Roman Catholic doctrine; for example, the Eucharist, where although Anglicans still believe the bread and wine are really the body and blood of Jesus (see p. 51), they do not accept the doctrine of transubstantiation and are reluctant to define in precisely what way Jesus is present, seeing this as a mystery. In addition, there was greater stress placed on the Bible and members of the Church of England were free to read and interpret the Bible for themselves. There is also remarkably little in the way of central authority in the Church of England, in contrast to the Catholic Church, where the teaching authority of the Magisterium in Rome pervades almost every aspect of the life of that Church.

In recent years the Church of England has sought to reunite with Rome but the discussions have not really progressed, largely on the issue of Anglican priestly orders, which the Catholic Church refuses to recognise. More recently, as we shall see, the Anglican Church has ordained women and, in some cases, has accepted homosexual relationships. These are stumbling blocks to reunification which will not be easily overcome.

Summary

By the end of the sixteenth century the divide between the Catholic Church on the one hand and an increasing number of Protestant churches on the other was clear. The divisions became more entrenched and these divisions were to be exported round the world. Even today, Germany and Switzerland are strongly Lutheran or Calvinist and, wherever Germans settled, there remains a strong Lutheran presence (South Australia is a good example). Anglicans are found in those countries which formed part of the British Empire, whereas Catholics tend to be found in places that were colonised by France, Spain and Portugal which, largely, remained Catholic countries. South America is, therefore, dominated by the Catholic Church. The United States has many Protestant groups which fled persecution in Europe and formed their own communities in the United States and which have, over the years, expanded. The legacy of the Reformation split, therefore, remains with us today, as do the other divisions within Christianity. These tensions and splits have, like the divisions in Islam and Judaism, been a tragic part of Christian history, yet despite them Christians are united in seeking to follow the example of Jesus of Nazareth, whom they all acknowledge as the second person of the Trinity who came to earth out of love for human beings, died on the cross and was resurrected on the third day.

NINE

The Rise of the Protestant Churches

The Reformation led to a tremendous growth in Protestant churches, with people being filled with a new sense of the importance of Jesus and of God's promises as revealed in the Gospels. The Enlightenment was a time of intellectual freedom and scientific enquiry, and across Europe people began to read the Bible for themselves and were not willing to accept ideas on the basis of authority or tradition alone. As a result, the old authority of the Catholic Church was challenged and Protestant Church membership grew. Prior to the Reformation, apart from the division between the Eastern and Western Churches, Rome maintained tight control of doctrine and liturgy and, thereby, held the Church together. However, once the authority of Rome was rejected and the central authority of the Church was swept away, fissures and splits occurred within Christianity. Initially many of the Protestant churches, such as the Church of England, were associated with nation states, and therefore were state churches – albeit with international links. Other new churches took their names from their founders such as the Hussites, the Lutherans and the Calvinists. The Catholic Church has, it must be admitted, sometimes been harsh in repressing dissent and what it saw as heresy, but the advantage of a strong central form of church government has been that unity has been retained. Once the power of Rome was rejected, any 'glue' that held Christians together dissolved and individual churches arose which often lacked the power to enforce what they saw as orthodoxy, and hence the door opened to fragmentation.

The Protestant churches emphasised the centrality of the Bible but also the individual Christian's relationship to God and Jesus in prayer. With the rejection of transubstantiation (see p. 113), the centrality of the Mass diminished, although most Protestant churches continued to have a Eucharist or Lord's Supper in response to Jesus' command to His followers that they should break bread and share wine in memory of Him. However, other forms of worship and praise began to develop. Protestants emphasised the importance of Jesus as personal Saviour and Redeemer (see pp. 54, 122) and praised Him for freeing them from the burden of sin and guilt. In some ways this was reminiscent of the people of Israel praising God for release from their imprisonment in Egypt but, for the new Protestant churches, praise was even more due to Jesus, who had taken the weight of human sin on Himself and had released every believer who had faith in Him.

Preaching the Gospel was vital in Protestant Christianity and the leader of a Protestant church service was expected to expound and to explain the Gospel reading or some other biblical text. Given the supremacy of the Bible for Protestants, it was to be expected that the exposition of Scripture, showing its relevance to the lives of believers, became a primary activity. Expounding the Gospel at Mass was also, of course, a responsibility of the Catholic clergy but the emphasis placed on the Bible amongst Protestants was much greater. Protestants also focused much more strongly on the salvation of each individual achieved by faith in the risen Lord Jesus, and also on the importance of the sacrifice of Jesus on the cross. The emphasis in Protestant Christianity came to be on Jesus' death on the cross as the single most important moment in Jesus' life, when He was seen as allowing Himself to be sacrificed for the sins of all. Catholics had tended to take a broader view, considering the whole of Jesus' life as being equally important.

Hymns came to be another distinctly Protestant way of proclaiming the Gospel. Hymn singing, prayer and exposition of the Gospel became the key features of Protestant services. Hymnals (books of hymns) were written with hymns for different times in the Christian year. Great European composers produced some of the most remarkable and beautiful liturgical music; from Beethoven to Mozart, from

Handel to Bach, music became a central part of praise and worship. However, for Protestants the emphasis was on the personal relationship of the individual with the risen Lord Jesus, as well as praise for Jesus' work as Saviour. For instance, one of the great Protestant hymn writers, Isaac Watts, emphasised a first-person approach to praise and thanks to God for all that God had done for the individual. Thus:

> *When I survey the wondrous cross*
> *On which the prince of glory died,*
> *My richest gain I count but loss,*
> *And pour contempt on all my pride.*

Whereas Catholics emphasised salvation through belonging to the Church and participation in the sacraments, Protestants emphasised the personal relationship of each individual with the risen Lord Jesus – a relationship that could be experienced when the Christian read the Bible, praised God or was at prayer. The personal relationship (which might be referred to as the individual 'God-relationship') of every Protestant Christian to God was, thus, essential.

Christianity was continually being renewed from the fifteenth century onwards, with new churches or sub-groups being formed which challenged existing churches when these were seen as no longer being faithful to the Gospel message. As always, the Bible provided the key litmus test and as churches grew and, perhaps, lost touch with their original roots, so new groups emerged. John and Charles Wesley (1703–91 and 1707–88) founded what was to become the worldwide Methodist Church, as they did not feel that the Church of England was any longer faithful to the Gospel message. Their fiery preaching and clear dedication led to Christianity emerging again with new vigour and energy.

Methodism was an attempt to revitalise the message of Christianity, which many felt had become institutionalised within the national Church. Although John Wesley himself said, 'I shall live and die as a member of the Church of England', he began unofficially ordaining priests and a split with the established Church became inevitable. The decision in 1795 by the annual conference of the new Methodist Church to provide what came to be called 'the Lord's Supper' in every chapel across the country effectively began the separate Methodist Church, and this brought Methodists into conflict with the Church of England. After John Wesley's death, there were a number of splits and then reunifications, and today Methodism is a relatively small but significant worldwide Christian movement. There are many similarities with the Church of England but also doctrinal differences which, in spite of many attempts, have led to a failure to bring the two churches together.

Presbyterianism was part of the Protestant, Reformed Christian tradition and particularly had its origin in Scotland. The name 'Presbyterianism' comes from the form of church government in which each church is led by elders or presbyters. Presbyterian theology is particularly influenced by John Calvin and John Knox. The emphasis is on the Bible and the grace of God. The Act of Union between Scotland and England in 1707 enshrined Presbyterianism as effectively the official religion of Scotland and most Presbyterian churches around the world have their historical roots in Scottish Christianity.

Baptist Christianity probably originated in 1609 in Amsterdam but spread to England and then to the United States. Baptists rejected infant baptism and instead argued for the need for adult baptism, often maintaining that this was only valid if the person to be baptised was fully immersed in water (in contrast to most other Christians who baptise children by pouring water onto the head). Divisions arose within the Baptist movement between those who held that Christ redeemed all people from the effects of sin (these were called 'General Baptists') and those who maintained that redemption extended only to those who had been correctly baptised ('Particular Baptists'). Today there are about 42 million Baptists and their churches are loosely grouped under the Baptist World Alliance.

The term 'Baptists' covers a wide diversity of churches but they are all committed to the rejection of infant baptism and the need for adult believers to make their own decision about whether or not to be baptised. Baptists have a strong biblically based faith but are not fundamentalist (although different strands within the Baptist tradition have varying views on how much interpretation is permissible). The Baptist tradition arose out of the Reformation, particularly among some in England who felt that the Church of England did not go far enough towards a full Protestant theology. John Smyth, in 1606, broke with the Church of England and in 1609 became pastor of the first Baptist church in Amsterdam. Baptists were often persecuted by more established churches and many went to the United States where different strands in the Baptist tradition are particularly strong.

The Salvation Army has between 1 million and 2 million members worldwide. The founders were Catherine and William Booth who saw the need for a militant Christianity dedicated to the relief of poverty amongst those who were marginalised and had nothing. However, the Salvation Army is concerned not just with the physical but the spiritual needs of the poor and vulnerable. It is present in over a hundred countries around the world and is to be found helping amongst those marginalised by society. It is organised like an army with military ranks and a firm sense of discipline but is a strongly Christian organisation with an emphasis on community service and a commitment to be present wherever the needs are greatest. It is often to be found, therefore, working in the poorest areas of cities, running food kitchens for people living on the streets, providing a bed and warmth for the night for those who are cold and hungry, and never turning its back on anyone in need, irrespective of their faith or lack of it. Members of the Salvation Army wear a uniform and it is based on military lines. Brass bands and music are a vital part of their outreach – these are often to be seen at railway stations, or other places raising money for the work of the Army. The initial converts were prostitutes, alcoholics and those living on the street – these were people who were often ignored by the regular and 'respectable' churches. In many countries, the Salvation Army has a very high approval rating among ordinary, non-Christian groups because of its active work with the poor.

Some groups split away from mainstream Christianity because they wanted to live more radically the message proclaimed by Jesus. The Society of Friends – or the 'Quakers', as they are called – were founded in the seventeenth century and live out a commitment to non-violence and to social justice. A young man called George Fox (1624–91) became convinced that it was possible to have a deep, personal relationship with the living Jesus Christ, and he travelled across England and other areas, including the United States, seeking to bring people back to what he saw as the original message of Christianity. He emphasised simplicity and avoiding luxury, and stressed the need to live a 'good' life in the deepest sense. Quakers have no institutional structure – they have no bishops or priests – and seek to live 'Godly' lives and never to resist evil. They will always, therefore, be pacifists, will refuse to fight in any conflict, and constantly seek to resolve tensions between different groups. They are at the forefront of attempts to prevent conflict and of social justice movements. Reconciliation is a key part of their teaching. Their meetings for worship are held in silence, with individuals speaking into this silence when they feel inspired by God to do so. Quakers have a minimal amount of doctrine, almost no liturgy or structure and tend to focus much more strongly on living the Christian message. They have high ethical standards and in the nineteenth century provided a lead in introducing modern factory and business methods combined with a strong ethical commitment and care for their workers. Companies such as Barclays Bank, Lloyds Bank, Friends Provident (the insurance company), Cadbury, Rowntree's and many others were all founded by Quakers. The worldwide influence of Quakers is still considerable considering how small their numbers are relative to other Christian groups.

Jehovah's Witnesses are a group who worship the single God – Jehovah. They reject mainstream Christian ideas of the Trinity but affirm the centrality of Jesus; because of this some Christians would not include them under the umbrella term 'Christian'. They refuse blood transfusions and have a strong commitment to the importance of the family. They consider secular society to be corrupt and seek to live pure lives as independently from this society as possible. They also reject any idea of hell, instead maintaining that those who reject God will pass out of existence. Jehovah's Witnesses do not celebrate Christmas, Easter or even birthdays, considering that such practices have their origins in pre-Christian pagan ceremonies.

Figure 1: The US dollar bill includes the words 'In God we trust'.

The discovery of the United States of America provided, literally, a new home for many dissident Christians in Europe who fled religious persecution of one form or another in their home countries. They made the dangerous journey across the Atlantic in search of a new life where they could follow their Christian convictions without persecution. It is not surprising, therefore, that the whole of the United States is in many ways founded on Christianity, and yet nowhere else does Christianity take so many varied forms. In almost every town there are many different churches and denominations with differences in doctrine and dogma that may appear small but are often fiercely held. Too often communities define themselves not so much in terms of what they are, but in terms of what they are not. So the growth of many different types of Protestantism often occurred on the basis of points of dogma or doctrine which became definitional for the new communities. In the United States there is a very strong separation of Church and State, so religious education is not allowed in State schools, although the motto of the United States is 'In God We Trust' and American Christians have been particularly active politically in seeking to ensure that they influence government policy, especially in the areas of ethics (notably abortion and homosexuality) and international relations. Not all Christians, however, consider that Christianity should have a political agenda and there are divergent views on this issue.

The move towards more evangelical forms of Christianity accentuated splits within Protestant Christianity and, indeed, different understandings of what it means to be a Christian. There is no single meaning to the word 'evangelical' and evangelical Christians can be found in every Christian denomination, but possibly the most important common features are that they emphasise the centrality of the Bible as well as the importance of a sense of personal conversion and a conviction of the presence of the risen Lord Jesus in their lives. They also see themselves as under an obligation to 'evangelise' or to bring others to share their faith. Evangelical Christian communities also see themselves as independent and reject the idea of being subsidised or supported by the State. The Lutheran and Calvinist Churches were State sponsored, as was – and is – the Church of England. Evangelical communities often saw this link with the State as a form of corruption (they often described themselves, therefore, as 'Free Churches') and they wanted to return Christianity to what they saw as its roots. Baptists and Pentecostal churches (see pp. 123, 216ff.) were examples of strongly evangelical communities but, to repeat, evangelical Christians can be found within every Christian church tradition. These issues will be further explored in Chapter 15.

TEN

The Bible

Since the mid nineteenth century a great deal of academic work has been undertaken on the Gospels. Among scholars there is a measure of agreement (although by no means unanimity) about the structure of the Gospels and how they came to be written. The Gospel of Mark has generally been considered to be the earliest. This is a bare and fairly sparse account, although it contains essential elements of Jesus' teaching and is far more sophisticated in its structure than many today realise. The Gospels of Matthew and Luke were written for different audiences but they both contain most of the Gospel of Mark as well as a common source which scholars have named 'Q' (from the German word *Quelle*, 'source'). The three Gospels of Matthew, Mark and Luke are referred to as the 'Synoptic' Gospels and they share much in common. Mark's Gospel was probably written about AD 60–80 and Matthew and Luke perhaps ten to twenty years later. The earliest Christian records are the letters or epistles written by Paul and others after Jesus' death. These are dated within fifteen to thirty years of Jesus' death and are the closest we have to a contemporary account. These give little detail about Jesus' life but they do serve to confirm many of the central theological ideas coming from the four Gospels.

The Gospel of Matthew was written for a Jewish audience and shows Jesus as the fulfilment of the prophecies in the Hebrew Scriptures. It therefore starts with a long genealogy, or list of descendants, establishing Jesus' identity as the descendant of King David through His adoptive father Joseph, and therefore establishing His credentials as the promised Messiah. It also includes many other references to Jesus fulfilling prophecies from the Hebrew Scriptures as a way of confirming to a Jewish readership that Jesus really was the person prophesied. There is no agreement among Christians about the historical accuracy of many of these accounts and it can be argued that the writer of Matthew's Gospel might have inserted some of them as a way of confirming Jesus' status in the eyes of the Jewish community. Many other Christians, however, would regard the stories as literally true. Matthew very probably used Mark's Gospel as a basis and then inserted material from 'Quelle', the common source shared with Luke.

The Gospel of Luke is generally agreed to have been compiled by a Greek doctor named Luke who intended his writing for a Gentile (non-Jewish) audience. He emphasises the gentleness of Jesus and His all-inclusive teaching and plays down the Jewish emphasis found in Matthew. Luke also uses Mark's Gospel and 'Quelle' but, again, includes his own unique material to provide an equally distinctive picture to appeal to a Gentile audience. It is important to understand that the picture of Jesus in both Matthew and Luke is essentially very similar (after all, they share much common material), but they nevertheless each provide their own individual slant on Jesus' life, and it is not surprising, therefore, that the early Church decided to retain both Gospels.

The whole tone of Matthew and Luke is different. Matthew's Gospel portrays Jesus primarily as a righteous Jew who was coming to restore Israel, and God as strict and demanding obedience to the letter of the Jewish law. Only in Matthew is Jesus recorded as saying that He comes not to abolish the Jewish law but to fulfil it (Matthew 5:17) and that not a 'jot or iota' of the law should be done away with; this would have been music to the ears of orthodox Jews. God is seen in Matthew's Gospel as being judgemental, with numerous references to people being excluded from God's presence, and there is much 'weeping and gnashing of teeth' (e.g. Matthew 13:42; 25:30 amongst others). Matthew describes how Jesus is rescued from King Herod's massacre of young children. Herod, the Jewish king, was frightened by a prophecy which said that the 'king of the Jews' had been born and saw this as a threat to his own throne (Matthew 2:1–7, 16–18). Matthew then portrays Jesus as fleeing to Egypt (Matthew 2:13–15). These stories would have appealed to a Jewish audience who would see the parallel with Moses, who was rescued as a baby from the Egyptians, and who later led the people of Israel out of Egypt, delivering them from slavery. Matthew is indicating that in a similar way, Jesus has come out of Egypt to rescue Israel.

Luke's Gospel has none of these elements. Luke is writing for an entirely different audience and his Gospel indicates this. Whereas Matthew was compiling material for a Jewish reader, Luke was writing for a Gentile or non-Jewish audience. Luke's Jesus, therefore, shows the love of God as being central; God cares for every individual, is always forgiving, and wishes to call back to faithful obedience everyone who has gone astray. Luke has no mention of the massacre of children or Jesus going to Egypt. Luke's Jesus comes to everyone and not just to the Jews; He associates with Samaritans (who were loathed by Jews), cures a Roman soldier's servant (Luke 7:1–10) and forgives a sinful woman (Luke 7:36–50). The whole flavour of Luke's Gospel is, therefore, much gentler than that of Matthew's.

The Gospel of John stands almost alone. It has little in common with the three Synoptic Gospels. The length of Jesus' ministry is only one year compared to three in the Synoptics, the timing of Jesus' death and resurrection is different and above all, John's Gospel is highly theological, portraying Jesus as the incarnate Word of God. The prologue of John's Gospel is profound:

In the beginning was the Word, and the Word was with God, and the Word was God. He was with God in the beginning. Through him all things were made; without him nothing was made that has been made. In him was life, and that life was the light of all mankind. The light shines in the darkness, and the darkness has not overcome it.

There was a man sent from God whose name was John.

He came as a witness to testify concerning that light, so that through him all might believe. He himself was not the light; he came only as a witness to the light.

The true light that gives light to everyone was coming into the world. He was in the world, and though the world was made through him, the world did not recognise him. He came to that which was his own, but his own did not receive him. Yet to all who did receive him, to those who believed in his name, he gave the right to become children of God – children born not of natural descent, nor of human decision or a husband's will, but born of God.

The Word became flesh and made his dwelling among us. We have seen his glory, the glory of the one and only Son, who came from the Father, full of grace and truth.

(John 1:1–14)

One of the central themes of John's Gospel is that God's Word, which was present at the creation and which came to the prophets throughout Israel's history, became incarnate in Jesus. God's very Word, effectively, took human flesh (became incarnate) to communicate the reality of God even more immediately than ever in the past. Here we have one of the most profound expressions of the fundamental Christian theological message – God's Word creates the universe and God's Word now becomes incarnate in Jesus. The prologue to John's Gospel tells of John the Baptist who prophesied the coming of the Messiah. Jesus is described as the 'light of the world' (a common expression used by Christians and often shown in paintings) but people were in darkness, which represented ignorance. They did not recognise Jesus for who He was. Jesus, as God, came to deliver every human being from the slavery of sin and to make them 'children of God', spiritually able to talk to God in prayer as 'Father'. To those who recognised Jesus, He was the Messiah, the chosen One who revealed God's full and final revelation in Himself. This is such a profound piece of theology that many commentators claim that it could only have been written much later than the other Gospels (probably around ninety to a hundred years after Jesus' death); and, indeed, this is the accepted wisdom amongst biblical scholars today. However, the 'accepted wisdom' is not necessarily correct. The writings of St Paul, which were undoubtedly written within twenty years of Jesus' death, are also theologically profound and a small minority of Christian commentators claim that John's Gospel was written much earlier than is generally supposed.

Figure 1: Jesus portrayed as The Light of the World by Holman Hunt (1853). Jesus is shown knocking on the door of the individual soul, seeking admittance, but the door is closed by weeds and resists His invitation to open.

There are few references to parables in the Gospel of John, none of the exorcisms recorded in the other Gospels and, above all, Jesus is portrayed as God's incarnate Word. Jesus is always depicted as being in control. Even when being taken to His crucifixion, events are unfolding as God would have them unfold. Jesus has foreknowledge of the death that awaits Him and goes to His death without any of the apprehension or fear recorded in Matthew's and Luke's Gospels. There is no idea of Jesus suffering in John and the human side of Jesus' nature is played down. Many biblical scholars consider that John's Gospel represents a later theological reflection on the person of Jesus and, therefore, can tell the modern reader little about His life. However, many ordinary Christians do not accept this academic explanation and give high priority to John's Gospel and its message.

There is probably no single issue that unites and yet divides Christians more than the Bible. Almost every division within Christianity can be explained through discussion of the Bible, and yet the underlying unity between all Christians is grounded in the Bible. Arguments about the status of the Bible have a long history, as we have seen, and disputes between science and Christianity have often been based on the status to be given to the Bible. Copernicus and Galileo both argued that, instead of the earth being the centre of the universe and remaining stationary, with the stars and planets moving round the earth, the earth moved round the sun. This was seen as challenging the authority of the Church as well as that of the Bible which, in a number of verses, seems clearly to imply that the earth is immovably fixed. For instance: *'The world is firmly established; it cannot be moved'* (1 Chronicles 16:30).

This fitted well with the science of Aristotle, who had held that the earth was the immoveable centre of the universe around which everything else moved, and was accepted by all Christians. Copernicus and Galileo were condemned because they questioned the authority of the Church, but even more, that of the Bible. In the nineteenth century, Darwin's theory of natural selection also seemed to challenge the Bible, as it maintained that human beings had evolved from lower forms of animal life rather than being created perfect by God in the Garden of Eden and then falling from this state of perfection as a result of the sin of Adam and Eve. Today most mainstream Christians accept evolution as well as Galileo's and Copernicus's views but, at the time, the challenge these ideas represented to the authority of the Bible was considerable.

Christians see God's Word as becoming incarnate in Jesus, so it is the person of Jesus rather than a text that is, for Christians, crucial. However, Christians know about Jesus through the written text – the New Testament. Also, in so far as Jesus was a Jew and is seen by Christians as the fulfilment of the Hebrew Scriptures, the text of what Christians call the Old Testament is also important.

The Protestant Reformation, as discussed in the previous chapter, placed increased emphasis on the primacy of the Bible, and the stress was on individuals reading the Bible for themselves and God speaking to them through the inspiration of the Holy Spirit. Preaching in Protestant church services tended – and still tends – to focus on expounding the Bible and its message. This stress on the Bible culminated, in the middle of the nineteenth century, in increasing academic study of the Bible, not simply as a way of understanding what was written but with increasing stress on when the Bible was written, and what the cultural contexts and influences were at that time. (This was undertaken through what became known as 'source', 'form', 'redaction' and 'literary' criticism of the biblical text.) It rapidly became clear that the Bible was far more complex than had previously been supposed. In particular, scholars focused attention on the sources of the Bible and these were found to be many and various. For instance, instead of the first five books of the Old Testament (the Jewish Torah) having been written down by a single person – Moses – as many Orthodox Jews still hold, it rapidly became clear that the stories in the Hebrew Scriptures were an amalgamation of different sources from various traditions. Even the God that they portrayed was different in different stories. This prompted a focus – which is still with us in terms of the way much academic biblical study is carried out – on what became known as 'biblical criticism'. This sought to reveal the many diverse sources that were brought together to form the Bible as Christians have it today. The word 'criticism' here should not be understood in a negative sense; rather it stands for an attempt to understand the various sources and origins of the Bible.

The academic work on the Bible led to increasing scepticism about what could actually be known about the person of Jesus. Thus began the 'quest for the historical Jesus': the attempt to work out who Jesus really was behind the Gospel accounts. There was an original quest (1840s onwards) and a 'New Quest' (1970s onwards) which brought together the finest biblical scholars and theologians. The most that these arrived at is that no certainty is possible. To what extent, therefore, does the Bible provide reliable knowledge about Jesus' life? This is one of the most important issues dividing Christians and biblical scholars today. There are two extreme positions:

1) The claim that the Bible is literally the dictated word of God – in the same way that the Qur'an is the word of God for Muslims. There is no serious European theologian at any major university who would hold this view. In the United States it might be a view held by a very small minority of academics. It is an approach, however, still held by many ordinary Christians who have not had the opportunity to think through the enormous intellectual problems with this claim, not least the many occasions when the Bible makes contradictory claims that cannot both be true.

2) The claim that the Bible can tell us nothing at all about Jesus of Nazareth, and all that it can show the modern reader or scholar is who Jesus was as seen by the early Church. On this view, the New Testament is a creation of the early Church and consists of stories about Jesus that were intended to make theological points regarding a first-century Palestine figure about whom nothing can be known. A small number of significant academic scholars have taken this view.

Neither of these are mainstream Christian positions. Almost every Christian would argue that the Bible is written by human beings who were inspired by God and that the Bible record can provide the Christian with sound and reliable knowledge about God and Jesus. However, the words 'sound and reliable' can be interpreted in many, many ways. The New Testament gives a theological picture of Jesus. It is, of course, influenced by those who wrote the Gospels or their sources, but the historical accuracy is less important than the soundness of the picture that it presents. If a group of people witness an accident or listen to a lecture, they will give different accounts of it if they are subsequently asked to recollect what happened. This does not mean that their accounts are inaccurate – just that they are partial.

When talking to Jewish commentators on Jesus, it is quite common to hear them say: 'Of course, Jesus was a good Jewish rabbi whose message was lost in its transmission to us. Christianity was invented by St Paul and the early Church and has nothing to do with Jesus himself.' This is a surprisingly prevalent view but it will not serve as an explanation of Christianity because, as will be made clear shortly, St Paul was writing within a very short time after Jesus' death and the message of St Paul is very largely the same as the message recorded in the Gospels about Jesus.

There are many Christian commentators who have, over the years, interpreted the New Testament in different ways, and various pictures of Jesus have emerged:

1) Jesus the misguided prophet who saw Himself as sent by God but was in fact deluded, and went to His death feeling deserted by the God whom He thought He had been serving – summarised in the last words from the cross when Jesus is recorded as saying, 'My God, my God, why have you forsaken me?' (Mark 15:34).
2) Jesus the prophetic revolutionary who wished to establish a new messianic kingdom. This sees Jesus as a failed revolutionary who wished to overthrow the power and might of Rome but, when this did not succeed, chose to go to His death as a way of overthrowing the established order and bringing the world to an end.
3) Jesus the Jew who wanted to convert people back to faith in Judaism as it was traditionally proclaimed.
4) Jesus as a social reformer who wished to introduce a new egalitarian world where everyone was equal.

5) Jesus as a political reformer who wished to overthrow the power structures of existing society and to establish a world where social justice reigned.

6) Jesus the feminist who wished to overthrow the power of a male-dominated establishment, who mixed freely with women and valued them equally and who prized love, compassion and forgiveness, but whose message was subverted by a male-dominated Church which silenced the voices of the female friends of Jesus who would otherwise have been the leaders of the new Church.

7) Jesus the hippie who wished to introduce a new order where money did not matter and love was the only rule.

All these are interesting perspectives but they often tell us more about the commentator who is writing about Jesus than about Jesus Himself. In all cases, these interpretations involve a highly selective reading of the text and a focus on a very small part of the overall tradition whilst disregarding other parts. It is important to recognise that within two decades of Jesus' death the Christian Church had already spread over much of the Roman world. Letters written by St Paul are recorded in the New Testament within a short time of Jesus' death and, at this time, many people who had known Jesus personally were alive and would have corrected any great distortion that crept in. Of course, stories about Jesus were written down by human beings and, like any such stories, these were not wholly accurate and emphasised different facets of his mission and message. This does not mean, however, that the stories can be disregarded or were wholly inaccurate.

Some writers argue that the 'quest for the historical Jesus' must now be abandoned. The real Jesus is lost in the mists of history and is completely inaccessible; all that can be known is what the Church constructed about Him. This was the view held by Albert Schweitzer – not surprisingly, it is not a Christian position.

Central to Christianity, throughout history, have been three fundamental claims:

1) That Jesus is God's Word become incarnate – Jesus is fully human and fully God. He has two distinct natures united in one human being. The person of Jesus is, therefore, the full and final revelation of God to human beings.

2) Jesus died on the cross to save people from their sins and to bring everyone to God. He rose again from the dead and calls all people to Him, to live lives of radical love and service to others. After death all human beings will be judged on how they have lived and will be accountable for their lives.

3) God is Trinitarian – three persons (Father, Son and Holy Spirit) in One. The Holy Spirit guides and inspires individual Christians and the Church. When Jesus was resurrected He specifically said that He was ascending to His Father and our Father and would send the Holy Spirit to be with His followers. This happened at Pentecost when the believers were gathered together and were aware of the presence of God, in the form of the Holy Spirit, coming to them (see p. 60). Christians maintain that, at baptism, the Holy Spirit is given to Christians if they will only be open.

If the essential Christian claims are true, then the accounts given of Jesus' life in the Gospels are fully in accordance with them. The historical details may in some cases be doubtful but this in no way invalidates the truth of the Gospel accounts. Within fifty years of Jesus' death many different stories and accounts of His life were circulating and some were judged by the early Church to be more reliable than others. Paul's letters were circulated, in collected form, around different Christian communities within seventy years of Jesus' death. It was the Church which decided which of the stories about Jesus and which of the letters and books recording the development of the early Church should be included in the 'canon' of the New Testament. In AD 180 Irenaeus refers to a 'canon' of four Gospels, which is the earliest reference to there being four agreed Gospels. By about AD 200 the twenty-seven books of the present New Testament were broadly accepted, although there were still disputes about Hebrews, James, 2 Peter, 2 and 3 John, and the book of Revelation. It should be clear, therefore, that acceptance of the present 'New Testament' was a process of much discussion, dispute and debate in the early Christian Church, but the Church finally decided on the twenty-seven books that presently form what all Christians regard as the New Testament. The role, therefore, of the Church is vital; the New Testament did not, as it were, descend from heaven fully formed. The material in the New Testament is written by human beings and represents the best early record of the life and death of Jesus of Nazareth. The early Christian communities had reflected on Jesus and had come to agreement on how His life and message could best be understood. The Bible, when seen in this way, provides a pivotally important part of the Christian understanding of Jesus and what it means to live life as one of His disciples.

Therefore, although the main differences between Christians may be based on how the Bible is interpreted, beneath this may lie another and more significant difference; namely, does the Holy Spirit inspire and guide individuals or rather, does it inspire and guide the Church which Jesus founded? Broadly, the latter position will be taken by Catholics and the Eastern Orthodox Church, whereas Protestant and Pentecostal churches will affirm the former. The latter position was affirmed by the Catholic Church at the Council of Trent when the importance of the Bible was clearly acknowledged, but only when correctly interpreted, and this interpretation had to be done by the Church. Source criticism, literary criticism, form criticism and the like all challenged the inerrancy of the Bible, and the Catholic Church felt compelled to reply to this and to assert traditional teaching. It did this in reaction to the 'Modernist' controversy.

The Modernist movement in Catholicism was not really a movement but rather a disparate group of British, French and Italian thinkers who took seriously the findings from academic scholarship about the Bible and were sceptical about some important parts of traditional Christianity, including some of Jesus' miracles. They argued that the Virgin Birth should not be regarded as historical and that understanding of the Bible could evolve over time. They challenged some of the teachings of the early Christian Church. George Tyrrell and Alfred Loisy (both Jesuits) were leading Modernists and were driven out of the Church as a result of their position. Loisy's most famous observation was that 'Jesus came preaching the Kingdom, and what arrived was the Church'. He said this with some regret but he rejected the Church as a seat of authority and did not believe that this was what Jesus intended. Further, he criticised some of the early Christian doctrines and argued that they were not what Jesus envisaged. He was excommunicated in 1908. Tyrrell said that commentators on the Bible stared down the well of history and only saw their own face reflected back to them. He was excommunicated in 1909 and refused Catholic burial.

Official Catholic opposition to Modernist ideas increased and in July 1907 the Catholic Holy Office (responsible for doctrine) published a broad condemnation of sixty-five statements which they regarded as stemming from Modernist writers and which they described as part of the Modernist heresy. In September 1910 Pope Pius X introduced the 'Oath Against Modernism' which had to be sworn by every Catholic priest and bishop, repudiating all the Modernist ideas. Today there is almost no Catholic theologian who would hold this view, and the oath was abolished in 1967 by Pope Paul VI.

Today Catholic and Protestant scholars work together as mutual partners seeking to understand more about the Bible and the study of biblical criticism is now a normal part of Christian theology. In this respect, Christianity differs from Islam, as almost all Islamic scholars still maintain that the Qur'an is the dictated word of God. Some Christians once took a similar position in relation to the Bible and, indeed, there are still Christians who hold to this today. It needs to be recognised that Christians who take the Bible as the literal Word of God would find any questioning of its status just as challenging as many devout Muslims would find Qur'anic criticism. However, all the major Christian churches (Catholic, Orthodox, Anglican, Methodist, Baptist, Lutheran, Calvinist etc.) would today affirm the need for a scholarly understanding of the complexity of the biblical material and would not see this as in any sense devaluing the importance and status of the biblical record.

It must be recognised that these issues are complex, but for those who are interested in exploring the issues that arise from study of the Bible in more depth, *Bible Matters* (Peter and Charlotte Vardy, SCM Press, 2016) provides a more detailed account.

ELEVEN

The Philosophy of Religion

Christianity has a long and rich intellectual tradition; reason and faith have always gone hand in hand. There have, as we have seen, been differences of emphasis. The Catholic tradition maintains the essential interdependence of reason and revelation, whereas for many Protestants it is the revelation in the Bible and in the person of Jesus that is primary and reason operates within faith. Nevertheless, almost no Christian would deny the importance of reason in their faith. This means that they have always engaged with the great religious questions:

1) Does God exist?
2) What is the nature of God? (Can God's omnipotence and omniscience be reconciled with human freedom?)
3) How can evil be explained?
4) What happens after death?
5) How can Jesus be both human and divine?

These questions have perplexed and engaged Christians across the centuries and different Christian groups have developed different answers. This chapter will explore some of these differences and the intellectual bases for them.

1. Does God exist?

There are various types of arguments for the existence of God:

Cosmological arguments

There are two types of cosmological argument:

The Dependency Argument

This argument seeks to show that the universe depends on God and that, without God, the universe would not remain in existence. It was clearly summarised by Professor Frederick Copleston SJ in a BBC debate with Bertrand Russell as follows:

1) Everything that exists is dependent on something else for its existence.
2) The universe as a whole is the sum total of dependent things and is itself dependent.
3) Therefore there must be something on which the universe as a whole depends which does not itself depend on anything else.
4) This is God.

The idea of dependency is crucial. Human beings are dependent for their continued existence on many things including gravity, the sun, oxygen, food and so on. Each of these things is itself dependent on something else. Copleston argues that one cannot go on for ever in a regress of causes and there must be an end to the regress; this is a cause that is self-explanatory and does not require any explanation outside itself. This cause, he argues, is God.

There are two major problems with this argument. Firstly, the second premise contains two claims: (i) that everything in the universe is dependent on something else (which seems reasonable) and (ii) that the universe is the sum total of dependent things and is itself dependent. This latter claim is the one that Bertrand Russell rejects. He argues that the universe itself 'just is' and requires no further explanation. In other words, the ultimate brute fact is the universe and we just have to accept that it exists. However, any child of five will, very reasonably, ask, 'Why, Mummy?' The Christian's reply will be that God is self-explanatory in a way that the universe is not – God, it is held, is *de re* necessary (*de re* is the Latin for 'of things' and means that God is necessary in and of God's self) – and cannot not exist. The critic will claim that the universe itself is the ultimate brute fact that does not require an explanation.

St Thomas Aquinas in the thirteenth century put forward five ways of seeking to argue for God. Four out of the five were derived from Aristotle but they all essentially seek to do the same thing – to arrive at God as the *de re* necessary explanation of the universe. The first three ways argue to:

- God as the prime mover (the first mover which explains all motion within the universe and is not itself caused to move by anything else).
- God as the uncaused cause (the cause on which all causes in the universe depend and which is not itself caused to exist by anything else).
- God as the *de re* necessary being. Everything in the universe is contingent (it might not have existed) and dependent (it depends for its existence on other things). God is necessary in that God is not contingent or dependent and everything else depends on the necessity of God's existence.

Aquinas developed these arguments as he did not think there was any way to prove that the universe came into existence. Aristotle had argued that the universe was without beginning and without end. Although Aquinas accepted that the world was created by God, based on revelation in the book of Genesis, he did not think that this could be demonstrated philosophically, so his arguments seek to show the dependence of the universe on God now and at all points in time. For this argument to succeed, one does not have to believe that the universe had a beginning and, therefore, this separates the argument from the second form of the Cosmological Argument.

The Kalam Argument

This argument derives from the great Islamic philosopher, Al-Ghazali (born *c.* AD 1058). Al-Ghazali rejected Aristotle's claim that the universe had always existed, since the Qur'an clearly teaches that God created the world. He therefore sought to produce an argument which depends on the world coming into existence. At the time Al-Ghazali was writing, there was no way that this could be rationally established but we now know that the universe did, indeed, come into existence (time and space came into existence about 13.7 billion years ago when the singularity began to expand in what has been termed the 'Big Bang').

The argument has been revised in a modern form by the Protestant philosopher of religion, William Lane Craig, and runs as follows:

1) Everything that begins to exist has a cause.
2) The universe began to exist.
3) Therefore the universe has a cause.
4) This cause is God.

The first premise would be widely accepted, although it is vulnerable to finding an uncaused event. It would only need one such event to be established by science for the first claim to be rendered invalid. Nevertheless, many would accept this claim is plausible.

The second claim is today generally regarded as being true. The evidence of red shift in the spectrum of light showing that the universe is expanding, as well as detection of the background radiation from the singularity, points to the universe having had a beginning as by far the most plausible scientific explanation.

The third claim follows from the first two – if the first two are true, then so will be the third.

The key step is the fourth claim, which is often unstated. Even if it is accepted that there is an explanation for the universe, this does not mean that the explanation is the personal God of Christianity. It might be argued that there is some prior state other than God that would explain the universe, although, against this, it does not actually make sense to talk of a 'prior state', as time and space did not exist prior to the singularity. If, therefore, the singularity occurred, and if it requires a cause, then this cause needs to be something that is necessary in and of itself and which does not require an explanation. This, of course, is precisely what many Christians consider God to be.

The central weakness of this argument is that, even if it succeeded, it would arrive at a deist rather than a theist God. A deist God created the universe but no longer has any interest in or involvement with it. Christians, Muslims and Jews have always been theists, and this argument does not demonstrate God's continued involvement with the universe.

Ontological arguments

These seek to move from a definition of God to the reality of God. Basically, if one analyses the statement 'God necessarily exists' this means that God has to exist – God cannot not exist. Alvin Plantinga argues that there are only three possibilities if this statement is considered:

1) It could be impossible. However, it is only impossible if the statement 'God necessarily exists' implies a contradiction, and there is nothing contradictory in the statement. If one says, 'Bachelors are female' then this is a contradictory statement, but 'God necessarily exists' is not like this.

2) 'God necessarily exists' could be possibly or probably true. If the statement was 'God exists', then this might, indeed, be possibly true. 'Unicorns exist' may be true or it may not – evidence would be needed. If 'God exists' was like 'unicorns exist' then it, also, might be possibly true; but the statement is not 'God exists' but 'God necessarily exists'. This cannot

simply be 'probably true' because of the claim that God is necessary. The statement must either be true or false.

If, then, the claim is that 'God necessarily exists' and if both 1) and 2) are ruled out, this leaves only the third alternative: 3) 'God necessarily exists' is true.

St Anselm of Canterbury was the first to formulate the so-called Ontological Argument. He maintained that once one has accepted the statement that 'God is that than which no greater can be conceived', then God must necessarily exist, since it is greater to exist both in the mind and in reality than it is to exist in the mind alone. So if someone has the *idea* of God and if God is, indeed, 'that than which no greater can be conceived', then God must exist both in the mind and in reality rather than in the mind alone.

The main trouble with this argument is that it assumes that the idea of a 'necessary being', a being that cannot not exist, makes sense – and Immanuel Kant thought that it was nonsense. Anything, including God, can either exist or not exist. 'Necessary existence' may relate to numbers and mathematics but cannot relate to anything in the real world. The weakness of Kant's challenge is that his claim certainly applies if God is a thing: another object in the universe. However, no serious Christian theologian thinks of God in this way. The whole point of the Ontological Argument is to show that God is *de re* necessary, necessary in and of God's self, and therefore is quite unlike any object in the universe. So to claim that God necessarily exists is to put God into a unique category.

The Design Argument

The Design Argument is possibly the oldest of all the arguments for God's existence. It was first put forward by Cicero but the best-known statement of it was by William Paley, archdeacon of Carlisle. His argument runs as follows: imagine you are crossing a heath and you come across a stone. You may well consider that it came there by chance. Now imagine you come across a watch (in Paley's time this would have been a mechanical watch with cogs and dials). You might not even know what the watch is for but it bears all the marks of contrivance and design, and it is more likely than not that there was a designer. Similarly, if we look around the world it, like the watch, shows all the marks of design.

Many critics today dismiss Paley as a naïve and bumbling clergyman who did not realise that an argument of this sort had been devastatingly criticised by the great atheist philosopher David Hume. However, this is a serious mistake. Paley was one of the greatest minds of his generation. Charles Darwin read Paley's most important book when he was at Cambridge and considered it one of the finest books he had read. Paley knew all about Hume. He knew that Hume had argued that the world is ordered but there is no evidence that it is designed; that if you look at the evidence in the world you would conclude that the designer was limited in power or not wholly good; and that if parallels were to be drawn between design within the universe and the design of the universe as a whole, this would point to many gods co-operating together rather than a single, all-powerful God. Paley understood Hume's arguments. However, what Paley was actually doing was far more subtle. He did not think that the Design Argument proved that God existed but that, if one looked at the incredible intricacies and beauty of the world, it was more plausible than not to conclude that there was an intelligence behind it rather than that the universe was the product of random forces. Richard Swinburne adopts a broadly similar approach when he argues that, if all the arguments for God are taken together, it is more probable than not that God exists.

This, perhaps, is the key to arguments for the existence of God. They can all be criticised, none are foolproof, but they are intended to make a persuasive case. When people saw what Jesus did (including miracles and His teaching), this was not a proof that He was sent by God – people had to make up their own minds. Indeed, some people thought that He was one of the great prophets of Israel who had come again, some that He was mad and some that He was sent directly by God and was the Messiah (Mark 8:27–30). Similarly, the arguments for the existence of God are not proofs in a scientific sense; they are intended to persuade people of the plausibility of God and to stake their lives on God's existence. However, they could always be wrong. St Paul recognised this when he said in one of his letters that if Jesus did not rise from the dead, then Christians were to be pitied more than anyone, as they had staked their life on a mistake.

2. What is the nature of God?

In Islam and Judaism no representations of God are allowed – neither statues, nor pictures nor any other kind of image. Christians take a different view. After a fierce argument in the ninth century in the Christian Church, it was agreed that, since God had taken

Figure 1: God is portrayed as an old man with a white beard, with Jesus and Mary, and the dove symbolising the Holy Spirit. Images such as these are unhelpful as they do not convey any realistic ideas that Christians have of God.

human form in Jesus, it was acceptable to make representations or pictures of God. This opened the door to the incredible religious art of the Middle Ages, but this art has actually been highly misleading. God is often portrayed as an old man. However, such representations are nonsense. Whatever God is, God is not anthropomorphic. No serious Christian theologian or philosopher thinks in these terms. The highest heavens cannot contain God, God is beyond human conceptualisation and yet, Christians maintain, God became incarnate as a human being out of love for human beings.

There are two essentially different understandings of God:

1) Firstly, God seen as being beyond time and space, wholly simple and utterly unchangeable. This is the God of mainstream Catholic theology.
2) Secondly, God seen as everlasting, without beginning and without end. This is the God of mainstream Protestant theology and also of the Franciscan tradition.

In both cases God is seen to be a Trinity of three persons in one (see pp. 78–9; 158–60), omnipotent, omniscient and wholly good. However, there are significant differences, not least in Christian understanding of the attributes of God. In the first model God is seen as acting in a single, timeless act which has a multitude of effects in the history of the universe, whereas the second model of God, since God is in time, sees God as acting in time: the future is future to God and the past is past. Many Protestants who support this latter view argue for what is termed 'openness theology'; the future is genuinely open and even God does not know what events have yet to occur. This position is necessary in order to safeguard human freedom.

There have been Christian thinkers, such as St Augustine, Calvin and Luther, who argue that human beings are not free and are in fact predetermined (see p. 109). This position is often referred to as predestination, as God predestines some people for heaven and some for hell. However, most Christians today do not accept this as, although it affirms the absolute sovereignty of God, it does so at the price of eliminating non-determined human freedom and makes the existence of suffering and evil very hard to explain.

3. How can evil be explained?

The classic rejection of belief in God comes from the existence of evil, particularly more recently, with the existence of horrendous evils which, it seems, no eventual good state of affairs could ever possibly justify. The problem can be put very simply:

1) God is held to be all good and all powerful.
2) An all-good God would want to get rid of evil.
3) An all-powerful God could get rid of evil.
4) Evil exists.
5) So God cannot exist.

The philosopher J. L. Mackie argued that belief in an all-good and all-powerful God as well as the existence of evil is an 'inconsistent triad'; in other words, all three beliefs (omnipotence, being wholly good and the existence of evil) cannot be held together. John Stuart Mill recognised the problem and argued that this did not rule out the existence of God, but either God could not be all good or God could not be all powerful. He chose (and it was a choice) to maintain that if God existed, God must be limited in power. This effectively eliminates the problem of evil, as whilst God wants what is good, and that includes the elimination of suffering, God is limited in power and does not have the ability to achieve this [3] above is rejected]. This approach, however, is not acceptable to most Christians, as to deny God's omnipotence is to deny a crucial attribute of God.

Two alternative approaches are taken within Christian philosophy to resolve the problem of evil. In very general terms, the first approach is taken within the Catholic tradition and the second approach is taken by many Protestant theologians and philosophers.

The Augustinian approach

St Augustine (AD 354–430) fully recognised the problem of evil and, outstanding philosopher that he was, he sought to resolve it. He drew on two sources: the book of Genesis (which he took relatively literally in a way that few theologians would do today) and the philosophy of Aristotle.

From Genesis, Augustine took the idea that God created the world good, free from sin, suffering and death. God created a perfect world in the Garden of Eden. He was influenced in his thinking by looking out of his study one day and seeing a woman breast feeding twins – one on each breast. As he watched one of the twins finished the milk on its side and tried to push the sibling away from the other breast. This had a profound effect on Augustine. If, Augustine reasoned, God created the world good, how come selfishness and greed were built in from birth? The answer he arrived at was 'original sin' – that is, that the disobedience by Adam and Eve in the Garden of Eden had disrupted the whole of the created order and that God's perfect world had been undermined by the introduction of sin into it. All human beings are, therefore, born in sin and affected by sin and, St Augustine argued, this could only be overcome by the grace of God which came from being baptised as a Christian and living the Christian life (see p. 76).

From Aristotle, Augustine took the idea that everything in the universe has a particular *telos* or nature. Anything that exists is actual in that it exists and it has a range of potentialities linked to what it is. Thus a tadpole exists and has the potential to become a frog. An acorn exists and has the potential to become an oak tree. It cannot become a rose or a swan. For many reasons, this potential may not be fulfilled (it may be eaten, it may not fall into good soil, it may fall in an area where there is too little or too much moisture and no nutrient in the soil). Similarly, human beings are actual in that they exist and they have the potential to become fully human (this is the basis for the Natural Law tradition of ethics which is dealt with on p. 164ff.).

Human beings can fall short of their true potential in two ways:

1) they may be physically defective – for instance, blind or maimed or unable to hear, or
2) they may use their free will to act in ways which diminish them and prevent them from fulfilling their true potential.

The second of these is due to human free will where human beings wilfully choose to fall short of the true potential which God has created for them.

For Augustine, anything that exists is good simply because it exists, but 'good' here is being used metaphysically rather than morally. A good acorn fulfils the potential of an acorn by growing into a perfect example of an oak tree; to the extent that it is less than perfect it is defective: it falls short of the true perfection of oak trees. An AIDS virus is good if it fulfils the nature of an AIDS virus, an earthquake is good if it does what an earthquake should do. This is, actually, a very modern view, as we now know that without earthquakes and the movements of the tectonic plates far beneath our feet, the enormous pressure that builds up from the Earth's molten core would have even more devastating consequences. For Augustine, moral evil arises because human beings use the freedom they have been given to be less than God intended them to be. God is not, therefore, to blame for evil; God creates a world that is wholly good but, because of the misuse of freedom by Adam and Eve and subsequently by every human being, evil enters the world.

Augustine's approach has a problem that he does not satisfactorily resolve, namely that he holds that human beings are determined, and this conflicts with the idea that human beings are free in a non-determined sense. Also, most serious theologians today do not take the story of Adam and Eve literally and this reduces the otherwise persuasive nature of his approach.

John Hick's Irenean theodicy

Although this approach is ascribed by the Protestant theologian John Hick to the second-century figure of St Irenaeus, this is not really accurate. Irenaeus hinted towards this approach, particularly in the way he used a key text from the book of Genesis. Genesis 1:26 says that God created human beings in God's 'image and likeness'. Hick separates these two and argues that God creates human beings in God's image with the potential to grow into God's likeness. He rejects Augustine's approach of taking the Adam and Eve story relatively literally and instead argues that this is a pre-scientific approach which no one who has understood Darwin's findings can accept. Hick maintains that God creates human beings imperfect and immature but with the potential to grow into the likeness of God. Sin and evil, therefore, instead of being a regrettable side-effect of a perfect creation, are actually the necessary conditions for human beings to grow into creatures of love and compassion. This world, Hick argues, is 'a vale of soul making' where we literally make or form ourselves during our life by our actions. Evil and suffering are the means that God deliberately uses to create our character.

Hick argues that we are created at an 'epistemic distance' from God – we cannot know that God exists. The world is created deliberately religiously ambiguous so that people are free to choose to reject God or

Figure 2: This image by William Blake can illustrate Hick's theodicy. God creates human beings imperfect – in the mud, wrapped round in sin (represented by the serpent) and unable to look at God – but human beings have the potential to grow to the likeness of God, and evil is a necessary condition of making this possible.

to accept God. If God's presence were more obvious, then we would be compelled to be obedient and freedom would be lost.

This approach strongly emphasises human freedom and rejects determinism. It maintains that the purpose of creation is so that human beings can grow into the likeness of God: people filled with compassion, love, who are non-judgemental and forgiving. There is no easy way to achieve this and the existence of evil is a necessary way of enabling people to grow. Without the possibility of great suffering there would not be the opportunity of great holiness and goodness.

This world is not a world for God's caged hamsters – where God creates them 'happy' – it is a world where God wants to develop a group of immortal, free beings who by their choices transform themselves into something extraordinary. The purpose of life is not to be happy but to grow into the image and likeness of God. Strangely, this is the approach taken in many modern movies where the heroes and heroines go through great suffering but, in the process, grow to what they have the potential to be at their best. This would not be possible without them enduring and overcoming evil and suffering.

4. What happens after death?

Catholics and Protestants differ about what happens after death. Generally, the Protestant position is the simpler one; this holds that Christians and whoever else God chooses go to a heavenly kingdom under the lordship of the risen Lord Jesus. This is a spiritual and social kingdom without end where the believer will be reunited with friends and family who have died. The alternative is eternal exile from God in what has traditionally been termed 'hell', although as God's mercy is infinite, many Christians tend not to emphasise this aspect of after-death survival. Precisely what survives is unclear: some hold that the soul survives death, some that there is a resurrected body, some that resurrection takes place immediately and some that it happens at the end of time.

The Catholic position is more complex. Catholics hold that the final end for believers is the Beatific Vision of God in which the faithful Catholic will become timeless and see God (God is timeless [see p. 150] and so is the Beatific Vision). This vision is wholly satisfying and time no longer passes. However, it is before then that the situation is less clear. Some will go to everlasting exile from God (hell) from which there is no escape. Faithful Catholics will go to purgatory which is an intermediate stage where the believer is cleansed of all the evil he or she has committed. Traditionally this has been regarded as a place of punishment but few Catholics take this view today and instead hold that purgatory is an intermediate state pending the final resurrection. There are, in the Catholic tradition, two judgements. A particular judgement takes place on death when the decision is taken whether the individual goes to purgatory or hell. However, for the believer, the pains and cleansing process in purgatory are mitigated by the knowledge that everyone in purgatory will eventually achieve the Beatific Vision which will take place after the second and final Judgement when Jesus returns.

The Catechism of the Catholic Church (published in 1992 and described by Pope John Paul II as 'a sure norm for teaching the Catholic faith') is the best single document to understand official Catholic teaching. Developments of doctrine and of teaching have occurred over the centuries and one of the areas that has been affected regards teaching on life after death. Hell is still affirmed, as was made clear by the *Catechism*, which describes hell as 'fiery eternal punishment for those who refuse to love God'. The *Catechism* says (1033–5):

> To die in mortal sin without repenting and accepting God's merciful love means remaining separated from him for ever by our own free choice . . . Jesus often speaks of 'Gehenna' or 'the unquenchable fire' reserved for those who to the end of their lives refuse to believe and be converted . . . Jesus solemnly proclaims . . . 'Depart from me, you cursed into the eternal fire!' . . . Immediately after death the souls of those

> *who die in a state of mortal sin descend into hell, where they*
> *suffer the punishments of eternal fire.*

However, as recently as 2007 the *Catholic Handbook for Youth* says that it is more accurate to see hell not as a place but as a state of exile from God. Many Christians today do not accept the idea of hell as a place of torture but rather see it as either non-existence or a place of permanent exile from God.

Catholics differ as to whether there is an immortal soul that survives death and then receives a new body (the view held by St Thomas Aquinas), or that the individual is resurrected with a new body, either immediately on death or at the end of time.

> *By death the soul is separated from the body, but in the resur-*
> *rection God will give incorruptible life to our body, transformed*
> *by reunion with our soul. Just as Christ is risen and lives for*
> *ever, so all of us will rise at the last day.*
> *(The Catechism of the Catholic Church 1016)*

Traditionally a soul was held to be implanted by God and it was this immortal soul that made human beings different from animals. However, in recent years this idea tends not to have been emphasised. Since Christians affirm that Jesus rose embodied, they have never been simple dualists (who argue that human beings are composed of soul and body and it is the soul alone that survives death). The Christian creeds (see p. 72) all affirm the resurrection of the body as a central element of Christian faith but the existence of the soul, perhaps as an intermediate state, remains a live possibility believed in by some Christians.

Orthodox Christians do not accept the idea of heaven and hell as places but rather see hell as a human creation: the result of an individual having chosen a life of pride, sin and self-assertiveness and thus becoming exiled from God's love. They also reject any idea of purgatory. Heaven is seen as dwelling in God's presence and since that state is held to be the end or purpose for which human beings are made, it is the only state that will represent true human fulfil-ment.

It is fair to say, therefore, that there is no single Christian position on life after death, except that belief in life after death is an abso-lute essential feature of Christianity. The precise form of this life after death is, however, less clear.

5. How can Jesus be both fully human and fully divine?

The doctrine of the Trinity is, without doubt, the greatest mystery at the heart of Christian thought and it is fair to say that it has never been clearly explained in a way that is rationally explicable. There is no differentiation between the three persons of the Trinity and yet the three persons are distinct. If this appears to be the ultimate mystery, then it is fair to accept that it is. Philosophically and rationally there is no easy (or complicated!) way to explain this. Some images can be helpful: a clover leaf has three parts but is still one; a triangle has three angles but is still one – but these are, frankly, far from precise. There are three leaves on the clover and these are not the same as each other even though the three parts make a unity. A human being has multiple organs, fingers, toes and so on but is a single human being. Neither image really explains how God can be both three and one.

Biblical passages can be used to support the claim. For instance, Genesis 1:26 refers to God in the plural: *'Let us make mankind in our image, in our likeness, so that they may rule over the fish in the sea and the birds in the sky, over the livestock and all the wild animals, and over all the creatures that move along the ground.'* One of the most important passages occurs when God visits Abraham in the desert to tell him that he and his wife will have a son, and God here appears as three persons. So God is sometimes described in the plural yet there are also clear references to God being one: *'Hear, O Israel: the* Lord *our God, the* Lord *is one'* (Deuteronomy 6:4). The oneness of God is fundamental to Judaism and Islam.

Biblical passages such as these do not really resolve the problem and the idea of the Trinity, absolutely central as it is to Christian belief, is nevertheless beyond human conceptualisation and analysis.

There are multiple New Testament references to the Trinity. For instance:

Therefore go and make disciples of all nations, baptising them in the name of the Father and of the Son and of the Holy Spirit . . .

(Matthew 28:19)

I and the Father are one.

(John 10:30)

Anyone who has seen me has seen the Father.

(John 14:9)

And if anyone does not have the Spirit of Christ, they do not belong to Christ.

(Romans 8:9)

Joseph son of David, do not be afraid to take Mary home as your wife, because what is conceived in her is from the Holy Spirit.

(Matthew 1:20)

The angel answered, 'The Holy Spirit will come on you, and the power of the Most High will overshadow you. So the holy one to be born will be called the Son of God.'

(Luke 1:35)

The problem is that modern biblical scholarship raises real questions about how many of these quotations were actually said by Jesus and how many were attributed to Him after He died. There is no way of resolving this issue but appealing to the Bible by itself as a 'proof' of the truth of a claim is now far more difficult that it was before the advent of biblical criticism. Few Christian theologians consider that the Bible is free of error and, therefore, relying solely on the Bible or the teaching of the different churches is increasingly problematic. As we have seen, Christian doctrines emerged over hundreds of years and the idea that Jesus was always an integral part of the Trinity which is God was not always accepted by many in the early Church (see pp. 72–5)

In a nineteenth-century book (recently made into a film) called *Flatland* the author, Edwin Abbott, asks us to imagine living in a two-dimensional world where there is only length and breadth and no height. There are different shapes (triangles, octagons, rectangles, squares etc.) but there is no idea of height; indeed, the very notion of height seems ridiculous to those inhabiting the Flatland world. We now know, through mathematics, that there are almost certainly at least nine dimensions (perhaps more). We cannot even conceive what these are. It may therefore be that much of reality as we understand it is beyond human conceptualisation, limited as we are (as Immanuel Kant recognised) by the prisons of our senses and our language. If this is the case, as it appears to be, then it is perhaps not surprising that the mystery of the Trinity should not be capable of rational analysis. The Jesuit Karl Rahner describes God as 'Holy Mystery' and perhaps this is as close as it is possible to get to a clear philosophical definition of God. Shakespeare's Hamlet says, 'There are more things in heaven and earth, Horatio, than are dreamt of in your philosophy' (*Hamlet*, Act 1, Scene 5). Christians maintain that this is undoubtedly the case, and attempting to understand God within the confines of human reason is simply impossible.

TWELVE

Christian Ethics

Before considering Christian ethics, there are meta-ethical issues that need to be addressed. Meta-ethics is sometimes referred to as 'high level' ethics as it addresses the broad issues such as: what is someone doing when they use words like 'good' and 'bad', 'right' and 'wrong'? Are there such things as absolute moral values or is all morality relative to culture and situation? What is the basis for moral decision making? Today many people are relativists; arguing that the days of absolute moral values are past and all ethical decisions are related to culture. Some, such as emotivists, argue that all a person is doing when they make an ethical comment is to express their emotional reaction (so 'abortion is wrong' would translate as 'I have a negative emotional reaction to abortion'). Many people today are post-modernists, arguing that all moral decisions are dependent on sexuality, gender and culture. Pope John Paul II in a 1998 encyclical (*Fides et Ratio*) argues that we live in a post-modern, relativistic and nihilistic world in which, for many, the days of absolute truths are a thing of the past. All Christians reject such a position; where they differ is around what grounds Christian ethics.

There is no single ethical system that can be regarded as Christian. Muslims will look to the Qur'an and Hadith in deciding on moral issues, seeing these texts as respectively dictated or inspired directly by God. Orthodox Jews will look to the Torah or Talmud. Both, however, will also need to use human reason to work out how even commands that are held to be divinely dictated are to be applied to the modern world. For Christians, however, who see God's Word becoming incarnate in Jesus rather than in a book, the problem is greater, as Jesus' life and message can be interpreted in many different ways. This means, therefore, that there are a variety of approaches to Christian ethics, no one of which will be accepted by all Christians. Unless one understands, therefore, the different bases of ethical decision making in Christianity, it will not be possible to understand why different Christians arrive at such varying conclusions on many contemporary ethical issues, even though they may agree on the broad meta-ethical principle that there are absolute moral values.

Theoretical bases for Christian ethics

This sounds complicated, but really it's not! Different Christian groups will have different starting points in working out how to act. They all have many features in common, not least their rejection of relativism and nihilism, but there are also significant differences:

Biblical ethics

Christians who base their beliefs mainly on the Hebrew and Christian Scriptures tend to be Protestant and Pentecostalist groups of various different types. Their starting point is what Luther described as 'the plain word of scripture' although, when it comes to ethics, biblical commands tend to be anything but clear and plain. If the Bible is taken as the Word of God then it follows, as in Islam and Orthodox Judaism, that what the Bible says must be true. The most obvious example is homosexuality, which both the Old and New Testaments clearly condemn. Those who base their ethics primarily on the Bible are, therefore, most likely to condemn homosexual practices as being contrary to God's command. The problems with this view, however, include the following:

1) Christians who support this position tend to be selective in the texts which they regard as authoritative – so, for instance, they will endorse the condemnation of homosexuality but will

ignore supposed commands from God about stoning one's son to death if he is disobedient; or Jesus apparently commanding his followers to cut their hands off if the hand caused offence; or the command to those who would follow Him to give all their money away to the poor; or, in the book of Leviticus, a brother being commanded to marry and sleep with his dead brother's wife; or the command that forbids wearing garments containing mixed fabrics. It is also not easy to apply the Bible to modern issues such as genetic engineering or stem cell research.

2) The context in which the Bible is written is important. This is a challenge for any religion that bases its teaching on a text: to what extent should the text be regarded as independent of time and space and to what extent should it be seen as culturally influenced or determined? All those religions which base divine revelation on a sacred text therefore have the problem of which parts of the text are to be regarded as authoritative.

3) The issue of inspiration is vital – all Christians see the Bible as being inspired by God, but this can mean many different things:

- Some Christians see the Bible as almost literally dictated by God – so God directly guides the authors of the various books of the Bible in what they will say. Inspiration of the writer is, therefore, direct and not mediated through the writer's own experience. The writers of the books are merely instruments in recording truth. This will lead to a literalist view of the Bible, with the problems that arise from having to be selective in the biblical texts, as set out above. This tends to be a minority view, although is particularly held by some groups within Protestant and Pentecostal Christianity.

- Other Christians consider that the writers of the Bible were, indeed, inspired but that they were also influenced by their cultural position and the time at which they wrote. Whilst, therefore, accepting the importance of the biblical message, they will see it as needing to be understood in context and will seek to apply it to today with a full recognition of the changed circumstances that now apply. Many mainstream Christians take this position.

- Other Christians see the reader of the Bible as being inspired by God when they read the Bible or say their prayers – the inspiration in this case is not so much of the writer of the text as of the reader of the text. Often Christians hold this view as well as one of the two views above.
- More liberal Christians will often argue that biblical scholarship can tell us very little about Jesus and that the Bible should be seen as a human document which seeks to reflect on the work of God in history. A general picture can emerge of Jesus, but detailed commands which will guide ethics today cannot be directly derived from the biblical account. These Christians will often base their ethics on one of the alternative bases set out below.

In practice, therefore, when Christians quote the Bible in support of their ethical views or seek guidance from the Bible, much is going to depend on the presuppositions they apply to the text. It is perfectly possible for two Christian groups to arrive at completely different approaches to divorce, abortion, euthanasia, stem cell research, sex, homosexuality, the position of women, social ethics or the nature of power and authority in Christianity, because they interpret the Bible differently.

The Natural Law approach to ethics

This is the approach adopted by the Roman Catholic Church. It was developed by St Thomas Aquinas in the thirteenth century and is largely based on the approach taken by the Greek philosopher Aristotle (see p. 98). God is seen as creating human beings with a common human nature. All human beings are actual in that they exist, but they also have the potential to become what they are capable of being at their best: in other words, to become 'fully human'. God wishes individuals to fulfil their human potential. Certain actions diminish us and lead us away from the potential that every human shares with every other human. These actions are 'intrinsically evil'; they are wrong in and of themselves and are therefore regarded as morally wrong or sinful.

St Thomas Aquinas argued that reason alone can work out what is morally right or wrong. Where philosophers talk of morally wrong actions, Christians would talk of sinful actions, but they are effectively the same. Both sinful and wrong actions, according to the Natural Law tradition of ethics, diminish human beings: make them less than they are capable of being.

Crucial to Aristotle's approach to ethics and to the Natural Law tradition as formulated by St Thomas Aquinas and held by the Catholic Church, is to work out the purpose of different species or different organs. The purpose of an acorn is clearly to grow into an oak tree, the purpose of a tadpole is to grow into a frog. In the same way, a human foetus has the potential to become a full, adult human being. The question becomes, of course, what it means to be fully human, and this is not always clear. The Catholic Church has traditionally argued that each part of a human being has a purpose, so the purpose of genitalia is held to be reproduction. Once this is accepted, then for a person to use their genitalia for any purpose that is not open to procreation becomes a wrong act: specifically, it becomes an 'intrinsically evil act' – an act that is wrong in and of itself, irrespective of the situation. This has led the Catholic Church, alone among Christian churches, to condemn all forms of artificial contraception (including condoms, the 'pill', the 'morning-after pill', the IUD device, implants, etc.) as these frustrate the purpose of genitalia. All sexual activity, for Catholics, must therefore be open to the possibility of procreation within marriage, as otherwise a person's genitalia are being used for a purpose for which they were not intended. It should be clear that much is going to depend on how purpose is defined, and there is no agreement on this.

Many Christians will hold that life is sacred from conception to death, but this depends on when personhood begins. Some Christians hold that, at conception, the embryo is alive and is human but is not a person until a later stage in foetal development. The status of the foetus is, therefore, a key issue; if the foetus is a person, then killing it would became an 'intrinsically evil act'. Pro-choice groups argue for the woman's right to choose what happens to her own body. Few Christians take this position, as it does not respect the rights of the foetus but some, such as Situation Ethicists (see p. 169), may consider that there are circumstances when abortion might be morally acceptable.

The Catholic Church also strongly affirms the sanctity of life from the moment of conception to death and therefore considers that, as well as abortion, assisted suicide and euthanasia are 'intrinsically evil': actions which cannot be justified, whatever the circumstances. In practice, many individual Catholics accept a more flexible approach whilst recognising that this is not in accordance with the teaching of the Church.

Under the Natural Law approach to ethics, sinful or wrong actions damage not only the individual by leading him or her away from fulfilling their full human potential, but also the community of which a person forms part. Sinful actions prevent the community from fulfilling its full potential. Biblical commands are seen by Natural Law supporters as commands which are fully in accordance with the Natural Law tradition. Reason can work out which actions are wrong but God also reveals in the Bible that the same actions are wrong and to be avoided. Revelation and reason therefore coincide. However, as we have seen, the Catholic tradition affirms the importance of the Church in interpreting the Bible, so there are none of the tensions with the modern world that sometimes arise with a purely biblical approach.

This tradition, as it is interpreted by the teaching authority of the Catholic Church, is said by some critics to lack flexibility. Actions are viewed as wrong in themselves, irrespective of the context or situation. This is criticised by supporters of Situation Ethics, as they argue that any sense of love or any flexibility is eliminated. However, this is not necessarily the case. St Thomas Aquinas himself argued for Natural Law to be flexible and to be subject to exceptions. M. J. Longford puts it like this:

It is true that Aquinas did also appear to hold some absolute moral rules, such as the one that disallowed lying . . . but this is not what is stressed in the account of natural law . . . His overall position is that there are what are called 'primary precepts' which are exceedingly general (such as the duty to worship God, and to love one's neighbour) and 'secondary precepts', which are more specific such as the duty to have only one husband or wife. However, the secondary precepts all have to be interpreted in the context of the situation, and it is here that the flexibility of natural law arises. At one point [Aquinas] argues as follows: 'The first principles of natural law are altogether unalterable. But its secondary precepts . . . though they are unalterable in the majority of cases . . . can nevertheless be changed on some particular and rare occasions . . .' Aquinas argues 'The more you descend into the details the more it appears how the general rule admits of exceptions, so that you have to hedge it with cautions and qualifications.'

(*The Good and the True: An introduction to Christian ethics*, SCM Press, 1985, p. 204)

This is important and not always recognised. Aquinas' admission that the 'the more you descend into the detail, the more the general rule admits of exceptions' opens up a degree of flexibility. Some Catholic theologians such as Bernard Hoose have developed what is seen as a modification of Natural Ethics called Proportionalism (although its supporters would not see it as a modification but as being faithful to the original intentions of Aquinas and others). Proportionalists argue that whilst some actions may indeed be wrong in and of themselves, sometimes there may be reasons of sufficient gravity that would make it right to do what, in other circumstances, might be wrong. Sometimes there may be a proportionate reason (this means a reason of sufficient seriousness) to cause an individual to do an action that would otherwise be wrong. Two examples would illustrate this:

1) It is wrong to lie, but if someone with a gun is intending to kill his wife because he thinks that she has had an affair, then lying might be the right thing to do if the gunman asks you if you know where his wife is. Lying is generally wrong, but it may be the right thing to do.
2) The Catholic Church condemns contraception and the morning-after pill, regarding both as intrinsically evil. However, if in a marriage the husband has AIDS, then using a condom may be the right thing to do because of the consequences of not doing so. Similarly, if a teenage girl is raped in war by a group of soldiers, then giving her the morning-after pill may be objectively wrong but may still be the right thing to do.

Proportionalism, therefore, introduces a flexibility into Natural Law teaching which many Western Catholics welcome but which has been condemned by the Magisterium – the teaching authority of the Catholic Church.

Pope Francis produced a letter to the Catholic faithful in April 2016 called 'The Joy of Love' (*Amoris Laetitia*) which affirmed traditional Catholic teaching on matters relating to divorce, remarriage, homosexuality and sex but also called for a more merciful (a key word he used) and a more open-minded approach by priests and bishops to the complex local situations in which individuals find themselves. In particular, he called for annulment of a marriage to become much easier (this is the process by which the Catholic Church declares a marriage to be invalid for various reasons, including that the couple did not really understand what Christian marriage was about or the importance of children) and also for local priests and bishops to be more open and sympathetic to allowing divorced and remarried Catholics to receive the sacraments (see p. 112). The Pope was not, therefore, changing fundamental Catholic teaching but was calling for a much greater emphasis on mercy and forgiveness as a central part of Christianity, and arguing that divorced and remarried Catholics, homosexual Catholics and others might be allowed to take the sacraments and to participate in Church life, even if the Church considered their behaviour to be wrong in itself.

Situation Ethics

Situation Ethics was developed by an Anglican theologian, Joseph Fletcher, in the 1960s, although he would claim that he was drawing on a long tradition. Fletcher was influenced by the culture of his time and also by the existential philosophy of Jean-Paul Sartre which called people to personal authenticity. Fletcher argued that Jesus did not come to found a particular ethical system but rather to proclaim the centrality of love to the universe. This is a central part of the Christian tradition. There are two commandments that are absolutely essential to Christianity and which, for Jesus, summarised the whole of the Jewish law and the teachings of the prophets. These were:

1) You shall love the Lord your God with all your heart and soul and mind, and
2) You shall love your neighbour as yourself.

For Jesus, love is a duty: it is a command. It is not a matter of loving one's husband, wife or partner, or one's friends or members of a particular social group. Still less is it a matter of loving only fellow Christians. The parable of the Good Samaritan (see p. 39) illustrates this well. Christian love means reaching out to those who are despised and rejected, those who are marginalised and excluded, and showing the love of God to everyone: even to lepers, thieves, robbers, liars, adulterers and sinners. St Francis of Assisi recognised this (see pp. 89ff.; 100) and sought to live by this message.

Fletcher rejects any absolute moral rules that claim to be

Christian and instead calls Christians to live lives based on a passionate commitment to love one's fellow human beings. Christian ethics, for Fletcher, is therefore about trying to decide what is the loving thing to do in the complex situation in which a person finds himself or herself. There are no absolute moral 'do's' or 'don'ts', no absolute commands. Instead the Christian is commanded to try to act as Jesus would have acted and to ask: 'What would Jesus have done in this situation? What is the loving thing to do?' Take, for instance, the question of assisted suicide. Many Christians would simply say, 'Assisted suicide is wrong', as it offends against the principle of the sanctity of human life. Situation Ethics would say, 'It all depends.' To assist someone to die because they are depressed or lonely is clearly wrong (as they could be shown love and support instead), but if someone is terminally ill, in great discomfort, has made his or her peace with family members, then it might be the loving thing to do. The same applies with divorce; instead of a firm rule which says 'Divorce is wrong', the Situation Ethicist would say, 'It all depends on the situation.' If the marriage has, really, completely broken down and is harming both parties and possibly their children, then divorce may be the loving thing to do. In the Second World War, Dietrich Bonhoeffer was a prominent Lutheran Christian and a pacifist, yet faced with the horrendous suffering caused by the war and the death camps, he took part in a plot to kill Hitler. He felt that it was what Jesus would have done in the particular situation in which Bonhoeffer found himself.

In the case of issues such as homosexuality, those who support Situation Ethics would look for the loving thing to do; in other words, what would Jesus have done? Many more liberal Christians, therefore, would have no difficulty with long-term, committed homosexual or lesbian relationships but all would reject casual sex or sex outside a committed relationship.

Opponents of Situation Ethics argue that it is isolating one element of Christian moral thinking – the law of love – and excluding all others. Also, as an ethical theory, it is not very effective, as two people faced with the same ethical dilemma may make totally different moral decisions. One weakness of Situation Ethics as expressed by Fletcher is, perhaps, that it focuses too much on love of neighbour and not enough on the love of God. If obedience to God is central in a person's life, and he or she is really seeking to act lovingly in the way that Jesus would have done, then, it might be argued, Situation Ethics is a part of the Christian tradition which is worthy of respect.

Orthodox ethics

The approach to ethics taken by the Eastern Orthodox Church is not monolithic and is grounded in the wisdom of the early Church Fathers, in the tradition of the Church, in community and in the relationship between the three persons of the Trinity. Since God is essentially relational within the Trinity, humans are expected to develop right relationships with families and the wider community. These relationships form the basis for ethics, and the accumulated wisdom of the Church and the early Church Fathers provides pointers towards this. Orthodox ethics are far less dominated by philosophy than Catholic ethics, largely because the Orthodox tradition seeks to remain faithful to the teachings of the early Church Fathers and resists any alteration of doctrine or approach not approved by the whole Church. The adoption, therefore, of philosophy and the work of St Thomas Aquinas by the Catholic Church is rejected by the Orthodox. This is significant when related to applied ethical issues such as abortion.

The Orthodox Church considers the whole of human life as a journey to God: from fertilised egg to the moment of death is all part of the same story of development. There is no idea, as there was in the Western Church, of God implanting a soul at a particular time and, before that, the foetus not being fully formed. The Orthodox Church has, therefore, always been opposed to abortion. In the early Church abortion was considered as equivalent to murder and the person aborting the foetus was excommunicated for life, although this was subsequently reduced to ten years. The foetus is considered as a distinct human person having its own rights and, therefore, any rights of the mother cannot override the rights of the foetus. Having said this, the Orthodox Church does recognise that there may be exceptional circumstances when an abortion may, although wrong, nevertheless be justifiable. Above all, the Orthodox Church always seeks to forgive and to reconcile people to God through forgiveness. Indeed, the centrality of forgiveness and the possibility of a new start may be one of the greatest differences of emphasis between approaches to ethics in the Eastern and Western Christian Churches.

Conscience

Ethical decisions, whilst they may be discussed in various theoretical ways, are in the end made by individuals. When faced with the reality of a particular situation, they have to decide how to act, and this applies to Christians as much as to any others. Whatever the general rules of a church may be or whatever the teaching of the Bible may be, the individual has, in the last analysis, to decide. Christians differ as to whether human beings are fundamentally good or not. There are two opposed positions:

1) St Thomas Aquinas and the Catholic tradition hold that human beings are fundamentally good and have a general orientation (called 'synderesis') towards doing what is good and right, implanted by God. People may, however, pursue what seems to them to be good but which is, in fact, not good at all. They may pursue an 'apparent good' – what appears to be good – rather than what is 'really good'. The role of ethical debate generally is to work out what is really good rather than what appears to be good. What is really good, as we have seen (see p. 165), is what is in accordance with the common human nature that all human beings share. In other words, good actions

are those that help an individual to be 'more fully human', more fully what they are capable of being at their best.
2) The other approach is to see human beings as fundamentally corrupted by the sin of Adam and Eve. This 'original sin' is built into what it means to be a human being and corrupts people to the very ground of their being. They are 'fallen' because Adam and Eve chose to disobey God, and all human beings are descended from Adam and Eve. Even human reason and rationality are fallen and, therefore, unaided human reason cannot bring people to work out for themselves what is right. On this view, it is only the grace and love of God which enables human beings to act correctly.

These are complex issues which cannot briefly be summarised, as Aquinas and the Catholic tradition also hold that human beings are fallen and need the grace of God. Nevertheless, whilst Protestants tend to reject reason as a way to understand God or, indeed, ethics and rely on revelation, Catholics affirm the importance of philosophy and reason and consider that these can be used to work out how a person should act.

This has a direct bearing on the role of conscience. For the Catholic tradition, conscience is 'reason making right decisions'; it is the ability of reason to be able to work out what is right or wrong, based, as set out above, on what it means to fulfil human potential. This is something that both Christians and non-Christians can do equally. All human beings need to reflect on what it means to live a good life, what it means to become fully human and to fulfil their common human nature. This can be done equally by a Christian, a Muslim or a Jew. It is quite possible, in this tradition, for an individual to seek to work out what is right but to be mistaken: to pursue, as we have seen, an 'apparent' rather than a 'real' good. Merely because someone thinks something is good does not, therefore, mean that it actually is. This raises an important question: Should conscience be what the individual works out as being good, using their own reason, or what the Catholic Church thinks is good, using the accumulated wisdom of the centuries? The issue is whose reason should dominate. The Catholic Church teaches that it is more likely that the Church, with its depth of theology and philosophy, should be able to work out what is right rather than the individual; therefore no Catholic should appeal to individual conscience against the teaching of the Church. However, this decision is, itself, a matter of conscience. It means individuals recognising that their ability to work out rationally what is right may be imperfect. They may not be sufficiently detached or may not be able to work out what is right on their own so, in conscience, they may decide to follow the teaching of the Church. As an example, an individual Catholic may feel that contraception is acceptable, but may, as a faithful Catholic, decide to follow the Church's teaching instead (although, in practice, many millions of Catholics do not do this) because the Catholic Church also teaches that its teaching is more likely to be rational. It seems fair to say that since the Second Vatican Council (see p. 215) and, in particular, since Pope Francis became Pope, the role of individual conscience has increased, allowing greater flexibility than might have been the case in the past.

In the Protestant tradition, by contrast, reason is often treated with suspicion and the focus is on the individual's relationship with God or with Jesus. The individual seeks to live a relationship of love with God. Conscience, therefore, comes from seeking to try to focus on the will of God when the individual is at prayer or when reading the Bible. Protestant Christians feel themselves to be guided by the Holy Spirit as well as their personal relationship with God, which enables them to work out what is right. This approach can be much more situational (see p. 169) and flexible, but it suffers from the difficulty of the individual having to separate what really is the will of God from what the individual would like to believe is the will of God – and this can be problematic at times.

As in so many other areas, therefore, Christians will differ on how conscience is applied.

Christian ethics today

It is fair to say that there is no single Christian view on most ethical controversies, such as:

- Homosexuality
- Divorce
- Abortion
- Euthanasia
- Stem cell research
- Genetic engineering
- Making large amounts of money
- Crime and punishment
- Environmental ethics
- Global warming
- Animal suffering
- Sex before marriage
- Contraception
- War

This makes it difficult in an introductory book such as this to set out 'the Christian position', as there is so much diversity as to what behaviour is morally right or wrong. For readers who would like to pursue these issues in more depth, *Ethics Matters* (SCM, 2015) by Charlotte and Peter Vardy seeks to achieve this.

There are, nevertheless, certain general positions on which all Christians would unite. These include:

A commitment to the idea of absolute Truth

This is a meta-ethical position and in today's post-modern and relativistic world this is deeply counter cultural. Either certain actions are right or they are wrong. There is a Truth at stake. Individuals have to stake their lives on Christians claims which could, in principle, be false. That is the nature of faith.

A commitment to justice in terms of relationships, family, society and the international dimension

This means being willing to stand for what is right rather than in favour of one's own interests, and to be willing to think more of the interests of others than one's own. It must be accepted that the record of many so-called Christian countries and individuals in these respects is not good and that Western society, in particular, has tended to put its own interest first and to 'use' or exploit those less fortunate or less able to exercise power. Christianity at its best and truest, however, stands against this. It was:

- Christians who founded hospitals and schools for the poor;
- Christians who devoted themselves to the care of the sick;
- Christians who stood against the evil of slavery and insisted on freedom for all;
- Christians who stood against the evils of *apartheid* in South Africa and insisted on the equality of all;
- Christians who fought for debt relief for sub-Saharan Africa;
- Christians who established food banks and low-interest loans for those in need;
- Christians who, in many cases, established labour unions to fight for the rights of ordinary working people.

It would be wrong and misleading to pretend that all Christians act in the interests of justice, but not to do so is a failure in Christian terms.

Love of one's neighbour

This means being willing to care for others as if they were your own close family, irrespective of race, skin colour, religion, sexual preference or disease. To love others is a Christian command, a Christian duty. Again, few Christians live up to this and many so-called Christians can be bigoted and condemnatory, but this is not what Christianity teaches. St Francis of Assisi, perhaps, exemplified this most clearly in going out to robbers, lepers and Muslims (whilst Christians and Muslims were at war) and expressing love and understanding (see pp. 91–2).

A commitment to social justice

This has been, perhaps, most clearly expressed in Catholic social justice teaching, but the idea of being committed to a just society is common to all Christians. There are five key principles in Catholic social teaching:

1) The sanctity of life and the dignity and value of every human being. Sanctity of life, of course, means Christians generally reject abortion and assisted suicide or euthanasia, but this can vary, depending on which ethical approach is taken (see above).
2) The search for the common good for the whole of society and not just for the wealthy and powerful.
3) Solidarity between all human beings, irrespective of race, religion, colour or sexuality.
4) 'Subsidiarity', which means that, as far as possible, decision making should be delegated to a lower level and that individuals and communities should be allowed to be free to make their own decisions.
5) An emphasis on the importance of ethics in business and international affairs, particularly focused on the issues of justice and fairness.

These principles are to be found in many papal documents (see p. 221) and most Christian churches have similar commitments. Social justice and business ethics are dealt with in more detail in Chapter 15.

Sexual fidelity in marriage

In the ancient Roman world, one of the clearest things that differentiated Christians from non-Christians was sexual fidelity. Roman society tended to be notoriously unfaithful and Christianity rejected this, as it does today. Christians are not prudish about sex and generally see it as a positive side of being human, but only if it takes place in its right context: in other words, within a committed marriage relationship. Marriage is seen by Christians as a sacred bond, expressed in the words of a typical marriage service: 'for better or worse, in sickness or health, for richer, for poorer, until death do us part.' Jesus is recorded as saying: *'what God has joined together, let no one separate'* (Matthew 19:6). Marriage is a lifelong commitment to another person, and giving oneself to them sexually is part of that. Catholic Christians therefore reject divorce and remarriage. Other Christians would see divorce as a failure, the breach of a solemn promise before God. Nevertheless, for many Christians, forgiveness and a new start are always possible and so remarriage may also be a possibility.

Compassion and forgiveness

This means being willing to stand in the shoes of another person: to be able to empathise with their positions, their sufferings and their aspirations. It means being willing to understand someone who is different and to care for them because they are a fellow human being, and for no other reason. It also means always being willing to forgive, time and time again (see p. 43).

Rejection of greed

Greed has always been condemned by Christianity and many Christians have had a negative view of the accumulation of wealth. However, this is certainly not the case in some parts of Protestant Christianity where the 'Protestant work ethic' had a profound influence. This included the idea that working hard and accumulating money was good and pleasing to God, although with this came a commitment to charity and caring for those who were poor, sick, orphans, widows or unable to look after themselves. In the United States, in particular, Christianity has been associated with a highly positive attitude to wealth creation, combined with a positive attitude to charitable giving. Business ethics is dealt with in Chapter 15.

Rejection of jealousy

Christianity has always seen jealousy or envy as one of the seven deadly sins (Lust, Gluttony, Greed, Sloth, Wrath, Envy and Pride). Jealousy is corrosive to the human spirit, it consumes people from within and also indicates that a person's life is not focused on God but on material ends. To be jealous of someone's wife or husband, boyfriend or girlfriend, car, house, job, mobile phone or 'success' indicates that the Christian order of priorities has been forgotten.

Rejection of anger

Christians are taught not to be angry, not to take revenge and always to be willing to forgive. However, there is one possible exception to this, based on the incident in the Temple in Jerusalem when Jesus drove out those who bought and sold animals to be offered as sacrifices there, or who changed money into the special coinage that was the only currency allowed in the Temple. These people were money-makers and Jesus drove them out with a whip. Anger, therefore, in a just cause is considered acceptable, but this always needs to be balanced with compassion and forgiveness where appropriate.

These are, however, ideals, albeit ideals to which almost all Christians would aspire. They would also aspire to the virtues (the early Church Fathers adopted the four cardinal virtues of Prudence, Justice, Restraint and Courage, and added to these what were termed the three theological virtues of Faith, Hope and Love, or Charity). These form the basis for 'Virtue Ethics' which sees the aim of the ethical life as being for each individual to develop into a person who practises the virtues and avoids vices. This idea stems from Aristotle and Greek philosophy, and whilst it has had a great influence on Christian thinking, it is not a specifically Christian approach. However, when it comes to more specific ethical dilemmas today, these general ideals may not offer a great deal of assistance.

If this chapter has left the reader unclear as to what 'the Christian position' is on many contemporary ethical issues, then this is good, because whilst many Christians may hold strong views on these issues, there is no consensus across Christian groups.

Spirituality and Mysticism

The Christian churches have, over the centuries, developed doctrines and dogmas, outlined creeds and formulated statements of belief. They have sought to ensure orthodoxy and to eliminate heresy and have tried to compress Christianity into categories that could be explained and understood. In doing this they have preserved something of the essential unity of Christianity and avoided too many splits, but the price paid has often been considerable. Yet, throughout two millennia, there has been another tradition – sometimes suppressed and regarded with suspicion by the institutional Church. This is the tradition of spirituality and mysticism in which people have sought (and often been sought by) God in individual encounters which have built, affirmed, reinforced and sometimes transformed their faith.

Mysticism has always been a central part of the Christian tradition, going back to the Hebrew prophets to whom the Word of God came in the desert, and also to the time of Jesus Himself, who constantly found the need to withdraw from the crowds that surrounded Him and to seek God in the wilderness. Many early Christians took a similar route, suffering hardship and hunger in order to devote their whole being to the search for God. This tradition has continued throughout Christian history and there has been a long, long list of major figures, both male and female, who have been directly aware of the presence of God. Sometimes this was in response to their search for God but, just as commonly, God came to them, often at the most unexpected and unlikely times. Many Christian groups have developed their own approaches to spirituality, including the classic Benedictine, Franciscan, Dominican and Jesuit spiritualities but, as we shall see, there are possibly even more significant contemporary spiritualities in Protestant Christianity, particularly when measured by the number of lives they affect in the contemporary world.

The great American psychologist, William James, argued in his seminal book, *The Varieties of Religious Experience*, that underneath all the creeds and dogmas of different religions lies the primacy of mystical experience. He identified four crucial marks of mystical experiences:

- They have a *noetic* quality – they provide knowledge that is not available by other means.
- They are *ineffable* – they cannot be described in normal language, so that the mystic has to resort to the language of paradox and contradiction to express a reality that goes beyond normal categories.
- They are *transitory* – the experiences last for a fairly short time.
- The individual is *passive* – individuals are 'grasped from without'; they do not seek the experience and hence are not active in looking for it.

Not everyone agrees with these features but they nevertheless represent a reasonable summary of what many consider Christian mysticism to involve. There are many different types of mysticism – particularly introvertive mysticism (which means God being found as part of an inner journey) and extrovertive mysticism (in which God is found in the everyday world). Some mystics are classed as introvertive and some as extrovertive, and academics vie with each other in attempting to classify and analyse mystical experience, but in a real sense, it resists rational analysis.

The mystic claims a direct experience of God and the reality of this experience is so great that it is overwhelming. The mystic is totally certain of the awareness of God and sometimes what he or she learns in these moments or states appears to run counter to the teaching of the Church. St Thomas Aquinas himself had a mystical experience towards the end of his life and wrote that everything he had written about theology and philosophy was 'as straw' compared to the reality of that experience. The authority of the mystics has sometimes been seen as a threat to the established order, as they can challenge existing practices and call people back to live a purer version of the life that Jesus preached. Seeing mystics as a threat particularly arises because they have often been women, and the Christian Church has not had a good record when it comes to the treatment of women or their insights into the nature of God and Jesus. Feminist writers in the twentieth and twenty-first centuries have argued that a male-dominated Church and clergy have often subverted and challenged the place of women in Christianity, starting from the earliest days (p. 30). Not everyone accepts this but it is undoubtedly the case that the insights of women mystics have often been treated with suspicion.

Many thousands of women were burnt as witches in the Middle Ages: something which all Christians would today condemn. Some of these supposed witches may have been mystics who sought God in prayer and by living a simple life, but who were seen as challenging the institutional Church. Others will simply have been 'wise women' who used herbs for healing; whilst still others were burnt for almost no reason at all other than that they were condemned by neighbours. Mystics were often simply silenced and marginalised and those that we know about today are a small minority.

By no means all mystics have been female, but the mystical tradition is particularly strong amongst women and some outstanding women provide good examples of the Christian mystical tradition and its importance. Among the most influential Christian mystics were the following:

St John Climacus (*c.* AD 525–606)

Climacus was a monk at St Catherine's monastery in Sinai – one of the most ancient in the Christian world. The monastery is incredibly isolated in the desert but the life of communal prayer, celibacy, abstinence, obedience and poverty was not enough for Climacus and he withdrew into a tiny hermitage at the foot of a nearby mountain range. He spent his time studying, particularly the lives of the saints, returning to the monastery about twenty years later. Climacus was a man of deep prayer and inward reflection who devoted his whole life to seeking God and to leading other people to God. When he was about seventy-five years of age he was persuaded to become abbot of the monastery. His reputation had spread throughout the Christian world of the time and he was spoken of with great respect. At the age of seventy-nine he returned to his hermitage to prepare for death.

Climacus's most famous book is called *The Ladder of Divine Ascent* and gives an account of how the Christian can seek to draw closer to God. It is based on the idea of a ladder reaching up to heaven, as Jacob saw in his dream (Genesis 28:10–17). Climacus describes thirty steps on the ladder, of which the first

Figure 1: St Catherine's monastery on Mount Sinai.

twenty-three give instructions as to how the pilgrim can overcome sin and vice, and the last three deal with developing the virtues. The idea of purging oneself of desire and the inclination to sin in order to draw closer to God is common on the mystical journey. Climacus's book is a manual on how to achieve union with God and it is intended for monks and others who have devoted themselves to God with their whole heart. It is probably the most widely read book by Orthodox Christians.

The Danish Lutheran philosopher, Søren Kierkegaard, wrote a number of books under the pseudonym John Climacus as, in a more modern world, he was also trying to show Christians how to draw closer to God.

The sixth-century Climacus has actually provided what is almost a self-help book on seeking God and, in the Orthodox Christian tradition, it is often not recommended to be read except by someone who is already quite advanced on the spiritual path and who is seeking God under the guidance of a spiritual advisor. A few extracts from *The Ladder of Divine Ascent* may give a flavour of the approach:

> *Remembrance of Jesus' passion will heal your soul of resentment, by making it ashamed of itself when it remembers the patience of the Lord. Some people have wearied themselves and suffered for a long time in order to extract forgiveness. By far the best course, however, is to forget the offences, since the Lord says: 'Forgive at once and you will be forgiven in generous measure' [Luke 6:37–38]. Forgetting offences is a sign of sincere repentance. If you keep the memory of them, you may believe you have repented but you are like someone running in his sleep. Let no one consider it a minor defect, this darkness that often clouds the eyes even of spiritual people.*

> *Love in its nature makes a human being like God, as far as is possible for a human being. The soul is intoxicated by the effects of it. Its characteristics are a fountain of faith, an abyss of patience, an ocean of humility. Love is the complete repudiation of any unkind thought about one's neighbour, since, 'Love thinks no evil' [1 Corinthians 13:5]. Love, unchangeable tranquillity and our adoption as children of God are different from each other only in name. As light, fire and flame are present in the self-same operation, so are these three manifestations of the Spirit. When someone is completely permeated with the love of God, the brightness of his soul is reflected by his whole being.*

St Benedict (*c.* AD 480–547)

St Benedict can be said to have founded Western monasticism (see pp. 81–2). He established the first monastery in Subiaco in Italy, the first of twelve to be founded by him. He envisaged each monastery as being independent and he established what has become known as 'the Rule of St Benedict' which is followed by many Christian monasteries around the world. Some Christians chose, and still choose, to live apart from the world and to dedicate their lives to God in prayer, study and work. They formed monastic communities for this purpose.

Those entering a Benedictine community take a vow of stability; they promise to stay a member of the monastic community for life. They must be obedient to their abbot or superior and they also promise to change their life so that it is focused on God in accordance with Benedict's Rule. Each day is carefully structured with set times for prayer, study and work. Benedict required all monks to work and monasteries have a long tradition of providing hospitality for travellers. This tradition continues but today people also visit monasteries for spiritual retreats under the guidance of a monk. The abbot has complete authority over the community and this can include assigning duties and even deciding what books may or may not be read. Obedience is a crucial part of monastic life and obedience to the abbot or superior is seen as equivalent to obedience to God. Much of Benedictine life is conducted in silence, with assigned times given for social interaction, although the practice varies between different monasteries. The whole of the Rule of St Benedict is structured so that the life of the monks (or nuns, in the case of a women's religious order) is planned round prayer and a focus on God.

Hildegard of Bingen (1098–1179)

Hildegard of Bingen lived through most of the twelfth century; this was a time of change when Europe was emerging from the Dark Ages. She was a powerful woman in a world dominated by men. She wrote music and poetry, preached, taught and established and ran Benedictine monasteries. She also battled with Church authorities. Her works were investigated and approved by the Pope's emissary, endorsed by scholars at the new University of Paris, and laid part of the foundations for Christian music. In her lifetime her works were read in abbeys across Germany and the Pope himself read out some of her works at a conference of bishops.

Hildegard focuses on the love of God and the central role of Christ in revealing God's love and justice. Creation is at the very centre of her theology and she may be seen as anticipating the creation-centred spirituality found in many feminist writers today. The old idea of 'fall' and 'redemption' is challenged by the new model that Hildegard provides. She is very positive about the whole universe being driven by God.

Hildegard wrote in a strongly patriarchal culture and Church. In a letter to St Bernard of Clairvaux she writes of the hardship she carries as a woman: '*I am wretched and more than wretched in my existence as a woman.*' She relates how, when she sought to cover up her visions, she was confined to a sickbed. Her decision to write about the visions got her out of her sickbed and provided energy and renewal. However, she was constantly aware of how insignificant she was as an individual:

> *Listen: there was once a king sitting on his throne. Around him stood great and wonderfully beautiful columns orna-mented with ivory, bearing the banners of the king with great honour. Then it pleased the king to raise a small feather from the ground, and he commanded it to fly. The feather flew, not because of anything in itself but because the air bore it along. Thus am I, a feather on the breath of God.*

Hildegard acknowledges that men and women are biologically different but also holds they are equal before God and equally involved in God's work. She writes: '*Man cannot be called man without woman. Neither can woman be called woman without man.'* Nevertheless, she does reject the idea of women priests and at times accepts that women should be obedient to men.

She had a series of visions which helped her to make sense of Christianity in a way which all her previous training had not achieved:

> *When I was forty-two years and seven months old, a burning light of tremendous brightness coming from heaven poured into my entire mind. Like a flame that does not burn but enkindles, it inflamed my entire heart and my entire breast, just like the sun that warms an object with its rays.*

Hildegard's visions continued, and her writing and art was an attempt to express these insights for others. Her visions are called 'illuminations' as she saw her life and mind being 'illumined' by the Holy Spirit. Hildegard portrays the Holy Spirit like fire. She writes: *'O Holy Spirit, Fiery Comforter Spirit, Life of the life of all creatures.'* And again:

> *'Who is the Holy Spirit?' 'The Holy Spirit is a Burning Spirit. It kindles the hearts of humankind. Like tympanum and lyre it plays them, gathering volume in the temple of the soul . . . The Holy Spirit resurrects and awakens everything that is.'*

The idea that the Holy Spirit is the life of the universe – full of energy, life-giving, life-enhancing, related to fire – is fundamental to Hildegard. She places strong emphasis on the Trinity:

> *This means that the Father, Who is Justice, is not without the Son or the Holy Spirit; and the Holy Spirit Who kindles the hearts of the faithful, is not without the Father and the Son; and the Son, Who is the plenitude of fruition, is not without the Father or the Holy Spirit. They are inseparable in Divine Majesty, for the Father is not without the Son, nor the Son*

without the Father, nor the Father and the Son without the Holy Spirit, nor the Holy Spirit without Them.

It is highly significant that in her art, which she commissioned to be drawn based on her visions, Hildegard does not, unlike so many painters, portray the Trinity as three human persons. Her understanding is far more sophisticated than this. She thus resists the anthropomorphism so common in the art of the Middle Ages.

Hildegard was strongly influenced by the Hebrew prophets and saw herself as belonging in this tradition. She called the female side of the Divine *Sapientia* (wisdom) and *Caritas* (charity or love). Wisdom,

Figure 2: *This extraordinary picture of the Trinity, painted at Hildegard's instruction, shows Jesus at the centre, surrounded by the fire of the Holy Spirit, and the outer circle represents God the Father.*

a feminine persona in the Hebrew Scriptures, is clearly identified with Christ (1 Corinthians 1:24). York Minster, England's second-most important cathedral, was dedicated to 'Holy Wisdom', as was the great Cathedral of Hagia Sophia in Constantinople (now Istanbul).

For Hildegard, *Caritas* and *Sapientia* are the bonds which unite Creator and creature. She normally uses masculine metaphors for God (Father, Son, King, Redeemer, Judge). The feminine metaphors relate to God's interaction with the cosmos. For Hildegard, the incarnation was the hinge of the whole of world history and feminine words are used to show the effects of the incarnation in God's relation to the world. *Scientia Dei* (the knowledge of God) is also female. Hildegard writes:

> *Scientia Dei is represented as a veiled woman with one hand raised in a gesture of forbearance. She is coloured entirely in gold leaf and set off by the backdrop of a starry sky. Suppliant angels surround her on either side. Flanked by a cluster of reverent people on her right and scoffers on her left.*
>
> (From *The Sister of Wisdom*)

The mystical writings, music and art of Hildegard have great contemporary relevance as they provide a highly positive understanding of the world and an affirmation that the feminine side of human experience is incorporated in God.

St Francis of Assisi (1181–1226)

As we have seen previously (p. 89), Francis of Assisi was the son of a wealthy merchant who felt called by God to renew the Church. He gave away all his possessions and founded a community of brothers (with a similar community of women being founded by Clare). Francis was particularly influenced by the words of Jesus in the Bible and was not an academic or philosopher, although members of the order he founded fitted into both categories (see pp. 89–93). Franciscan spirituality is characterised by a life of poverty, love of nature, and giving charity to those in need. Francis' spirituality sees love at the heart of God; there is a dynamic, loving relationship between the three persons of the Christian Trinity, and this overflows in love for creation. Love is self-diffusive and God's love underpins the whole universe.

More than any other part of the Christian tradition, Franciscan theology has beauty as its focus. It sees the beauty of the natural world as pointing to God, and love and beauty are intimately related in the Godhead. Prayer was central to the life of Francis (as it is to every mystic) and Franciscan spirituality focuses on living as Jesus would have lived: a life of gentleness and service to others in poverty and simplicity.

Julian of Norwich (1342–1416)

Julian of Norwich is one of the greatest English mystics, although little is known about her apart from her writings. Julian was a hermit living in a tiny cell attached to a church in Norwich and spending her entire time in prayer. She suffered from a series of illnesses and, at the age of thirty, was in great pain. During this time she had incredibly intense visions of Jesus Christ, which she recorded about a year later when she had recovered from her illness and the visions ceased. She wrote about them once again about twenty years later, albeit with greater theological reflection. Her book, *Revelations of Divine Love*, was written around 1393 when she was about fifty years old and is the first book to be written by a woman in the English language.

Julian had a highly positive attitude to the world in spite of her suffering and she constantly speaks of God's love in terms that were alien at the time. The contemporary Church emphasised duty and obedience to the Church. God could seem harsh and judgemental and the penalties for sin were strongly emphasised. By contrast, Julian's writings are full of joy at the all-encompassing love of God. She believed passionately that God's love was universal and that God wished to bring every human being into a love relationship with God. Today this does not seem radical but Julian wrote at a time when early death was common. A plague called the Black Death swept across Europe and killed a significant percentage of the population, and popular piety saw this as a judgement by God for sin. Churches were full of preaching on the fires and suffering in hell. Julian's understanding, coming from her mystical experience of God, rejected this picture and emphasised the universal love of God – with some modern commentators arguing that she considered every human being was destined to be with God, whether or not they were Christians.

Julian wrote of the Holy Trinity in very personal terms. She compares Jesus to a mother who is loving, wise and merciful and she speaks of God in relation to conception, nursing a baby, labour and bringing up a child. What is more, she argues that God is both Father, Mother and Lord. Again, this ran against Church teaching and ideas, which have tended to speak of God exclusively in male terms – although Julian's view goes back to one of the early creation stories in the book of Genesis, where women and men are both spoken of as being created in the likeness of God.

Possibly the saying for which Julian of Norwich is most well known is: *'All shall be well and all shall be well and all manner of thing shall be well.'* This is far removed from the negative, judgemental, patriarchal picture of God which dominated among contemporary writers, and emphasises the positive and, above all, hope-filled message of Christianity.

St Ignatius of Loyola (1491–1556)

The founding of the Jesuit order by Ignatius of Loyola (see pp. 110–11) has already been dealt with, but the Jesuits have developed one of the most influential forms of spirituality in the Catholic Christian tradition. Ignatius created a thirty-day programme which is referred to as the *Spiritual Exercises*; these are intended to help the individual *'to conquer oneself and to regulate one's life in such a way that no decision is made*

Figure 3: This is the symbol of the Society of Jesus. The letters 'IHS' are an abbreviated form of the name of Jesus; the cross is the central Christian symbol; the three nails are the nails with which Jesus was attached to the cross; the blazing sun is a reminder that Jesus is the light of the world.

under the influence of any inordinate attachment.' The aim, therefore, is that the person who takes the *Exercises* will be given freedom from his or her own desires and inclinations. Crucial to this is developing a process of 'discernment' to work out what God really wants them to do.

Ignatius said that human beings are *'created to praise, reverence, and serve God Our Lord and by this means to save their soul.'* This is the 'First Principle and Foundation' of the *Spiritual Exercises*. Ignatius declares:

> *The goal of our life is to live with God forever. God who loves us, gave us life. Our own response of love allows God's life to flow into us without limit . . . Our only desire and our one choice should be this: I want and I choose what better leads to the deepening of God's life in me.*

This is an excellent definition of Christian spirituality, although there may be various ways in which it can be achieved, and this gives rise to the different forms of spirituality within Christianity. Ignatius emphasised an ardent love for the Saviour, Jesus. In the *Exercises*, Ignatius devoted the last weeks of the programme to the contemplation of Jesus: from infancy and public ministry, to His passion and lastly His risen life. In the *Spiritual Exercises* this is summed up in the prayer: *'Lord, grant that I may see thee more clearly, love thee more dearly, follow thee more nearly day by day'* (104).

Ignatius recommends that, every day, the individual should take time to reflect on what God is really calling him or her to do so that personal inclination should be resisted and God should be master of every aspect of the individual's life. Self-awareness is central and individuals are recommended to have a spiritual director who can guide them on a path closer to God. For Ignatius, spirituality and God are not to be found in renouncing the world in the way that St Benedict and the monastic tradition tended to emphasise. Instead God is to be found in all things; this led Jesuits to embrace science and education and to be active in every walk of life. God is to be found in the everyday. What is needed is a change of heart by the individual so that they recognise this.

St John of the Cross (1542–91)

John of the Cross wrote soon after the Council of Trent (see p. 111ff.) and the Catholic Counter-Reformation. He was educated by the Jesuits, who were a new religious order at the time, and came from a poor family who had converted from Judaism. He entered the Carmelite order and in his twenties began to consider becoming a Carthusian monk; this was a very strict monastic order devoted to silence and contemplation of God. He worked closely with a Carmelite religious sister – Teresa of Avila – who persuaded him not to enter the Carthusians but, instead, to embark on a process of reform of the Carmelites to bring them back to their original vision. Teresa sought to make similar changes in the Carmelite women's order. The proposed changes were strongly resisted by the superiors in the Carmelite order who imprisoned John and sought to force him to conform to the existing standards of the order. He suffered terribly in this period, although he managed to escape after nine months of imprisonment and resumed his reformation of the order. This was to lead to a split in the Carmelites between those who accepted John of the Cross's reforms and those who did not. Importantly, John talked of the 'dark night of the soul': a period in which, even for the person who desires God most, God seems absent. The soul desires God and seeks to be united with God and is desolate when God seems even further away. It is not that God does not exist but that God seems at an impossible distance and all seems hopeless. Eventually the soul overcomes the terror of the dark night and is united with God. This insight, that God can often only be found through times of terrible suffering, has been an important element in Christian spirituality.

St Teresa of Avila (1515–82)

St Teresa of Avila is one of the best examples of an introvertive mystic. She spent seventeen years on the mystic path and she outlined the progressive stages of the mystic's journey towards what some call the vision of God.

The first stage is an awareness that there is more to life than is currently experienced. It may be gradual or sudden but the individual realises that the world is imperfect, that all love is imperfect or that they themselves are imperfect.

The second stage is awareness of sin and is marked by the mystic being aware of the distance between themselves and God. This leads them to try to eliminate some of the obstacles between themselves and the divine. They may engage in simplifying their lives, controlling and disciplining themselves. This is sometimes called purgation.

If the individual is sufficiently strong and develops the virtues needed, they may then reach the third stage – that of illumination. This stage is usually accompanied by a deep and joyful sense of the presence of God.

In between the stage of illumination and the next stage – ecstasy and rapture – there is often a stage called the 'dark night of the soul'. This phrase comes from St John of the Cross and is understood by some mystics as a phase which is necessary for the individual to go through before the true spiritual union may be achieved. During this stage the individual is often convinced that God has abandoned them; they feel totally sinful and close to despair. St Teresa experienced this: God seemed completely absent and to have deserted her.

In the final stage, the prayer of illumination reaches a higher stage when the mystic is subjected to ecstasy and rapture. During raptures the mystic cannot attend to anything in the world, but is, rather, taken out of the world. The mystic does not have the strength to resist it, even if it comes at an inconvenient moment when in public. The mystical journey is often an isolated and painful one but the mystic attempts to see God with the whole of his or her heart and to put all distractions to one side.

Evelyn Underhill (1875–1941)

Evelyn Underhill was an Anglican, albeit one who felt herself to be part of the continuous catholic tradition in England. In a book entitled *Mysticism: A Study of the Nature and Development of Man's Spiritual Consciousness*, she outlines the universal mystic way, the actual process by which the mystic arrives at union with the absolute. She identifies five stages of this process. First is the awakening, the stage in which one begins to have some consciousness of absolute or divine reality. The second stage is one of purgation which is characterised by an awareness of one's own imperfections and finiteness. The response in this stage is one of self-discipline and mortification. The third stage, illumination, is one reached by artists and visionaries as well as being the final stage of some mystics. It is marked by a consciousness of a transcendent order and a vision of a new heaven and a new earth. The great mystics go beyond the stage of illumination to a fourth stage which Underhill, borrowing the language of St John of the Cross, calls the dark night of the soul. This stage, experienced by only a few individuals, is one of final and complete purification and is marked by confusion, helplessness and a feeling that God's presence has been withdrawn. It is the period of the final lack of concern with the self as well as the surrender to the hidden purposes of God. The final and last stage is one of union with God. Here the self has been permanently established on a transcendental level and liberated for a new purpose. Filled up with the knowledge of God, the individual will wish to return to this world in order to show something of God's purposes in the world: to try to show others the way to God.

In her book *The Grey World*, Underhill tells the story of a young boy who dies and realises that there is a life after death but it is, for most people, grey, tedious and devoid of meaning or purpose. He is then born into another body and remembers his previous experience of life after death. He can no longer accept the 'real', everyday world since he has experienced something radically different. He sees through the tedium and meaninglessness of the real world and the superficiality of the lives of almost everyone around him, including his new family, but none of them can understand him. He realises that the barren nature of the after-death reality that he has experienced is the product of the way most people choose to live. On rare occasions he seeks to communicate what he knows from his own experiences but he is mocked and marginalised. No one takes seriously what he is trying to communicate. They are all concerned with mundane practicalities. He knows that there is a transcendent world, that death is not the end and that he and everyone else are, in fact, immortal spirits. However, in a practical and scientific world no one can comprehend, still less accept this. Finally, he comes to fully understand the folly of prizing all those things that everyone else considers so important and he retreats to a small cottage in the country where he lives a life of simplicity and prayer as a book binder. He has seen through the emptiness of the world around him and comes to understand a little of the transcendent nature of reality. Expressed like this, Underhill's book can appear trivial but it points to a truth that mystics have always claimed: that focusing on the world of practicality, on business success, on buying, selling and acquiring things, is empty and, ultimately, will disappoint and be seen as a delusion.

Marian spirituality

One division that needs to be recognised amongst Christians focuses on the mother of Jesus – Mary. All Christians see Mary as a remarkable woman who was willing to be obedient to God and to carry the baby Jesus, God incarnate, in spite of the scandal this would have caused, because she was an unmarried girl when the Angel Gabriel came to her (Luke 1:26–38) to tell her of her forthcoming pregnancy. The Catholic tradition has, however, raised Mary's position so that she is a pivotal figure for the spirituality of many Catholics. She is seen as pre-eminent among women and described as 'the Queen of Heaven' and generally referred to as 'the Blessed

Virgin Mary', and prayers addressed to her are held to be particularly effective. Many churches are dedicated to the Virgin Mary and there have been many appearances of Mary to faithful Catholics over the centuries. Statues of her appear in almost every Catholic church. Catholics see Mary as having herself been conceived without sin (since, in traditional Catholic theology, the sexual act itself is a product of desire and is itself wrong, although necessary for procreation [see p. 230]) and, therefore, God specifically kept her free from the original sin which is seen as being passed on through the sexual act. (This is a position that few, if any, Catholics would hold today.) All other human beings are affected by original sin (see pp. 76, 152) but Mary is held to be an exception.

Protestants tend to be sceptical about the elevated status of Mary, as there is little biblical evidence for it and many see the emphasis on Mary's lack of sexuality as stemming from a negative attitude to women's sexuality on the part of the institutional Church with a male-dominated clergy. They also see Mary as being elevated to her present status because the Church needed a feminine figure to balance the idea of God, who is portrayed as male. Jesus was, of course, also male.

There are four key Marian doctrines held by the Catholic Church:

1) Mary was a perpetual virgin before, during and after the birth of Jesus.
2) Mary was the mother of God.
3) Mary, from the moment that she was conceived, was free from original sin (see p. 27).
4) Mary was assumed directly, body and soul, into heaven.

The last of these was only promulgated as an official teaching of the Church in 1950 and is required to be accepted by

Figure 4: A traditional statue of the Virgin Mary.

every faithful Catholic (it is what is termed a 'dogma' and is one of the very few papal teachings that is held to be infallibly true). More than this, some Catholics argue that Mary should be regarded as co-redeemer with Jesus. This could be the next doctrine to be promulgated by the Catholic Church. It holds that Mary was 'co-redemptrix', that she participates in the process of the redemption from sin of all human beings by giving birth to Jesus. Discussion on this is ongoing but so far it is not a requirement for Catholics to accept this teaching. Orthodox Christians view such additional claims with considerable caution as they consider that there should be no development in Christian doctrine beyond that agreed by the united Christian Church in the early centuries of the faith, although they also revere Mary as the mother of God. Protestants are sceptical about all except the second of the above claims. An emphasis on Marian spirituality, therefore, tends to be found primarily amongst Catholics and Anglicans who are close to the Catholic position as well as, to a lesser extent, among Orthodox Christians. It tends not, however, to have a similar prominence amongst most other Christians.

Mysticism in a broader context

Perhaps in the modern world mysticism can be seen as pointing to a broader vision of the nature of reality. The everyday world, according to the mystic, is only a part of reality and there is a need for human beings to see through the veil of illusion to glimpse something of the transcendent reality that lies beyond. Death is not the end and those false gods that most people prize so highly are ephemeral, transitory and of little account compared with the greater reality that the mystic has experienced.

Contrary to popular opinion, mysticism is not confined to a small group of elite religious individuals: it is part of a wider spectrum which includes religious experiences of different kinds. Tens of thousands of people throughout the world have attested to this broader vision of the nature of reality which, once glimpsed, places the rest of the world and its striving for material success in an appropriate context. The mystic does not reject the everyday world but does call people to realise that it is relatively insignificant when seen under the auspices of eternity. There is a real sense, therefore, in which mysticism challenges the everyday world of 'common sense'. It points to a transcendent reality, to a meaning and purpose for life that goes beyond our everyday concerns and is in many ways in tension with the common-sense way of looking at the world. In that sense it is deeply subversive.

FOURTEEN

Outward Expressions of Inner Realities

All religions combine an inward transformation with external manifestations of belief. People make decisions in their individual lives
and circumstances and these are obviously influenced by their faith.
Christians seek to orientate their lives towards God in prayer and
solitude, as well as in community action and their everyday decisions.
However, their beliefs are also expressed through forms of ritual,
praise and worship which are outward manifestations of their inner
beliefs. These outward manifestations of religious belief can, in some
cases, become an end in themselves without any connection with
an internal change: religion then becomes a matter of social convention (see Amos 5:21-24). This happens in Christianity and in all
religions. It is very easy for 'being a Christian' to become a matter
of 'going to church'. If this happens, something significant has died
and what has survived does not in any sense represent what is
important.

Throughout Christian history there have been important times
of year when certain events in Jesus' life are remembered and when
certain practices are undertaken to remind the Christian that their
life is anchored on belief in the risen Lord Jesus. These outward
manifestations are important in the life of a Christian but they are
merely outward expressions of an inward spiritual journey. They
are meant to help individuals to remain focused on the central
features of the Christian message. The most important of these in
the main churches are the following:

Advent

Advent is the church season that precedes Christmas (the word 'Advent' means 'coming' or 'arrival'). It is not celebrated by all Christians. Some Protestant groups argue that the season does not have its roots in Scripture.

The Orthodox Church has a forty-day period of preparation called the Nativity Fast, beginning in mid November, which involves fasting from meat and dairy foods and sometimes also from fish, wine and oil. The fast is seen by Orthodox Christians as a spiritual journey and a way of purifying and preparing themselves for the joy of Christmas.

However, many of the mainstream Western churches do celebrate Advent and would see it as the beginning of what is termed the 'liturgical year' ('liturgy' means the church services that take place throughout the year and which are governed by the 'liturgical calendar' – at least in the more traditional churches). Advent begins on the fourth Sunday before 25 December, falling sometime between 27 November and 3 December. This is, for Christians, a time of preparation for the joyfulness of Christmas. In the past this has been a time for fasting and for Christians to prepare themselves to remember the birth of the Christ-child. However, the focus of Advent is not simply about remembering events 2,000 years ago. The season also has an eschatological dimension; it looks forward to what Christians believe will be the second coming of Christ as the end of time.

In churches that use liturgical colours to mark the seasons, the predominant colour of Advent is purple, which symbolises preparation and penance. The well-known custom of the Advent calendar has become increasingly secular to the point where it is almost completely disconnected from Christian themes. For many Christians, their religious symbols in Advent are focused around light and darkness and are linked to a belief in Jesus as the Light of the World. Most familiar among these would be the Advent wreath which is made of evergreen and traditionally has three purple candles and one pink one. On the first Sunday of Advent the first purple candle is lit, then two candles on the second Sunday so that the light gradually increases as Christmas approaches. The pink candle of the third Sunday symbolises the joy of the season.

Christmas

No one knows when Jesus was born. The early Christian Church, therefore, took over what was previously a pagan festival which marked the turning of the northern hemisphere year from midwinter to longer days, and used this to commemorate Jesus' birth. Christmas is one of the most important moments for Christians – it is a time of joy and celebration that God has become incarnate (become human) out of love for human beings. Sadly, today, Christmas has become commercialised and any connection with Christianity can easily be forgotten, but the origins of Christmas lie solidly in it being a major Christian festival.

Not all Christians celebrate Christmas on 25 December. In Orthodox Churches, which still use the old Roman (Julian) calendar, Christmas is celebrated on 7 January. There are some regional differences but for many Orthodox Christians, celebrations begin with a service of readings and communion on Christmas Eve morning. Then people fast until sunset when they may have a special twelve-course meal (one course for each of the twelve apostles). This is followed by a Nativity vigil with Scripture readings and an anointing with oil. On Christmas Day, people return to church for the Feast of the Nativity and the following day there are special services to honour the Virgin Mary.

Some Christians do not celebrate Christmas at all (see p. 126), arguing that it is essentially a pagan festival and that many of the customs associated with it are also pagan.

Epiphany

This is part of the Christmas season but is a particular time following the Christmas festival. In Western churches it is celebrated on 6 January and commemorates the visit of the Magi (wise men) to the infant Jesus:

> *After Jesus was born in Bethlehem in Judea, during the time of King Herod, Magi from the east came to Jerusalem and asked, 'Where is the one who has been born king of the Jews? We saw his star when it rose and have come to worship him.'* (Matthew 2:1–2)

The visit of the Magi – who, according to Matthew's Gospel, travelled to Bethlehem from foreign lands – represents Christ being revealed to the wider world.

The Orthodox Church calls this feast Theophany: the appearance or manifestation of God. In Orthodox churches using the Julian calendar it is celebrated thirteen days later than in the Western churches.

Epiphany/Theophany celebrates the baptism of Jesus:

> *At that time Jesus came from Nazareth in Galilee and was baptised by John in the Jordan. Just as Jesus was coming up out of the water, he saw heaven being torn open and the Spirit descending on him like a dove. And a voice came from heaven: 'You are my Son, whom I love; with you I am well pleased.'* (Mark 1:9–11; see also pp. 27–9)

Orthodox Christians believe that the divinity of Christ was revealed at his baptism, so their celebrations on that day include a blessing of the baptismal water and in some places a blessing of a nearby river, lake or sea.

Lent

Lent is a period of forty days (plus six Sundays) before Easter and is one of the most solemn times of the Christian year, as Christians anticipate the remembrance of Jesus' death on the cross. This is, of course, far more than remembrance of an unbelievably horrific death; this is Jesus as God, the second person of the Divine Trinity, willingly going to His death in obedience to God the Father's will in order to save all human beings from the effects of sin and to open the doors of heaven to all who will trust in Him. The idea of sacrifice is an alien one to modern culture. Sometimes people talk of those in the armed forces sacrificing their lives, but Christians see Jesus as the ultimate sacrifice: God in God's self suffering with human beings. In Liberation Theology (see p. 223ff.) God is seen as suffering with the poor and the oppressed, but all Christians see the suffering of Jesus on the cross as the supreme sacrifice by the God of love, who is willing for God's own Son to die in a horrific manner to atone (or to pay the price for) the sins of the whole world. Lent is the time when Christians remember this sacrifice and many Christians either fast or give up things that they would normally enjoy in order, in a very small way, to remind themselves of the sacrifice of Jesus. This is a solemn time in the Church year as Christians think forward to 'Good Friday' – the day when Jesus is remembered as dying on the cross. The Orthodox Church has a much stricter fast for 'Great Lent' and Orthodox Christians are asked to avoid meat, fish, eggs and dairy, olive oil and alcohol during the fast. Married couples are also supposed to refrain from sexual relations. Unlike the Roman Catholic Church and many other churches, the Orthodox Church also practises what is called a eucharistic fasting, which means that the Eucharist or Divine Liturgy is not celebrated on weekdays in Great Lent.

As with other seasons in the Christian year, the Lent fast is not an end in itself but is seen as a way of renewing one's relationship with God. It is meant to be accompanied by almsgiving and prayer, and all Christians are urged to do their fasting secretly and joyfully:

But when you fast, put oil on your head and wash your face,
so that it will not be obvious to others that you are fasting,
but only to your Father, who is unseen; and your Father, who
sees what is done in secret, will reward you.

(Matthew 6:17–18)

The last week of Lent, leading up to Easter, is commonly called Holy Week and is the most solemn week of the year for most Christians. It begins with Palm Sunday, when many Christians attend special services to commemorate Christ's entry into Jerusalem, riding a donkey. Processions often re-enact this event, along with a blessing of palm branches.

In the Orthodox Church there is a service of anointing and confession of sins on the Wednesday of Holy Week, called the Sacrament of Holy Unction.

On the Thursday evening of the same week, Christians who use liturgical worship gather to celebrate the Eucharist and to remember the Last Supper Jesus shared with his followers. In some churches the priest or minister re-enacts the Gospel scene where Jesus washed the feet of His disciples, by washing the feet of some of the congregation (see p. 33). This day is called Holy or 'Maundy' Thursday, from the Latin word *mandatum*, meaning 'commandment'. It refers to the commandment Jesus gave to His disciples: '*A new command I give you: love one another. As I have loved you, so you must love one another*' (John 13:34).

It is traditional in some churches to strip the altar at the end of this service and to leave the church bare of decoration until the first celebration of the resurrection (often at an Easter Vigil on Saturday night). Some churches will also keep a vigil of prayer into the night, to remember how Jesus went to the Garden of Gethsemane to pray with His disciples prior to His arrest there.

Good Friday services in general are sparse and sombre affairs, to remind the congregation that they are there to commemorate the death of Jesus. Bible readings tell of the story of Jesus' death. Some churches will have processions carrying a cross, and sometimes

Christians of different denominations join together in an ecumenical walk of witness around their local area. Roman Catholic and Orthodox churches also include veneration of the cross, when members of the congregation come forward to kiss the cross or offer some other gesture of respect. Sometimes services on Good Friday afternoon last for the three-hour period during which Jesus was on the cross. In the Orthodox Church the body of Christ is also removed from the crucifix, wrapped in a white cloth and placed in a symbolic tomb.

Easter

From a Christian perspective Easter is the most important festival of the year and is therefore celebrated by most Christians. One notable exception is the Society of Friends, who do not celebrate festivals at all:

> *Another testimony held by early Friends was that against the keeping of 'times and seasons'. We might understand this as part of the conviction that all of life is sacramental; that since all times are therefore holy, no time should be marked out as more holy; that what God has done for us should always be remembered and not only on the occasions named Christmas, Easter and Pentecost.*
>
> (Janet Scott, *Quaker Faith and Practice*, 1994, 27.42)

Easter (known as Pascha in the Orthodox Church), when the resurrection of Jesus is remembered, is the most joyous day of the Christian year. The contrast with the bleakness of Good Friday is extreme. Churches are full of light and decoration and the atmosphere is jubilant. Christians will often greet each other by saying, 'Jesus is risen', to which the standard reply is, 'He is risen indeed.' Many churches begin their Easter celebrations with an Easter vigil beginning on the Saturday night. A fire is lit and the new Paschal (Easter)

Candle is lit from it and carried into a darkened church. Members of the congregation light their candles from the Paschal Candle until the light – representing the resurrection of Jesus – spreads throughout the church. In the early Christian Church, Easter would have been the time when new members were initiated (and Lent would have been their final stage of preparation for baptism). Some churches, such as the Roman Catholic Church, still receive new adult members at Easter, when they are baptised, confirmed and receive communion for the first time.

The custom of giving Easter eggs is a commercialised way of representing the new life that results from the resurrection. Easter has now become a time when large amounts of chocolate are consumed with little awareness of the day's religious significance. Today it is difficult to understand the significance of Easter and the hope it brings for Christians unless one understands it as the culmination of the period of Lent following the despair of Good Friday. The date for Easter varies each year, as it is calculated from the moon and falls on the Sunday after the full moon following the Spring Equinox. In practice, this means that Easter always falls somewhere between 22 March and 25 April, except for Orthodox Churches following the Julian calendar, for whom it is later.

Ascension

This is celebrated forty days after Easter and ten days before Pentecost and is the date when Jesus is commemorated as ascending to heaven. After He died, He rose from the dead and appeared to His disciples (p. 57) and others on a number of occasions before ascending to be at one again with God the Father. So the Ascension commemorates the end of Jesus' earthly ministry.

Pentecost

Some Christians see Pentecost as the 'birthday' of the Christian Church, in the sense that it was at Pentecost that the followers of Jesus began to go out and spread His message to other people from around the world. This has always been an important part of the Church year, but for evangelical Christians it is particularly significant. Pentecost is the occasion when the Holy Spirit descended on Jesus' followers in the early Church. The Acts of the Apostles records the occasion as follows:

> *When the day of Pentecost came, they were all together in one place. Suddenly a sound like the blowing of a violent wind came from heaven and filled the whole house where they were sitting. They saw what seemed to be tongues of fire that separated and came to rest on each of them. All of them were filled with the Holy Spirit and began to speak in other tongues as the Spirit enabled them.*
>
> (Acts 2:1–4)

At Pentecost Christians remember the centrality of the Holy Spirit which dwells in their lives and represents the presence of God with them. Jesus told His disciples that when He ascended they were not to be afraid:

> *If you love me, keep my commands. And I will ask the Father, and he will give you another advocate to help you and be with you forever – the Spirit of truth. The world cannot accept him, because it neither sees him nor knows him. But you know him, for he lives with you and will be in you. I will not leave you as orphans; I will come to you. Before long, the world will not see me any more, but you will see me. Because I live, you also will live.*
>
> (John 14:15–19)

In the Orthodox Church, Pentecost is also known as Trinity Day because the coming of the Holy Spirit is seen as the time when the Trinity was fully revealed to human beings. Often icons showing both the Spirit descending as tongues of fire and the Trinity itself are placed in the centre of the church on this day. Pentecost is not seen simply as the celebration of a historical event, but is a reminder of the belief that the Holy Spirit comes to all Christians.

This idea is also shared by Pentecostal Christians who believe that they need to be open to the Holy Spirit every day and that it can give them gifts of healing, tongues and prophecy, just like the disciples in the Bible account.

Between these key periods of the Church year is what is called 'ordinary time' (particularly in the Catholic, Methodist and Anglican/ Episcopalian Churches); this refers to church services which are not in any one of the 'special' periods set out above.

Symbols

Symbols are meant to speak. They are carriers of meaning, outward expressions of an inner reality. The problem is that they have widely different and sometimes conflicting interpretations. Some might argue that there are universal symbols (e.g. water, light) which can still speak powerfully to people of different backgrounds, but often believers need to be initiated into the symbols of their community in order to understand them. A further problem can arise if the symbols become an end in themselves rather than expressions of a deeper truth or reality. Such symbols become empty, which is why some groups of Christians are wary of using them. At their best, they can enrich the experience of Christian life, enabling people to touch on some of the key aspects of Christian belief, not only intellectually but through the senses.

Churches are places full of symbols that are of deep significance to Christians. There are many Christian symbols but the most important of all is the cross.

Crosses

The cross exists in a multitude of different designs which reflect different aspects of the faith of the Christians who use them.

A cross with a figure of Jesus on it is known as a crucifix. Most commonly found in Roman Catholic churches, or as icons in Orthodox churches, it focuses on the sacrificial love of Jesus through His death on the cross.

Many Protestant churches prefer a plain cross, which is used to symbolise the resurrection: the belief that Christ has overcome death on the cross and has risen to a new life.

The Orthodox cross has two extra horizontal beams. The top beam is often said to represent the inscription placed by Pontius Pilate on the cross which said, 'The king of the Jews'. The bottom beam represents the foot support that was used in crucifixions. There are various explanations for this being a diagonal beam. One popular idea is that the side slanting upwards points towards heaven and the other side points down to hell.

There is no single interpretation of the Celtic cross (see p. 82), which is a cross with a circle around the centre and often with elaborate Celtic knot-work designs. Some have a three-pointed knot which could represent the Trinity.

The Coptic cross is depicted on p. 69.

The Jerusalem cross consists of a large cross surrounded by four smaller ones. As with the other crosses, there are various interpretations of the symbolism. Some argue that the crosses represent the wounds of Jesus on the cross; or that the four smaller crosses represent the four evangelists, Matthew, Mark, Luke and John; or that the design represents Christianity reaching out to the four corners of the earth.

All the above symbols and forms of worship are important, but they are outward manifestations of an inner transformed reality, whereby the Christian has anchored himself or herself not on worldly concerns but on the centrality of God and the risen Lord Jesus.

FIFTEEN

Christianity Today

There are about 2 billion Christians in the world and Christianity is, by a significant margin, the largest world religion. Very roughly, 34 per cent of Christians are found in North and South America, 24 per cent in Europe, 25 per cent in Africa south of the Sahara and 17 per cent in the rest of the world. The fastest growth, however, is in Africa south of the Sahara and, surprisingly, in China (albeit from a low base). In Europe and North America, numbers of Christians are falling. However, these broad figures mask a considerable lack of unity among different Christian churches, communities and groups, who often each see their own version of Christianity as the only right one, in some cases leading to intolerance between Christian groups.

The Catholic Church accounts for about 60 per cent of the total number of Christians, with the rest being split between a wide variety of denominations. The Orthodox Church tends to be focused in particular nations – for instance, the Russian, Syrian, Greek, Serbian and other Orthodox Churches – although recently more Orthodox churches have been opening in other European countries and in Australasia and North America. The Coptic Church is mainly centred in Egypt and Protestant churches in various forms are present in every country of the world. The World Council of Churches is an umbrella body that brings together many different churches and acts as a place for discussion. (However, the Catholic Church, even though it believes greater unity is desirable, has always declined to participate, as it holds that the 'fullness of salvation' can only be found within the Catholic Church.) Nevertheless, beneath the diversity, the

Christian churches are nearly all united in the central Christian claims outlined in this book: that Jesus of Nazareth was crucified under Pontius Pilate, died and rose from the dead; that Jesus is the second person of the Divine Trinity; and that all those who have faith in Jesus and entrust their lives totally to God will be forgiven and brought to God's heavenly kingdom. Almost all affirm the importance of baptism and all try to follow Jesus' example. Almost all Christians take part in communal worship and the church or chapel will be an important part of their lives. So, to an extent, being a Christian means belonging to a Christian community, but it also means a personal transformation as the individual seeks to be faithful to the Gospel message and to live as Jesus would have wished. The mainstream Christian traditions established in the past mostly continue today, but Christian worship takes different forms, with some groups emphasising hymn singing and praise, some emphasising the sacraments (see p. 112), some focusing more on active service amongst the poor, and others making stillness and silence central. All aim, in spite of their different manifestations, to place God at the centre of their lives.

The divisions from the past still remain, with Catholics continuing to place the Church, the Mass and the other sacraments at the centre of their lives, whilst Protestants continue to emphasise the role of Jesus as the personal Saviour of every Christian and, therefore, Protestant services are full of praise and thanksgiving. The Anglican or Episcopalian Church remains in the middle, with some wings of that church identifying more closely with the Catholic tradition whilst others identify more with Protestant Christianity. Anglicanism has always prided itself on being a 'broad church' that accepts a very wide range of theological positions.

Within Catholic Christianity there have been three great recent (in the last 500 years) Councils of the Church. The first was the Council of Trent (see p. 111ff.) and the second was the First Vatican Council. This was called by Pope Pius IX and was held between 1869 and 1870, and particularly addressed issues arising from the rise of liberalism, materialism and biblical criticism. This Council also affirmed papal infallibility, which is a dogma with a more limited scope than many people understand. It does not mean that everything that a Pope says is necessarily true and must be accepted; it only claims that when the Pope is speaking *ex cathedra* and laying down doctrine, then his statements must be accepted by the faithful. There are very few such infallible doctrines but they include the doctrine of infallibility itself and the claim that the Virgin Mary was assumed, body and soul, directly into heaven without passing through purgatory (see pp. 94–5; 156). Orthodox and other Christians do not accept this doctrine of papal infallibility, and this is one of many reasons why there continue to be marked divisions between Christians today.

The Second Vatican Council (1962–5), like its predecessors, addressed issues of contemporary concern. The Council was called by Pope John XXIII but due to his unexpected death in 1963, Pope Paul VI presided over the proceedings. The Council brought together cardinals, bishops, theologians and some lay people and addressed areas of great relevance in the modern world. It emphasised the importance of the role of lay people in the Church and the principle of 'subsidiarity': that local cardinals and bishops should have greater autonomy. It also affirmed the importance of individual conscience reigning supreme, as well as introducing important liturgical changes such as the Mass being celebrated in local languages rather than in Latin. However, certain matters agreed by the Council also faced real opposition from more conservative Catholics who bemoaned the increasing freedom that the Council seemed to have introduced and also the idea that after nearly two millennia the Mass, which is at the heart of the life of a faithful Catholic, was no longer to be said in the universal language of the Church (Latin) but in local languages.

Some more conservative Catholics felt that the Second Vatican Council had gone too far. A small number of groups insisted on continuing to celebrate Mass in Latin whilst others played down the role of individual conscience by arguing that no faithful Catholic could appeal to individual conscience against the clear teaching of the Church. Catholics needed to inform their conscience by Church teaching and Cardinal Ratzinger (later to become Pope Benedict) said that, because of this, no faithful Catholic could use individual conscience to reject the clear teaching of the Church. Nevertheless, for many, the Second Vatican Council was liberating and introduced the Church to the modern world in a new and more relevant way. Most modern married Catholics, for instance, use contraception even though the Church's teaching rejects this, and many infertile Catholic couples use IVF even though this, also, has been condemned by the Church. The issue of conscience (see pp. 172–3) is central to understanding the current tensions within the Catholic Church on some contemporary issues, not least those arising from Pope Francis' 2016 Encyclical, *Amoris Laetitia* ('The Joy of Love'; see p. 168).

The Anglican Church has been beset by splits and divisions, and similar divisions have occurred within many Protestant churches including the Methodists, Baptists and Lutherans. The two most important of these contemporary divisions revolve round the role of women in the Church and the issue of homosexuality (which is discussed later in this chapter). Very broadly, more conservative Christians have insisted that priests can only be male, as Jesus only chose male disciples and, since the priest represents Jesus, the priest has to be a man. Dissenting voices have rejected this and have argued that Jesus came to earth as a human being and His gender was not significant, whilst the disciples were male because the culture at the time would only have accepted male leaders.

Whilst the long-established Christian churches have all continued and mostly grown (particularly in the developing world), perhaps the most important new movement in Christianity in the last hundred years is a movement strongly based on individual spiritual experience and God's Holy Spirit, which is seen to be at direct work in the community: this is Pentecostalism.

Pentecostalism has been influenced by the tremendous growth in African-based Christian churches originally developing from the preaching of missionaries in Africa but, perhaps more importantly, deriving from the experience of slavery in the southern half of the

United States and the plantations in the Caribbean. Christianity adapted to the oppression and suffering of the African people and was seen as having a political and social agenda, leading oppressed people to freedom from white domination. African Christian churches tend to be Pentecostal and to emphasise the giving of the Holy Spirit at Pentecost. Personal witness tends to be vital, with individuals coming forward to testify about the power of the risen Lord Jesus in their lives. Sermons are often long and are directly related to Gospel themes, and many will focus on the need to recognise individual sin and to repent. Services appeal to the emotions and the participants can reach something close to a religious frenzy. It is fair to say that Pentecostal worship tends to be much less restrained and much more communally based than services in more traditional churches, where the role of liturgy and the centrality of the priest tend to be more important. Passionate and beautiful communal hymn singing is almost always a central part of African Christianity, and 'Gospel music', in which the Christian Gospel is expressed through song, originated in Pentecostalism. Pentecostal Christians feel inspired by the activity of the Holy Spirit working through individuals and communities, and the passion, commitment and enthusiasm this generates have a profound effect.

Pentecostal services tend to be long with a focus on worship and praise of God, hymn singing and preaching on the text of the Bible and the need to avoid sin and to live as the Spirit of God directs. However, personal testimony to the power of Jesus in an individual's life is also common and there is often a highly charged emotional atmosphere. Pentecostal Christianity emphasises the importance of the 'full Gospel' message, which is sometimes referred to as the 'four square Gospel' as it contains four crucial points:

1) Jesus saves the individual Christian, according to John 3:16.
2) Baptism with the Holy Spirit is essential, in accordance with Acts 2:4.
3) The individual Christian is healed bodily, provided they have faith, as promised in James 5:15.

4) Jesus will come again to receive into heaven all those who are
   saved, as declared in 1 Thessalonians 4:16–17.

Pentecostalists believe that the Bible is the Word of God and that
in terms of both faith and doctrine, obedience to the Bible is central.
However, the sending of God's Spirit is not confined to the time of
the early Church, and miracles and 'Spirit-filled' individuals occur
just as often today. The power of the Holy Spirit is constantly at
work to heal people and to save them. God is seen to speak directly
to individuals as they pray and particularly when they read the
Bible. Salvation comes through faith in Jesus as one's personal
Saviour, and the grace of God is essential in terms of God acting
to wipe out individual sin and to bring people to salvation. Salvation
is not something that can be earned by good works; it is a free gift
of God given to the undeserving individual out of God's love and
care, and all that God requires is thanksgiving and obedience to
God's Word in the Bible and to follow in the footsteps of Jesus.
Most Pentecostalists would have little time for biblical exegesis or
interpretation (see p. 219). They would also focus on the power of
prayer. Testimonies of healings and miracles that have occurred as
a result of prayer are frequently given during church meetings.

Pentecostal churches are growing faster than any other single
group and have much in common with each other. Across mainstream
Christian denominations, African churches have developed that have
an energy, independence and enthusiasm rarely found within those
denominations. Some Pentecostal churches in the United States have
huge numbers of adherents and their political influence can be
considerable. They often tend to be conservative in matters of ethics,
as was seen in Chapter 12.

The 'Toronto Blessing' was a manifestation of the Spirit of
Pentecost which occurred in 1994 at the then Vineyard Church at
Toronto Airport. The manifestations of the Spirit could include
laughter, speaking in tongues and crying, and there was certainly a
significant emotional element. This type of ecstatic experience is not
new but it is a particular feature of Pentecostalist churches.

The Assemblies of God is one of the largest groups of Pentecostal churches, and in their 'Statement of Fundamental Truths' they set out their core beliefs, which are consistent with the mainstream Christian message taught down the centuries, namely that 'The Lord Jesus Christ is the Eternal Son of God.' Moreover, concerning Christ the Scriptures declare:

- His virgin birth (Matthew 1:23; Luke 1:31, 35).
- His sinless life (Hebrews 7:26; 1 Peter 2:22).
- His miracles (Acts 2:22; 10:38).
- His substitutionary work on the cross (1 Corinthians 15:3; 2 Corinthians 5:21).
- His bodily resurrection from the dead (Luke 24:39; 1 Corinthians 15:4).
- His exaltation to the right hand of God (Acts 1:9, 11; 2:33; Philippians 2:9–11; Hebrews 1:3).

The biblical base of the Pentecostal churches is clear here, as is the accord between Pentecostal belief and mainstream Christian belief. Pentecostal Christians emphasise Jesus dying on the cross as a substitute for the punishment due for the sins of individual human beings, and they also emphasise the Holy Spirit at work within the lives of individuals. Pentecostal Christians differ, therefore, from other Christian groups more in their manner of worship than in the fundamental nature of their beliefs.

Quakers continue to be a small but disproportionately influential minority, with their emphasis on stillness, silence and 'waiting on God'. Their meetings are conducted in silence unless someone feels prompted to speak into it, and they have no place for hymn singing or liturgy. They have, effectively, stripped back Christianity to an attentive 'waiting on God' and seeking to live simple lives caring for others. In particular, Quakers are passionately committed to the principles of justice and non-violence.

'House churches' or 'cell churches' have in recent years become relatively common. These are not generally affiliated to any denomination and members meet in each other's houses, as was the custom amongst the earliest Christians. Some members argue that meeting in homes is a more intimate and effective way of spreading the Christian message and it has even been argued that this was the intention of the early Christians. There are also financial issues, with the cost of maintaining expensive church buildings becoming an increasingly onerous burden for established churches, which means less money is available for helping the poor and marginalised or for outreach to non-Christians.

Charismatic Christianity is a common phenomenon today in mainline Christian churches. It is an approach to Christianity that can be found in almost all church communities. It may best be seen as a renewal movement. Charismatics generally maintain that the institutional side of normal Christian churches lacks the fervour that faith in the risen Lord Jesus should engender. They therefore draw on the Spirit of Pentecost (Acts 2:1–4) to enliven more traditional forms of worship. However, this has provoked some tensions within traditional institutions and sometimes this has led to the formation of new Charismatic churches. Today the boundaries between the various Pentecostalist and Charismatic churches are far from clear, but the emphasis on the active work of the Holy Spirit is common to both. Charismatic Christianity is to be found in Catholic, Protestant and Pentecostal churches as well as others. Orthodox Christianity has tended to be more sceptical about this approach, as it seems to depart from worship and practice as found in the early Church.

The issue of homosexual relations has been dealt with in Chapter 12, but it raises the issue of homosexual priests. Clearly, if homosexuality is wrong, then it would not be possible to be a priest and also to be in an active homosexual relationship. It is important, of course, to distinguish between an active homosexual relationship and a homosexual inclination. It is perfectly possible to be celibate and to be either heterosexually or homosexually inclined.

Sadly, these divisions have been given too much attention by many Christians and have eclipsed the broader vision and challenge of Christianity. Perhaps this is particularly the case in the United States, where being a Christian has become closely associated in the minds of many people with being against homosexuality and against abortion. Pope Francis, in his visit to the United States in September 2015, sought to take the emphasis away from these issues and instead to focus on issues related to social justice (an uncomfortable subject in the United States, where the profit motive and capitalism are strongly part of the American way of life). Whilst homosexuality and abortion are important and divisive issues, any understanding of the history of Christianity would make clear that Christians should be giving greater emphasis to issues of social justice and the dedication of an individual's life to God.

Social justice

Perhaps one of the key ways of understanding Christianity today is in its commitment to social justice. Some elements of Christian social ethics have been outlined in Chapter 12, but this aspect of Christianity is of enormous contemporary relevance and is (or perhaps should be) the central feature of much mainstream Christianity today. Social teaching is, perhaps, expressed and defined most clearly within the Catholic tradition but the commitment to social justice is central to almost all parts of the diverse Christian tradition. Pope Pius XII, during the Second World War, spoke out strongly against the war and Pope John XXIII issued papal encyclicals (*Pacem in Terris* – Peace on Earth; *Mater et Magistra* – Mother and Teacher) condemning war and calling for an end to the arms race and for a ban on nuclear weapons. The second document also dealt with issues of economic injustice affecting the developing world.

Pacem in Terris argued that the values that individuals are called to live by – justice, solidarity with others and a commitment to truth – should also guide relationships between nations and communities. Politics, it argued, required a blend of charity and justice. Pope Paul VI argued in *Populorum Progressio* (On the Progress of

Peoples) that economic development without a commitment to seeking the development of the whole person was wrong, and he criticised what he termed the 'idolatry of the market place'.

In mainline churches there has been an increased attempt to merge both work for social justice and the contemplative side of Christianity. In 1968 there was a gathering of Catholic Latin American bishops for a congress in Medellín, Colombia. The bishops identified many of the problems – social, political and economic – which beset their continent and called for radical change. They were critical of violence, and also of forms of capitalism and Marxism which contributed further to oppression of the poor. They also recognised that the Church had not always been perceived as being on the side of the poor:

> *And incidents are not lacking in which the poor feel that their bishops, or pastors and religious, do not really identify themselves with them, with their problems and afflictions, that they do not always support those that work with them or plead their cause.*
>
> (*Poverty of the Church*,
> statement of the Latin American Bishops,
> Medellín, Colombia, 6 September 1968)

However, they also called for positive and practical action. They committed themselves to reform the way the Church operated so that it would be in greater solidarity with the poor. They placed themselves firmly on the side of the poor and oppressed and called all Christians to fulfil their responsibility to transform society:

> *The Lord's distinct commandment to 'evangelize the poor' ought to bring us to a distribution of resources and apostolic personnel that effectively gives preference to the poorest and most needy sectors.*
>
> (*Poverty of the Church*)

As the Dominican Giles Hibbert OP says:

> *The traditional role of the Church had been to support this oppression. ('Be submissive; offer up your sufferings, and great will be your reward in heaven.')*

The preferential option for the poor

The idea of a 'preferential option for the poor', as articulated by the Latin American bishops at Medellín, came from a letter written in 1968 by Pedro Arrupe SJ who was Superior General of the Jesuit order. It is an idea also developed by liberation theologians such as Gustavo Gutiérrez. Liberation theologians read the Hebrew Scriptures and the Gospels and concluded that God was always on the side of the poor and the outcasts – not on the side of the powerful, the priests and the institutions. They therefore saw the function of theology as being to change people's lives and, specifically, to make an 'option for the poor'.

'The option for the poor' was seen as an important part of Catholic Christianity. Nevertheless, there was nervousness by the Magisterium (the teaching authority in Rome) over the apparent links between Liberation Theology and a perceived Marxist analysis. There was a real tension, as Marx had criticised religion generally as favouring the wealthy and keeping the poor marginalised. He described religion as 'the opium of the people', as ordinary people were taught to keep quiet, accept their poverty and hope for a reward in heaven. Marx rejected this and called for social change. When, therefore, liberation theologians made a similar call for social change, many conservative Catholics saw them as having been influenced by Marx. Nevertheless, liberation theologians argued that Jesus Himself called for His followers to care for the weak and marginalised in society and, therefore, that challenging structural injustices that kept the poor in poverty whilst the rich became more and more wealthy was a central Christian duty.

On 24 March 1980, Archbishop Romero of El Salvador celebrated Mass in the small chapel at the cancer hospital of Divina Providencia, where the sisters had given him a small and very basic apartment. Just after he had finished his sermon, he spread his hands for the next prayer. A shot was fired from a military jeep that had crept up unnoticed outside the open front doors. Romero hunched forward slightly on the impact, then collapsed backward, his heart literally exploded by the single mushrooming bullet.

At the time El Salvador was ruled by a small wealthy elite who were reluctant to give up power. People who spoke out against the government or who worked for political change and land reform were brutally repressed and the majority of the population lived in desperate poverty. Romero was initially appointed as he was seen as a figure who would not cause any unrest. However, shortly after his appointment a close friend of his, the Jesuit Rutilio Grande, was assassinated by the regime after working to help the poor campaign for free elections. As he listened to the stories of poverty, torture, deaths and disappearances Romero became more outspoken and began to challenge the regime. In his fourth pastoral letter, in August 1979, he said:

The church, then, would betray its own love for God and its fidelity to the gospel if it stopped being the voice of the voiceless, a defender of the rights of the poor, a promoter of every just aspiration for liberation, a guide, an empowerer, a humaniser of every legitimate struggle to achieve a more just society, a society that prepares the way for the true kingdom of God in history. This demands of the church a greater presence among the poor. It ought to be in solidarity with them, running the risks they run, enduring the persecution that is their fate, ready to give the greatest possible testimony to its love by defending and promoting those who were first in Jesus' love.

(Fourth Pastoral Letter of Archbishop Romero, 6 August 1979)

He was well aware of the risks he was taking in speaking out, but he continued to do so, whilst always advocating a non-violent approach to the struggle. After his death, El Salvador endured many years of violence and unrest. Six Jesuit professors at the Central American University (UCA) in San Salvador were the intellectual leaders of Liberation Theology. They were therefore considered leaders of revolution against the government. Because of that, they were murdered. One morning the Jesuits were taken from their quarters and dragged into the garden. They were shot in the brain with exploding bullets because they were 'the brains of the people's movement'. Some Christians, as a result of this violence, decided that the only way to overcome the injustice endemic in many South American countries was to join the revolutionaries and to take up arms but, however understandable this might seem as a reaction, it is a position that has always been condemned by Church leaders.

The Brazilian Leonardo Boff has been a leading figure in Liberation Theology, drawing on his Franciscan roots. He has received awards for his work for human rights, but his criticism of Church hierarchy has made him a controversial figure within the Catholic Church, which has sought to silence him on more than one occasion. In 1985 he was suspended from his religious duties by the then Cardinal Ratzinger, after publication of his book *Church: Charism and Power*, although this was lifted after a year. However, when a second attempt was made to censure him in 1992, he left the Franciscan order and the priesthood. Boff continues to work among poor communities including the Base Christian Communities in Brazil and particularly seeks to integrate ecology with Liberation Theology. In an article in January 2016 ('The Earth Will Defeat Capitalism') he said that we have now reached:

> *the day when the Earth no longer has the capacity, by herself, to meet human demands. She needs a year and a half to replace all that is taken from her in one year. She has become dangerously unsustainable. Either we restrain the voracity of wealth accumulation to let her rest and replenish herself, or we must prepare for the worst.*

Jürgen Moltmann, a German Lutheran theologian, in a book entitled *The Crucified God*, argued that God suffers in and with those who are poor and who are outcasts of society. The suffering of Jesus on the cross is a good picture of the present suffering of God whose people suffer. This therefore calls Christians to relieve this suffering by social action to change an economic system that favours the rich and wealthy and tends to keep the poor in poverty. Structural change is therefore needed.

Helder Camara's famous words summarise the challenge of Liberation Theology: *'When I seek to relieve the suffering of the poor I am declared a saint. When I ask, "Why are they poor?" I am accused of being a Communist.'*

Although the term Liberation Theology is commonly used to refer to the ideas that grew out of Latin America in the 1960s and 1970s, in its broadest sense it refers to other situations of oppression, such as the oppression of black people and of women. James Hal Cone is an ordained minister in the African Methodist Episcopal Church and is Professor of Systematic Theology at Union Theological Seminary in the city of New York. He did his doctoral thesis on Karl Barth and this influenced his early work. His theology is rooted in the experience of African Americans and the racism they experience. However, he did not feel that traditional theology spoke to those experiences. His 1969 book *Black Theology and Black Power* expressed the distinctive theology of the black Church. His other works include *A Black Theology of Liberation* (1970) and *God of the Oppressed* (1975).

He turned to Scripture to find answers to the questions, but has also used African American writers and resources. In response to criticism by black women, he developed his ideas to include greater consideration of gender issues. Cone argues that theology is tied to its specific historical context. His theology of liberation and his interpretation of Scripture come out of the context of the black experience of oppression. Jesus identifies with the poor and oppressed, and the resurrection is an act of liberation. Cone also talks about the 'blackness of God':

*If the Church is to remain faithful to its Lord, it must make
a decisive break with the structure of this society by launching
a vehement attack on the evils of racism in all forms. It must
become prophetic, demanding a radical change in the inter-
locking structures of this society.*

(Black Theology and Black Power, 1969)

In his 2011 book *The Cross and the Lynching Tree*, he writes:

*And yet the Christian gospel is more than a transcendent
reality, more than 'going to heaven when I die, to shout salvation as I fly.' It is also an immanent reality – a powerful
liberating presence among the poor right now in their midst,
'building them up where they are torn down and propping
them up on every leaning side.' The gospel is found wherever
poor people struggle for justice, fighting for their right to life,
liberty, and the pursuit of happiness.*

Pope Francis has taken a dramatic lead in emphasising the importance
of the Christian commitment to the poor. He has been highly critical
of unrestrained capitalism and the search for profit at the expense of
social justice and has been criticised by some from within his own
Church for taking a stance that is too 'socialist' and not in favour of
the profit principle. He himself came from South America and was
influenced by Liberation Theology, although initially he was sceptical
about it. However, he has increasingly placed the commitment to
social justice and the rejection of the evils of greed, capitalism and
environmental damage at the centre of his concerns. He has been an
outspoken critic of countries and governments that fail to take seriously the threat of global warming and the disastrous consequences
this is going to have for all people, particularly the poor.

Pope Francis' 2015 encyclical *Laudato Si* (subtitled 'Care for Our
Common Home') is a very important document in relation to the
environment. In comparison with his predecessors, he seeks to live
a simple life and Francis of Assisi (after whom he took the name

of Pope Francis) has clearly been a major influence on him. Other Christian leaders such as Justin Welby, the Archbishop of Canterbury, have followed the Pope's lead and some Anglicans in England are at the forefront of seeking to identify with the poor: for instance, by running food banks or loan clubs to provide cheap financial help to those at the bottom of society who would otherwise be forced into the hands of loan companies charging exorbitant rates of interest. Anglican bishops have also united in criticising British government cutbacks to assistance for the poor, the disabled, single mothers and others.

There is nothing new in Christian terms about a commitment to social justice but it must be accepted that the radical nature of the call to live a simpler life, and to put the needs of others before one's own prosperity, is an uncomfortable and challenging idea. Nevertheless, it is hard to deny that it is a central part of the Christian vocation.

Business ethics

Christian concern for ethics in business arises from concern for social ethics. Whilst acknowledging the need for profit and efficiency, Christian social ethics calls for equal importance to be given to caring for workers, suppliers, customers and the environment: in other words, to standing up for a broadly understood commitment to justice. For too long, the only measure of success in business has been financial, and this is argued to be a denial of the values for which Jesus always stood. Reference has already been made (see p. 125) to the great Quaker businessmen and businesswomen of the past, but Christian business ethics today is a feature of all Christian churches. It calls people back to caring for a wider group than simply those who own, control and profit from business. In recent years, those who were already wealthy have seen their wealth increase dramatically, those on high salaries have seen their salaries increase still further, whilst ordinary workers, teachers, civil servants and others have slid into relative poverty. This situation, it is argued, is unacceptable for a Christian.

One of the best examples of this is the 2008 financial crisis. The major banks around the world were 'deregulated' (this means that most government controls were removed) and the result was that unrestrained greed took over in a very large number of the biggest banks. Traditionally banks were respectable, did not take risks and were regarded as prudent: safeguarding the interests of savers and borrowers. In the years leading up to 2007 this no longer applied. The banks speculated with money entrusted to them and bankers paid themselves huge bonuses. The result was a financial disaster, with governments across the world having to invest billions (not millions) of dollars, pounds, euros, yen and other currencies to 'bail out the banks', in the process massively increasing government debt which has, in the end, to be repaid by ordinary taxpayers. Having brought the Western economic system to the point of near collapse, the bankers, once they were saved by governments, continued to pay themselves huge amounts of money whilst hundreds of thousands of ordinary workers were either made redundant or had their wages cut in real terms. This, by any standards, was and is ethically unacceptable and Christian leaders have challenged the basic assumptions of a capitalist economic system which fails to care for those who are powerless.

The rewards of business must be fairly distributed and whilst this should, rightly, include recognising the contributions of business leaders and shareholders, Christian churches maintain that the wealth of companies and other organisations should be shared with workers and with wider society in pursuit of 'the common good'.

Feminism

Many feminist theologians argue that the early Church undermined the central role of women and subverted their importance by introducing a male-dominated institutional structure. Jesus had many very close female friends who supported Him from their own wealth. Having women priests, some argued, restores the equality between male and female which Jesus always seemed to affirm. Many Protestant churches as well as the Anglican churches have ordained women to the priesthood and in 2015 the Church of England accepted female bishops. The Lutheran church is divided over the issue. However, the role of women is still a controversial one and there are dissenting voices who do not accept the ordination of women within the Anglican, Lutheran and other churches – whilst, of course, the Catholic and Orthodox churches completely reject it.

Modern voices have been raised which challenge the selection of the books which formed the 'canon' of the New Testament. Feminist theologians, for instance, hold that the early Church deliberately 'selected out' those records which gave a central place to women and, particularly, Mary Magdalene in the development of the early Church (see pp. 56–7; 231). These feminist theologians argue that the early Church quickly became dominated by men and sought to present a male, patriarchal understanding of God and the Church. So priests could only be male and maleness as an image of God was regarded as the norm. Female vocabulary tended to be resisted and a feminist reading of the Gospels, which would see a pivotal role for women in Jesus' ministry, was all too often neglected or deliberately suppressed.

The suppression of the role of women (who seemed to have a vitally important role during Jesus' life), and the way the Church has in the past suppressed women's sexuality, is a stain on the history of Christianity. In the area of sexuality, in particular, St Augustine's views cast a long shadow. He blamed the Fall in the Garden of Eden largely on the figure of Eve and saw women as using their sexual attractiveness to lure men away from morality. He had a distinctly negative view of sex, which was shared by many Christian thinkers, seeing it as solely for procreation with almost no emphasis on its positive side.

This illustration, from the Missal of Bernhard von Rohr (1482), shows three female figures. One is a naked Eve, representing female

sexuality, which is associated with evil and death (indicated by the skull in the tree). A second figure is the Virgin Mary: an example of a pure virgin who is associated with Jesus and Christianity (represented by the cross in the tree). The serpent, representing the forces of evil, comes out of the third, naked woman's genitalia, thus associating female sexuality with sin, evil and death. Today all Christian churches reject this negative view and emphasise more strongly the 'unitive' role of sex within marriage, bringing the couple together in intimacy and love. Many Christian writers now link sex, at its best, with spirituality.

Elizabeth Stanton's *The Woman's Bible* was published in 1898 and might be regarded as the start of modern feminism, although there is no fixed date. Almost all feminist theologians see a leading role for nature in spirituality and for the concept of a woman giving birth to new life in a way that a man cannot, thus providing parallels with the concept of God as creator. All reject male images of God and all consider that leading Christian figures, such as Mary Magdalene, have been distorted by Christian leaders. As we have seen, Mary Magdalene is a good example, as it is clear from the Gospels that she was a strong, independent woman who was a close friend of Jesus and who, with others, supported Him and His followers financially. However, in a sermon in AD 591 Pope Gregory identified Mary Magdalene with another figure, also named Mary, who was taken in adultery. Feminists point out that there is no basis for this in the biblical text, but it enabled Mary Magdalene to be portrayed by the Church as a prostitute and sinner, thereby marginalising her influence. Paintings of Mary Magdalene in the Middle Ages depicted her as a prostitute, gazing up to heaven in penitence, often with a skull representing death beside her. Generally, she is portrayed with ginger hair, as this was a common motif to indicate prostitution at the time. In 1969 the Catholic Church stated that Mary Magdalene's saint's day (22 July) relates to the woman who saw the risen Lord Jesus (see pp. 56–7) and not to the woman mentioned by Pope Gregory, thereby effectively refuting the wrongful link between the two Marys. Nevertheless, many popular Western films today still identify Mary as a prostitute, for instance, Martin Scorsese's film adaptation of Nikos Kazantzakis' novel *The Last Temptation of Christ*, as well as Andrew Lloyd Webber's *Jesus Christ Superstar* and Mel Gibson's *The Passion of the Christ*. The position they take is a popular one, albeit with little academic basis and held by few serious Christian thinkers today.

Feminist theologians tend to place considerable emphasis on religious experience and mysticism as a way to know and understand God, and many may be regarded as 'nature mystics': seeing God's presence in the natural world and in beauty as a key part of the immanence of God. Interestingly, St Francis took a very similar position. Key figures in this connection include Hildegaard of Bingen (see p. 186), Julian of Norwich (p. 191), Teresa of Avila (p. 195) and Evelyn Underhill (p. 196), among many others. All feminists lament the marginalisation of women over the centuries and regret that the wisdom of so many Christian women is not accessible today, as few of their writings have been preserved.

Feminist approaches to Christianity and theology are diverse but the main ones are:

1) Some feminist writers accept the Bible and traditional Christianity but consider that it has been distorted by men to suppress the role of women. Many of these theologians wish to maintain the essentials of the Christian tradition and to call people back to Jesus' original vision, which saw all people as equal, irrespective of gender or race. They would regard themselves as evangelical feminists. Almost all wish to stop using

the masculine pronoun when referring to God, as God is beyond gender. Some suggest referring to God as 'she', or using the names 'Sophia' or 'Holy Wisdom' as exemplifying the female side of God. Some refer to God as 'Thea' rather than 'Theos'.

Elisabeth Schüssler Fiorenza has been one of the most influential feminist writers. She seeks the transformation of the Western Christian tradition through a response that recognises the importance of gender and sexual difference and argues that a male reading of texts and a male understanding of Christianity is no longer defensible. Her key works include: *In Memory of Her*; *Bread Not Stone: The Challenge of Feminist Biblical Interpretation*; *But She Said: Feminist Practices of Biblical Interpretation* and *Jesus: Miriam's Child, Sophia's Prophet: Critical Issues in Feminist Christology*.

Schüssler Fiorenza wished to remain within the Christian Church community. In a keynote address to the Women's Ordination Worldwide conference in 2005 she explained why:

It is no wonder that I am often asked: Why do you as a feminist stay in this church? Why do you still call yourself a Catholic theologian? These questions are serious challenges but in my view they are wrong-headed because they presuppose that the hierarchy is the church rather than that we the people of G*d are the church whom the hierarchy is called to serve. To move out of the church rather than to continue the struggle within it would mean giving up our birth-right and abandoning our people who are Catholic wo/men.

She claims that since Western Christianity has been so clearly 'implicated in the continuing exploitation of wo/men and other non-persons', feminist studies must continually challenge its 'willingness to participate in social movements for change'. She challenges what she terms the 'kyriarchal' relationships of authority and power that underpin Western history and tradition, arguing that it is pointless to try to integrate wo/men into existing academic and church systems; rather, it is necessary instead to transform those systems and religious practices. The word 'kyriarchy' translates as 'the rule of the lord, master, father, husband' and Schüssler Fiorenza uses it as a tool to reject the patriarchal understanding of the Christian Church.

She speaks instead of the 'ekklēsia of wo/men' as a place from which 'the voices from the margins [can] seek to destabilise the centre'. The term 'wo/men' is intended to be inclusive of both women and men.

Rosemary Radford Ruether, Professor of Feminist Theology at Claremont Graduate University, maintains that the term 'feminism' should be seen as a rejection of sexism of any kind. She sees women as fully human and fully equal to men in every respect. She argues that religion, psychiatry and philosophy seek to marginalise and dehumanise women and that such movements need to be resisted wherever they are found. Feminism is about the equality of both women and men. She does not see feminism as seeking to put down men but rather as affirming the fundamental equality of the sexes:

Feminism is about both women and men. It affirms women's full humanity, but it is not a putdown of men's humanity. Rather it is a critique of patriarchy as a system that distorts the humanity of both women and men. Men are distorted by patriarchy both in being socialized into aggression, but also shamed when they seek their other creativities. Feminism critiques both distortions, and liberates men as well as women.
('What is Feminism and Why Should We Do it?',
24 June 2011)

I think Christians today of all traditions, but specifically Catholics, need to see this issue as non-negotiable. We need to insist on women's capacity for ordained ministry and the validity of their call to such ministry by God. This means that we need to continue to pursue parallel paths to women's ordination as long as the Vatican refuses to acknowledge the truthfulness of this claim. We will not be deterred by escalating blows of

spiritual violence from the Vatican. As long as we are firm in
our convictions, such blows finally cannot harm us. This perhaps
is the deepest fear of the Vatican, to recognize that its most
powerful weapons against this dissent are finally impotent.

('The Vatican's Spiritual Violence Against
Women's Ordination', 22 July 2011)

Ruether has a strong commitment to environmental concern and
she talks of God as the ground of our being or the cosmic womb
that gives rise to all of reality. In *Women and Redemption: A*
Theological History (1998) she writes:

God is not a 'being' removed from creation, ruling it from
outside in the manner of a patriarchal ruler; God is the source
of being that underlies creation and grounds its nature and
future potential for continual transformative renewal in
biophilic mutuality.

Ruether developed the word 'God/ess' to reject the masculine asso-
ciations of the word 'God' and also to emphasise that we have no
adequate language to describe God. Interestingly, she argued that
Christian theology developed along anti-Jewish lines (a theme developed in *Bible Matters* by Charlotte and Peter Vardy, 2016). She also
argued for the development of a feminist Christology which recognised that Jesus made no distinction between males and females.

2) This second approach includes those who see the Bible as
   corrupted by the influence of males, not least in the way in
   which a male-dominated Church suppressed feminist writings
   at the time when the Bible was brought together as a unity.
   Books such as *The Gospel of Mary* were, they argue, deliberately omitted, as these gave too positive a role for women and
   the male-dominated Church could not accept this. There is a
   spectrum of views here, ranging from those who wish to recover
   the neglected feminist tradition in the Bible by looking at key

figures from the Hebrew Scriptures such as Deborah, Ruth and Esther, to those who consider that the Bible is so affected by male domination that it has become irrelevant.

Mary Daly (1928–2010) might be an example of the second of these positions. She was highly influential in feminist theology and became increasingly strident, claiming that to call God 'Father' is to make fathers gods – implicitly leading to totalitarianism and even sanctioning abuse within families. In *Beyond God the Father* (1973) she wrote: *'The character of Vito Corleone in* The Godfather *is a vivid illustration of the marriage of tenderness and violence so intricately blended in the patriarchal ideal.'* She wanted to cause offence, on some occasions banning men from her lectures in Boston College, the Catholic university where she worked. She argued that this paralleled the way that women have been banned from leadership positions in the Church. She said: *'"God's plan" is often a front for men's plans and a cover for inadequacy, ignorance, and evil.'* Daly saw the Church as overtly oppressive of women:

We understand deeply that until all women are free no man can be free. Even when we believe that we've taken everything into consideration we acknowledge that we may be behaving as badly and as foolishly as our forefathers. We are learning to recognize this as a culturally inherited blind spot that leads inevitably to the destruction of women and all life on Earth, including ourselves.

Critics of Daly's position argue that *Sophia* (Wisdom) has always been regarded as female and that the Holy Spirit is not suggested anywhere in Christian theology as being male. However, Daly would argue that Jesus was a man, all His disciples were men and the idea of God as *Sophia* lost out in the early Church to God as *Logos* (Word), which is male rather than female. Daly moved beyond orthodox Christianity and yet she still wished to maintain a degree of relevance for the Christian stories. In 1996 she wrote:

Ever since childhood, I have been honing my skills for living the life of a radical feminist pirate and cultivating the courage to sin. The word 'sin' is derived from the Indo-European root 'es-,' meaning 'to be.' When I discovered this etymology, I intuitively understood that for a woman trapped in patriarchy, which is the religion of the entire planet, 'to be' in the fullest sense is 'to sin.'

('SIN BIG', *The New Yorker*, 26 February 1996)

3) Some post-Christian feminists argue for multiple gods, both male and female, whilst others look to the female gods of ancient pagan traditions. However, it is questionable whether such feminists can any longer be regarded as Christian.

The decision by Pope Francis in 2016 to open the door to the discussion of women deacons in the Catholic Church is a significant forward step, although even this faces strong criticism from more conservative members of the Church. The issue of women priests, according to the Catholic Magisterium, is not even allowed to be discussed by faithful Catholics. A bishop in Australia was removed for even suggesting, in a parish newsletter, that it might be discussed.

The challenge of the new atheism

Atheism is not new. The word 'atheist' comes from the Greek *atheos* (ἄθεος) which means 'denying the gods, or the ungodly'. Socrates was accused of being an atheist because he did not believe in the state gods of Athens. David Hume was almost certainly an atheist. In the nineteenth century, many key figures were atheists including Ludwig Feuerbach, Freud, Schopenhauer, Nietzsche and Marx. In the 1930s, figures such as A. J. Ayer and the logical positivists argued that statements about God could not be verified by sense experience and were, therefore, meaningless. Bertrand Russell was a lifelong atheist and so was Anthony Flew, until he was convinced late in his life by science to become a deist (a deist believes that God was responsible for starting the universe but, unlike a theist, does not believe that God continues to sustain or interact with the universe).

However, the new atheist movement in the beginning of the twenty-first century represents a sustained attack on the 'evils' of religion, prompted possibly by the claimed religious motivation behind the 9/11 attacks on the Twin Towers in New York. Sam Harris's book *The End of Faith* launched the new atheism. There are four key figures behind the movement, sometimes referred to as 'the Four Horsemen of the new atheism' (referring to the Four Horsemen of the Apocalypse in the Christian tradition): Richard Dawkins, Daniel Dennett, Sam Harris and Christopher Hitchens.

The key features of the new atheism which distinguish it from previous atheist positions are:

1) The strident tone of the new atheists is notable – there is a passion and conviction in their writings that is new.
2) The critiques of religion by the new atheists tend to be based more on science than philosophy – indeed, some of the new atheists disparage the value of philosophy when it comes to debates between religion and faith. Daniel Dennett is an exception here, and in *The God Delusion* Richard Dawkins makes an attempt to produce some basic philosophic arguments against God.
3) Darwinian natural selection is held to be able to produce a total and complete explanation for the existence of the diversity of the natural world as well as the existence of human beings. Dawkins argues that the hypothesis of God and the hypotheses in science are similar, and scientific evidence is required for both. Naturally, he argues that this evidence is lacking in the case of religion.
4) Belief in life after death is dismissed and religion is seen as a psychological prop to prevent people having to deal with the meaninglessness of the universe. Daniel Dennett, in particular,

sees religion as a response to a psychological need (there are clear echoes of Sigmund Freud here), and altruism and other features of religion can be explained in terms of the protection of the human gene pool.

5) Morality, altruism and aesthetics are held to be explainable in psychological and sociological terms.

6) The popularity of books by the new atheists is also new. Whereas previous books by authors such as A. J. Ayer and Bertrand Russell were popular, none can match the popularity of the new offerings by authors such as Daniel Dennett, Richard Dawkins and Christopher Hitchens.

7) Whereas previous atheist writings have been relatively individual affairs, the new atheists are much in accord and unleash a sustained and multi-faceted broadside against religion.

8) Religion is attacked not just for being false but for being positively dangerous and for being the cause of suffering and evil.

Sam Harris claims not to be a fan of the word 'atheist'. In his 2006 book *An Atheist Manifesto* he says:

Atheism is not a philosophy; it is not even a view of the world; it is simply a refusal to deny the obvious. Unfortunately, we live in a world in which the obvious is overlooked as a matter of principle. The obvious must be observed and re-observed and argued for. This is a thankless job. It carries with it an aura of petulance and insensitivity. It is, moreover, a job that the atheist does not want.

It is worth noting that no one ever need identify himself as a non-astrologer or a non-alchemist. Consequently, we do not have words for people who deny the validity of these pseudo-disciplines. Likewise, 'atheism' is a term that should not even exist. Atheism is nothing more than the noises reasonable people make when in the presence of religious dogma.

In *The End of Faith* (2004) Harris claims that religion is not simply irrational and outdated, but dangerous. He argues:

> *Our technical advances in the art of war have finally rendered our religious differences – and hence our religious beliefs – antithetical to our survival. We can no longer ignore the fact that billions of our neighbors believe in the metaphysics of martyrdom, or in the literal truth of the book of Revelation, or any of the other fantastical notions that have lurked in the minds of the faithful for millennia – because our neighbors are now armed with chemical, biological, and nuclear weapons. There is no doubt that these developments mark the terminal phase of our credulity. Words like 'God' and 'Allah' must go the way of 'Apollo' and 'Baal' or they will unmake our world.*

He is critical not just of fundamentalist approaches to religion, arguing that religious texts do not stand up to scrutiny, contradict each other and often advocate behaviour that most twenty-first-century people would find unacceptable. He is also critical of moderates, arguing that their moderate views are the result of both secular knowledge and scriptural ignorance, and that they betray both faith, by being selective about which sections of Scripture they follow, and reason, because they accept beliefs uncritically.

The title of one of Richard Dawkins' earlier books was *The Blind Watchmaker* (1986), referring to William Paley's argument (see pp. 147–8). Dawkins claims that natural selection is 'blind' – it has no aim, no purpose:

> *Evolution has no long term goal. There is no long term target, no final perfection to serve as a criteria for selection . . . The criteria for selection is always short term, either simply survival or, more generally, reproductive success. The 'watchmaker' that is cumulative natural selection is blind to the future and has no long term goal.*

Dawkins follows Hume and describes approaches like Swinburne's probability arguments for the existence of God (see p. 147) as 'arguments from personal incredulity'. Dawkins' view is that the hypothesis of God is entirely superfluous and that order is due to natural selection alone: a 'blind, unconscious, automatic process' which is completely without purpose. Hence the title of his book, *The Blind Watchmaker*.

In *The Selfish Gene* (1976) Dawkins claims that humans only act so that their genes may survive. All we are is mechanisms to pass on our genes in competition with other species. We are simply the means used by our genes to replicate themselves: '*We are survival machines – robot vehicles blindly programmed to preserve the selfish molecules known as genes.*'

In *River Out of Eden* (1995) Dawkins says: '*We cannot admit that things might be neither good nor evil, neither cruel nor callous – but simply callous: Indifferent to all suffering, lacking all ideas of purpose.*'

He quotes Prince Philip, Duke of Edinburgh, who (in a seminar at Windsor Castle addressed by Dr Peter Atkins) said: '*You scientists are very good at answering "how" questions. But you must admit that you are powerless when it comes to the "why" questions.*' Dawkins rejects this: there is no why, except that anything that happens can be explained in evolutionary terms. There simply is no wider meaning or purpose. However, what science and evolution can explain is the mechanisms which bring about states of affairs.

Dawkins understands human beings strictly in terms of biology. We have about 5 billion cells each containing 46 chromosomes and 23 base pairs. Each chromosome contains tens of thousands of genes. Dawkins describes DNA as follows:

It is raining DNA outside. On the banks of the Oxford canal at the bottom of my garden is a large willow tree and it is pumping downy seeds into the air . . . not just any DNA but DNA whose coded characteristics spell out specific instructions for building willow trees that will shed a new generation of

downy seeds. These fluffy specks are literally, spreading instructions for making themselves. They are there because their ancestors succeeded in doing the same. It's raining instructions out there. It's raining programmes; it's raining tree-growing, fluff-spreading algorithms. This is not a metaphor, it is the plain truth. It couldn't be plainer if it were raining floppy discs.
(*The Blind Watchmaker*, p. 111)

Dawkins claims that our coming to self-consciousness so that we can understand ourselves is wonderful. Evolution can explain a skylark and also a Shakespeare sonnet. He claims that the spotlight of consciousness shines not just on the here and now (as it does with animals) but enables us to place ourselves in a broader setting:

The spotlight passes but, exhilaratingly, before doing so it gives us time to comprehend something of this place in which we fleetingly find ourselves and the reason that we do so. We are alone among animals in being able to say before we die: Yes, this is why it was worth coming to life in the first place . . .
(*Unweaving the Rainbow*, 1998, pp. 312–13)

On this basis, we can come to understand the truth about ourselves, and for Dawkins this consciousness that has arisen in us is a thing of wonder. It has no purpose but we can understand why we are here, and this is something at which we may wonder and about which poets can muse.

In his 2007 book, *God is not Great: How Religion Poisons Everything*, Christopher Hitchens argues that we no longer need religion and that it was a product of a more ignorant age. He says it is complicit in, if not responsible for, cruelties and atrocities throughout history:

There still remain four irreducible objections to religious faith: that it wholly misrepresents the origins of man and the cosmos, that because of this original error it manages to combine the

*maximum of servility with the maximum of solipsism, that it
is both the result and the cause of dangerous sexual repression,
and that it is ultimately grounded on wish-thinking.*

*Religion comes from the period of human prehistory where
nobody – not even the mighty Democritus who concluded that
all matter was made from atoms – had the smallest idea what
was going on. It comes from the bawling and fearful infancy
of our species, and is a babyish attempt to meet our inescap-
able demand for knowledge (as well as for comfort, reassurance,
and other infantile needs). Today the least educated of my
children knows much more about the natural order than any
of the founders of religion, and one would like to think –
though the connection is not a fully demonstrable one – that
this is why they seem so uninterested in sending fellow humans
to hell . . . All attempts to reconcile faith with science and
reason are consigned to failure and ridicule for precisely these
reasons.*

Most of the arguments by the new atheists are not new, and the
general rejection of philosophy tends to mean that there is an implicit
assumption that science and verificationism are the only ways in
which knowledge can be sustained. Few of the authors are versed
in theology and, therefore, there is a tendency to argue against a
naïve version of Christianity; for instance, assuming that Christians
believe that God is another object, a type of 'thing' in the universe
(Dawkins likens belief in God to belief in an undiscovered teapot
floating round the planet Pluto). There is also a tendency to take a
relatively literalist view of the Bible, not least of the account of
creation in the book of Genesis.

The responses of Christians to the new atheism vary from a
simple dismissal to one or more of the following:

1) A rejection of the view that science and verificationism are the
only ways to attain knowledge or to justify claims to knowledge.

2) A rejection of what is seen as a faith claim that Darwinian natural selection can provide a complete explanation. There is held to be an unjustified leap from saying that natural selection can explain a great deal (which most Christians would accept) to the claim that it can provide a total explanation (which they would reject).

3) A rejection of the literalist view of the Bible taken by the new atheists (see Chapter 10).

4) A claim that God provides a more plausible total explanation for the beginning of the universe than any of the alternatives (such as the multiverse or the claim that the universe 'just happened').

5) A claim that religious experience is too quickly dismissed and can provide a sound pointer to the existence of God, not least when coupled with the other philosophic arguments which seek to show the probability of God.

6) A claim that beauty, justice, goodness and truth are not merely a matter of convention and can be discovered rather than created. In some cases these are linked to mathematical realism.

7) A claim that lack of proof is not the same as lack of truth. Most Christians tend to be modest in their convictions. They will accept that there is a lack of proof for God's existence and that, in principle, the new atheists could be right but, against this, they will claim that their whole experience and the experience of countless others through the generations is so real that they are willing to stake their lives on the claim to truth.

8) The idea that 'reality' is simply material is now recognised by all scientists as nonsense. At the most basic level of reality, the Plank scale, there are not even electrons – just potential electrons. Reality at the quantum level is totally 'other' than the material universe we experience and some Christians, at least, argue that this new scientific paradigm opens up ways of understanding 'God' and theology that are relevant, liberating and exciting. Religion may have a great deal to offer in terms

of this new understanding.

9) Some Christians, particularly in the United States, argue for 'intelligent design' (see especially the work of Michael Behe). This aims to show not the existence of God but the need to postulate an intelligence to explain the complexity of the universe. The new atheists, naturally, have no need for such an hypothesis.

The popularity of the new atheism has put Christians on the defensive and its influence has been considerable. Consumerism, materialism and the secular culture have also become more influential, with the result that Christianity, in the West at least, has become somewhat marginalised in some countries.

Worship and practice

It is probably true to say that Christians who see worship as the only important aspect of their Christian practice, totally disconnected from everyday life, have misunderstood the teachings of their own churches. In many churches an emphasis is placed on Sunday worship and the centrality of the Eucharist, but worship is not an end in itself. It is true that Christians are called to come together as a community in worship. Here they acknowledge and ask forgiveness for their failure to live up to Jesus' teachings; they listen to the Word of God in Scripture, reminding them what it means to live a Christian life; and often they share a eucharistic meal. But to truly fulfil Jesus' commandment to 'do this in memory of me' requires more than attendance at a weekly church service. Many services end with a command to the worshippers to 'go in peace to love and serve the Lord'. Effectively, this is sending Christians out into the world to share in the mission of the first apostles. The shared worship and Communion are the source of inspiration and strength which enable Christians to go out and put the teachings of Jesus into practice in their everyday life. So, as Jesus explained to the teacher of the law, love of God and love of neighbour are both essential:

> *On one occasion an expert in the law stood up to test Jesus.*
> *'Teacher,' he asked, 'what must I do to inherit eternal life?'*
>
> *'What is written in the Law?' he replied. 'How do you read it?'*
>
> *He answered, '"Love the Lord your God with all your heart and with all your soul and with all your strength and with all your mind"; and, "Love your neighbour as yourself."'*
>
> *'You have answered correctly,' Jesus replied. 'Do this and you will live.'*
>
> (Luke 10:25–28)

SIXTEEN

Conclusion

As this book has made clear, Christianity is multi-faceted, and whilst it is right to recognise its weaknesses and the extent to which it has been misused by those interested in power rather than service to God, nevertheless its essential message is a profound and abiding one: that God exists and is real and loves every single human being and wishes to bring them into a love relationship with God, grounded in lives of love and service to others, and that God loved human beings so much that God was ready to sacrifice God's only Son to redeem them from the effects of sin and evil and to bring them home to God.

Jesus came not to those who are righteous but to sinners and outcasts, those whom respectable society despised and rejected. Christianity is a religion for failures, those without hope and without strength, those who have failed time and time again and consider themselves useless and unworthy of love or acceptance. It is to these people that Christianity comes with its message of God's unconditional love and forgiveness. Christianity teaches that God is personal and loves every individual, no matter what they have done and no matter how they have lived, and God wants nothing more than to forgive people for past mistakes and to welcome them back into close relationship with God. This is incredibly hard for many people to accept as most people consider that, in order for them to be loved, they must be lovable. Yet most people know that, if anyone really knows them very well, they would see that they have fundamentally unlovable characteristics: they are sometimes jealous, full of pride, liars, deceivers, or maybe adulterers and thieves. Christianity teaches that it is precisely such people whom God loves most and whom God wants to welcome back into a close personal relationship. The image of God as the Father welcoming back the prodigal son who has gone astray is a very powerful one and is at the core of Christianity. God's love is unconditional and God's capacity for forgiveness unending. This does not mean that Christians believe that morally wrong behaviour should continue – only that the door is always open to genuine repentance and a new start.

It is precisely here that the challenge this book faces comes into clearest focus. It is so easy to concentrate on the divisions, on the disagreements, on the arguments and the abuses within Christianity but fail to see that, beneath these, there is a unity which cannot be clearly expressed. It is rather like a rainbow made up of many different colours: none are the same but, somehow, taken together, they create something of great profundity and something which inspires people across the world. So it is with Christianity. It has been abused, distorted, manipulated, used for selfish ends and to achieve power and dominance but it also, at its heart, contains claims to deep Truth, and this applies as much in the area of ethics as anywhere else. The irrevocable importance of every human being, irrespective of race, gender or sexual orientation, as a precious child of God is absolutely essential to Christians and anyone who rejects this cannot be considered to be taking Christianity seriously.

Christianity holds that it is only in centring one's life on God that true human fulfilment lies – anything else will lead to despair. Focusing on money, power, reputation, fashion, technology, relationships, sex or anything else will lead to disappointment and emptiness. Only God remains when everything else changes and falls apart. When death approaches, it is only the person who has centred their life on prayer and service to God who will be able to face death peacefully and without fear. This life is but the prelude to eternity and nothing can really hurt those who have centred their lives on God; they stand on the other side of a boundary line. The world can mock them, they may lose their possessions, their relationships may fail, they may get ill and they will eventually die but, in the final analysis, the world cannot hurt someone whose life is truly built on God. They have grounded themselves on a foundation that cannot be moved and that will stand fast, no matter what storms the world throws at them.

Above all Christianity is a religion of hope. In a world which can often seem bleak and dark, Christianity holds that good will triumph over evil, light will triumph over darkness and love will conquer hatred. Christians will recognise that even in the moments of the most profound despair there is always hope and that, in the end, goodness will win, even though it may not seem like that at the time. Hope is a central feature of a true Christian life: hope in spite of the evidence pointing to everything being hopeless; hope when the world seems dark and bleak and when the forces of betrayal, greed and evil seem to triumph; hope when giving up and being hopeless seems the most appropriate reaction. This hope extends not only to this life but also to life after death; all Christians are committed to the view that human potential is fulfilled after death. This life is not the final end. Because of this hope, Christians should be willing to endure suffering peacefully and without complaint. This does not mean accepting injustice, inequality or the forces of evil and selfishness; these need to be resisted and this is part of the Christian's life journey. However, suffering is inevitable for those who take God and Christianity seriously. They will be marginalised by many, mocked and 'written off' by most people. In an age dominated by materialism, shopping and capitalism, Christians are called to march to a different drummer, to centre their lives on God and not on the ephemeral things in this world.

Christians have always been called to suffer for their faith. Jesus died on the cross in the most horrific manner, Christians were persecuted and martyred across the Roman world and have been similarly persecuted down the ages, including today in many (not all) parts of the Islamic world. Indeed, it may be true to say that real Christian faith is best seen in times of oppression and persecution when individuals are forced to depend on God alone and not on their own efforts. It must be recognised that God's power was shown most clearly not in thunderbolts from the sky, as in some pagan religions, but in the power of love to conquer evil. Christians are proud of the symbol of the cross, although for Romans crucifixion was the ultimate degradation. It is through the powerlessness of the cross that Jesus overcame and defeated death and opened the kingdom of heaven to all those who choose to follow Him.

This does not mean that Christians seek suffering but that, standing firm for the values that Jesus proclaimed in a world obsessed by power, money, materialism and consumerism, the true Christian life will always face persecution and opposition. People will laugh at and mock those who take Christianity seriously and will accuse them of not focusing on the worldly goods that everyone else considers so important. Jesus Himself recognised that this would be the case and said that it was impossible to serve God and earthly values at the same time – one or the other must be given priority (Matthew 6:24). Christians have always been willing to challenge the world's way of looking at things and when they conform to worldly expectations, it is probable that they are not being faithful to the message of their Founder.

Some will, of course, ask, 'But is Christianity true?' The answer is that there can be no proof, no way of verifying the truth or falsity of Christianity by the sort of tests that scientists would accept. However, lack of proof is not the same as lack of truth. Either there is a God or there is not. Either Jesus was God or Jesus was not. Either Jesus rose from the dead or He did not. Either human beings will survive death or they will not. Individuals must decide for themselves. That does not mean that truth becomes a matter of opinion. Today we live in a relativistic and post-modern world where every truth claim is seen as of equal value. (Pope John Paul II recognised this in a wonderful encyclical in 1998 entitled *Fides et Ratio*; see p. 161). Christianity makes claims that are not like this. It makes a claim to ultimate Truth and, perhaps, only those who embrace this claim and try to live it out in their daily lives will really come to understand this Truth. Christianity calls people to stake their lives on things that cannot be proved but are neverthe-

250

less the most important issues that any human being can face: Has life any meaning? Is there hope in the face of despair? Is faith a delusion? Countless hundreds of millions of people across the world embrace Christianity's truth claims and seek to live them out and, in so doing, find a meaning and purpose which many others would reject. Are they wrong to do so? Are they naïve and ignorant? This may be the case, but equally, some of the most intelligent scientists, mathematicians, academics, historians and countless others have claimed that they are not wrong, that they have found something incredibly important and of incalculable value. They have found 'the pearl of great price' (Matthew 13:46 KJV).

Søren Kierkegaard, the great nineteenth-century philosopher, psychologist and theologian, told a parable which emphasised the importance of action in the Christian life. It can be summarised as follows (adapted from C. Stephen Evans, *Kierkegaard: An Introduction*, Cambridge University Press, 2009):

In a farmyard there was a church made up of ducks. Every week they would waddle to the Sunday services, open the duck holy book, sing duck songs, and listen to the duck preacher expound on the meaning of being a duck. One particular Sunday all of the ducks waddled in and the service began. Shortly afterwards, the duck preacher opened the duck book and began to preach. The message was essentially the same every Sunday. With determination and fire in his eyes, the duck preacher proclaimed with confidence:

'We are ducks!'

'Amen!' said all of the other ducks.

'We have waddled too long!' he continued. 'We have wings! We can fly!' he shouted as all of the ducks joined together in a resounding 'Amen!' and they quacked throughout the duck congregation. The service came alive as all of the ducks began to see their potential. 'We have been confined to this mundane existence of waddling for far too long!' exclaimed the duck preacher. 'We can spread our wings and fly!' The service continued with enthusiasm for over an hour as shouts of 'Amen!' and 'Preach it, brother!' filled the duck church.

When the duck preacher concluded the service, the congregation of ducks applauded and closed their duck books. And they all waddled home.

However, one of the younger ducks really took the message to heart and instead of going to the duck services, he focused on really trying to fly. It was very difficult and he tried again and again, devoting all his energies to flying. One day he succeeded and he flew over the farmyard and called the others to do likewise, but they would not listen. They would not even look up to see what he was doing.

Similarly, it is not words that make someone a Christian but really trying to live out the Christian message.

> *I hear of nothing but perfection on every side, so far as talk goes; but I see very few people who really practise it. Everybody has his own notion of perfection. One may think it lies in the cut of his clothes, another in fasting, a third in almsgiving or in frequenting the sacraments, in meditation, in some special gift of contemplation, or in extraordinary gifts of graces – but they are all mistaken, as it seems to me, because they confuse the means, or the results, with the end and cause.*
>
> (St François de Sales, quoted in Aldous Huxley,
> *The Perennial Philosophy*, 1945)

> *For my part, the only perfection I know is of a hearty love of God, and to love one's neighbour as oneself. Charity is the only virtue which rightly unites us to God and man. Such union is our final aim and end, and all the rest is mere delusion.*
>
> (Jean-Pierre Camus de Ponte Carré, quoted in
> Aldous Huxley, *The Perennial Philosophy*, 1945)

Postscript

Many people have influenced me indirectly in writing this book and, in a sense, it is invidious to mention individuals. Nevertheless, there have been key figures who have helped me to understand Christianity better, and not simply in an academic sense: the Revd Henry Bettenson and 'Kipper' Leask at my schools; the Revd Robert Corbin, the Revd Gordon Dowden, Margaret Bishop and Marjorie Fryer from Selborne in Hampshire; Fr Gerry Hughes SJ, Fr Michael Barnes SJ; Fr Paul Rout OFM and Fr Peter Gallagher SJ at Heythrop College, University of London, where I was an academic for nearly thirty wonderful years. Many impressive students have taught me a great deal, particularly Felicity McCutcheon, the Revd John Hanford, the Revd Rodney Ward, Sr Anne-Marie Quigg, Sr Beverley Zimmerman, Rhys, Caroline Martin and many, many more.

I am particularly grateful to Moira Siara for her help in editing this book prior to publication.

If nothing else, this book aims to try to show the relevance of Christianity for today. The splits, divisions and abuses must be acknowledged but, beneath these, the Christian message challenges the contemporary world by asking fundamental questions about the nature of reality, the meaning of life and survival of death. In so doing, its relevance is enduring, as is the message of hope that it brings.

Peter Vardy
Bracken Ridge Farm, Upper Nidderdale, Easter 2016

List of illustrations

List of illustrations

List of illustrations

Index

The reference 'webPoC' below indicates where relevant supplementary material (at no cost) can be found at www.puzzleofchristianity.org. Much other material is also available, so use of the site to provide supplementary material for students is recommended.

Index

Index

Index